HELL & HIGH WATER

For my parents, Colin and Kay Goddard

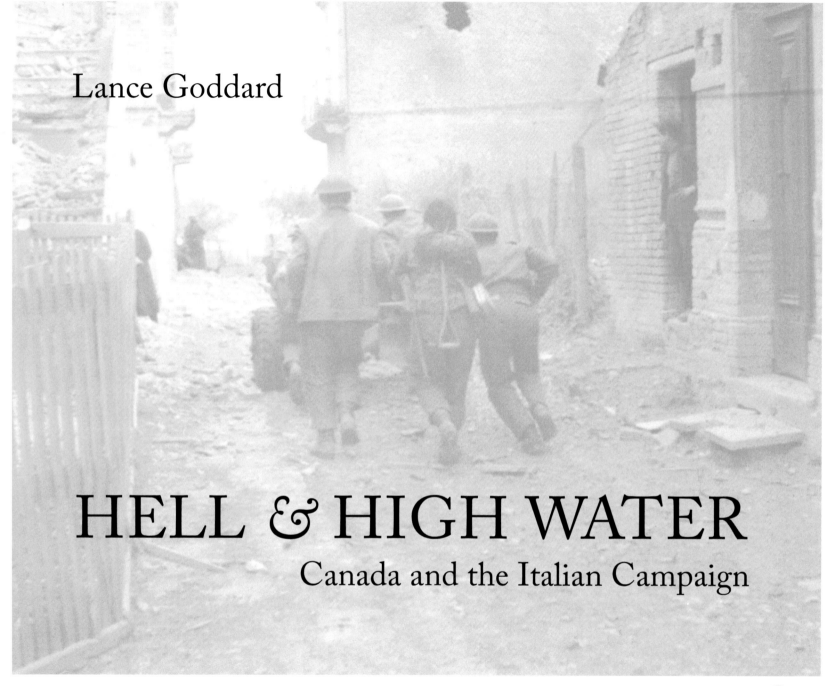

Lance Goddard

HELL & HIGH WATER

Canada and the Italian Campaign

The Dundurn Group
Toronto

Copy-editor: Andrea Waters
Designer: Jennifer Scott
Printer: Tri-Graphic Printing Ltd.

Library and Archives Canada Cataloguing in Publication

Goddard, Lance
    Hell and high water : Canada and the Italian campaign / Lance Goddard.

ISBN 978-1-55002-728-0

    1. World War, 1939-1945--Campaigns--Italy. 2. Canada. Canadian
Army--History--World War, 1939-1945. I. Title.

D763.I8G63 2007   940.54'215   C2007-904659-2

1   2   3   4   5   11   10   09   08   07

We acknowledge the support of the **Canada Council for the Arts** and the **Ontario Arts Council** for our publishing program. We also acknowledge the financial support of the **Government of Canada** through the **Book Publishing Industry Development Program** and **The Association for the Export of Canadian Books**, and the **Government of Ontario** through the **Ontario Book Publishers Tax Credit** program and the **Ontario Media Development Corporation**.

Care has been taken to trace the ownership of copyright material used in this book. The author and the publisher welcome any information enabling them to rectify any references or credits in subsequent editions.

J. Kirk Howard, President

Printed and bound in Canada
www.dundurn.com

Dundurn Press
3 Church Street, Suite 500
Toronto, Ontario, Canada
M5E 1M2

Gazelle Book Services Limited
White Cross Mills
High Town, Lancaster, England
LA1 4XS

Dundurn Press
2250 Military Road
Tonawanda, NY U.S.A.
14150

TABLE OF CONTENTS

INTERVIEWS

Sydney Frost (Princess Patricia's Canadian Light Infantry)
Fred Scott (Perth Regiment)
Al Sellers (Governor General's Horse Guards)
John Richardson (Ontario Regiment)
Peter Routcliffe (Governor General's Horse Guards)
Herb Pike (48th Highlanders)
Gord Outhwaite (48th Highlanders)
Jim Holman (48th Highlanders)
Joseph Reid (Calgary Regiment)
Harry Fox (Hastings and Prince Edward Regiment)
Albert Wade (Royal Canadian Dragoons)
Lloyd Williams (Royal Canadian Navy)

FOREWORD | *Colonel Sydney Frost*

C.D., Q.C., B.Sc. Mil., LL.B., LL.D.

THIS IS LANCE GODDARD'S THIRD BOOK describing the actions of Canada's soldiers in the Second World War. Having recorded the critical role of the Canadian Army in D-Day and the Liberation of the Netherlands, he now tells the story of the forgotten Italian Campaign.

Hell & High Water follows the format of his earlier books, which was so effective: a concise description of each operation by the author, followed by graphic recollections of veterans who tell it like it was. The many photographs add to the realism of their stories.

The Italian Campaign has never been given the respect it deserves, and its history is not widely known. The invasion of Sicily was the largest amphibious invasion ever to take place. The campaign was the longest engagement in ground combat for Canadians in the Second World War. Almost one hundred thousand Canadians served in Italy.

They battled not only some of the best formations in the German Army but also the hell of Sicily's heat, the rugged mountains of central Italy, and the mud and flood waters of northern Italy.

They suffered terrible casualties from enemy action and sickness, including malaria, jaundice, and dysentery. More Canadians were killed in Italy than in any other country in the Second World War. More than 5,900 Canadians are buried in eighteen war cemeteries in Italy.

Left and above: *Colonel Sydney Frost.*

They were denied reinforcements, ammunition, and supplies that went to the Second Front. After Normandy, the press relegated stories from Italy to the back pages. The Canadian Corps became the forgotten legion.

Then came the insults — snide references about the idle troops in the 8th Army. They were said to be basking in the sun while the armies of Eisenhower were forging prodigious feats of valour on their way to Berlin. They were a scruffy, undisciplined, drunken bunch, filled with venereal disease. They were, indeed, D-Day Dodgers, deliberately avoiding the Second Front in France, where the real war was.

Lance Goddard deals with these slanderous remarks in his usual effective manner. He shows how the troops in Italy sloughed off these ridiculous charges and responded to the D-Day Dodgers canard by composing a song that described what a fine holiday they were really having in sunny Italy — always on the vino, always on a spree, free beer, German bands to cheer them on, bathing in the Po River.

In the view of Lance Goddard, the Italian Campaign should be a source of national pride for Canada. The soldiers who helped to ensure victory there have not been given their due. His fine book will go a long way to set the record straight. It is a story that should be read by every Canadian, especially those of the younger generation.

PREFACE

I HAVE A PERSONAL CONNECTION TO the Italian Campaign, as my grandfather, Stephen Goddard, served in Italy with the British Royal Artillery. His unit was the 58 (Kent) Heavy Anti-Aircraft Regiment RA, and he had fought in the Battle of Britain and across North Africa prior to being sent to Italy in July 1943.

My grandfather always had incredible eyesight. I remember going to the airport with him to watch the airliners land at Toronto, where he would be able to make out the distinguishing features of the aircraft with his naked eye before I could with a pair of binoculars. I couldn't believe that he could see that well, and yet he was right every time. That was when he was in his sixties. When he joined the military as a young man this must have been a factor, as he was assigned to be an anti-aircraft gunner.

Stephen Goddard, 58 (Kent) Heavy AA Regiment RA.

Left: *Stephen Goddard in Italy, 1944.*

Right: *Anti-aircraft crew during the winter.*

During the dark days of the Battle of Britain he was stationed along the white cliffs of Dover, shooting down every German aircraft passing by. With a wife and baby (my father) back in London, he felt especially motivated to stop every enemy aircraft he could. Who knew which one might bomb his family? With his incredible eyesight, he would have been a definite asset to his regiment. He rose to lance corporal and was at one point offered the rank of sergeant, which he turned down.

There is a great story that he used to tell of when he was on leave in Rome and he had just

British soldiers on leave in Italy. Stephen Goddard is second from the left.

Group photo during leave in Rome. Stephen Goddard is second from the left in the front row.

sent off a letter to my grandmother. In the letter he wondered how his brother-in-law Horace Hollingsworth was doing and if they would possibly meet in Italy. He knew from letters from home that Horace was somewhere in the country and had fought at the battle of Monte Cassino, but it had been years since they had seen each other. My grandparents had vacationed together with Horace and his wife, my grandfather's sister Lil. As the story went, my grandfather had just posted the letter and turned the corner when who should he run into? Horace! They spent the rest of the day together catching up and marvelling at what a small world it was.

My grandfather served in Italy to the end of the war and then returned to England and his family. They immigrated to Canada in the mid-1950s, settling in St. Catharines, Ontario. My grandfather never talked a lot about his time in the service, and when he did, it was mostly to me. He left me his medals, which I now have mounted and framed along with his picture, cap badge, and stripes. It is proudly on display in the foyer of my home, as a reminder that our

family was involved in the great struggle for freedom. My sons are growing up proud in the knowledge that their great-grandfather helped to fight the Nazis, and they connect with him despite never having had the chance to meet him. We honour him in this way. With this book I hope to honour our Canadian soldiers who did their part in winning the Second World War and protecting the freedom that we all enjoy today.

Top left: *Stephen Goddard and friend on leave in Rome, 1944.*

Top right: *Stephen Goddard's anti-aircraft crew in action.*

Left: *Battery group photo of the 58 (Kent) Heavy AA Regiment RA. Stephen Goddard stands in the middle of the group.*

INTRODUCTION

THE WATER WAS CHOPPY AS THE landing craft ploughed through the waves. Volley after volley of artillery fire roared overhead as the Canadians prepared for their landing on the beach. Behind them were thousands of ships and craft filled with men and *matériel* to ensure that this grand attack would succeed. It was the largest amphibious invasion to take place in history, and three nations led they way — Great Britain, Canada, and the United States. For the Allies, it was the long-awaited return to Europe to battle the Nazis and to liberate the continent.

To many, this would sound like a description of D-Day, June 6, 1944, yet this invasion took place almost a year earlier. It was not along the Normandy coast but along the sandy southern shore of Sicily. It was the beginning of an arduous twenty-month campaign for the Canadian Army, one where almost one hundred thousand Canadians would play a major role. It would be the longest engagement in ground combat for the Canadians in the Second World War, through some of the fiercest fighting of the war under horrible conditions.

Sadly, this important part of Canadian history is not widely known by many of its citizens. The glory goes to D-Day and the battles of northwest Europe that led to VE Day. Like the great heroism of the Canadians at the Battle of Hong Kong, the Canadian role in the Italian Campaign is all but forgotten, with fragments of knowledge scattered here and there amongst a few interested parties. Yet the Italian Campaign should be a great source of national pride for

Canada. It represents one great victory after another for the Canadian Army, often against the best that the Germans had. Canadian soldiers provided bravery and heroism in the battle to reclaim Europe from tyranny, and they fought through some of the worst extremes in the war. They suffered through the hell of the Sicilian summer and brutal battles such as Ortona, to the high waters of the innumerable flooded rivers that they had to cross. The Italian Campaign was a pivotal part of the Second World War, yet the Canadians who helped to ensure victory there have not been given their due. This book is in honour of those men.

PLANNING

EARLY IN THE SECOND WORLD WAR the Nazis took control of Europe, driving the Allies across the English Channel into England. The Nazis were in a comfortable position defensively. They had allies, neutral countries, or shorelines on their borders. The Soviet Union was a possible threat, but Hitler had signed a non-aggression pact with Stalin to eliminate that eventuality. In 1941 Germany broke its pact and invaded the Soviet Union, and the future of the world was being decided along the Eastern Front. Stalin looked to his allies to create a second front to relieve the pressure from his armies, who were suffering monumental losses. At that time many of the Allies felt that the second front should be in Western Europe, but the problem with an amphibious invasion there was twofold: the coastline was heavily fortified by the Atlantic Wall and the seas were controlled by German U-boats. The difficulty of such an invasion was underscored by the disaster at Dieppe on August 19, 1942.

That same month, Winston Churchill proposed another option for the second front: to attack in the Mediterranean. That would force the Germans to divide their troops between the Russian Front, the Atlantic Wall, and the south, weakening them on all fronts. This would assuage Stalin's demands for a second front and would increase the chances of success for an eventual invasion of France by reducing the defensive units there. Churchill presented his idea to Stalin during his August 1942 visit to Moscow.

As that year progressed, the Allies started to turn the tide of the war, defeating the Germans in North Africa. The momentum was in their favour. The next question was: how to exploit it?

In January 1943 the Allies met at the Casablanca Summit to determine the next course of action. The Allies were spread thin, conducting a war against Germany and Japan at the same time, so it was decided to focus their efforts on defeating Germany first, and then to mass their forces against Japan. To launch the effort against Germany, they considered the idea of attacking somewhere in the Mediterranean as Churchill had suggested. This concept exposed a philosophical divide between the British and the Americans. The British wanted to systematically weaken the Germans by forcing them to spread out their troops to defend several areas simultaneously and to bomb them continually to wear down their resolve. The Americans preferred more decisive action through a large-scale attack. The Americans had several other factors to bear in mind while making this decision. First, they had a large proportion of their combat troops and air force in the Pacific theatre, so they were limited in the size of attack that they could launch. Second, they were relatively new to the war, and with public opinion not in favour of joining the war prior to Pearl Harbor, the Americans needed victories to maintain support for the war effort.

The campaign in North Africa played a role in the decision. There were large numbers of troops there from the desert campaign, and moving them to another part of the Mediterranean made more logistical sense than returning them to England to prepare for a landing in France. The British opposed an invasion of France at that point since the Allies did not have superiority in the air and on the sea, and they could not guarantee the supply lines. While the British were unified in their position, the Americans were not, and as a result, the decision was made to make the next move in the Mediterranean.

The next debate was about the specific location of the invasion. Initially there were plenty of choices: southern France, Sardinia, Sicily, Greece, or the Balkans. The first consideration was ensuring proximity to existing air bases for support and maintaining supply lines to ensure the ongoing success of the invasion. The Allies had bases in Malta and Tunisia, which narrowed down the options, leading to Sicily as the target of choice. The island was key to the shipping lanes in the Mediterranean, and it would provide air bases to launch attacks against southern Europe. An attack on Sicily and then Italy would not only force the Germans to commit troops that could be utilized elsewhere but would possibly drive Italy out of the Axis. The Germans would then have to defend the front in Italy on their own, plus they would have to commit even more troops to the Balkans to replace the Italians there.

Sydney Frost (Princess Patricia's Canadian Light Infantry)
Well, the Allies were looking for some kind of victory. They had a terrible time at Dieppe and at Hong Kong and so they wanted to make this one a proper victory without too many casualties. They decided on Sicily, that being the soft underbelly of Europe.

Sydney Frost of the Princess Patricia's Canadian Light Infantry, 2006.

The Germans were discovering that it is easier to take land than it is to defend it. Like the western coastline of Europe, the Germans could not hope to defend every inch of the southern coastline. Sicily provided a dilemma for the Germans: should they defend it or not? It would take a lot of men to defend, yet was it worth it? The Germans were also uncertain about the Italians, both as soldiers and as allies. To lose Italy would be to lose control of the Mediterranean, and German command could not agree about the plan of defence. Field Marshal Albert Kesselring was the Supreme Commander in the Mediterranean, and he believed that all of Sicily and Italy could be defended. The biggest problem for the Germans was that they did not know where the invasion was going to take place, much less if there was even going to be one in the Mediterranean. Similar debates were held over defensive strategy for all segments of the southern coastline from France to Greece. They simply had more shoreline than men to defend it, so they determined the most likely locations for an invasion and proceeded to prepare defensive positions there.

To disrupt the Germans' defensive plans, the Allies developed a subterfuge that would make it appear that the invasion was to take place in Greece. A body was left on the Spanish shoreline with fake plans for an invasion. The Allies knew that any intelligence that fell into the hands of the Spanish would be quickly passed on to the Germans.

Joseph Reid (Calgary Regiment)
They planted this dead man with the information that the assault from the sea will be on Greece. Sure enough, the body was picked up and was used to a great deal of effect. As a result, we didn't have as tough a time as we might have had. Now in addition to that, where in Sicily would we land? They used some deception as to where we would land.

Joseph Reid of the Calgary Regiment, 2006.

Part of the bogus plan was a feint on Sicily. The Spanish turned this information over to the Germans, and they believed that they had the intelligence that they needed to repel an Allied invasion of southern Europe. They immediately transferred a Panzer division from France to Greece and sent two hundred aircraft from Sicily to reinforce their position there. While the Germans expected a buildup of invasion forces off the coast of Sicily, they did not expect them to land, so they did not make any special preparations there for defence.

At that time, Sicily was defended by the Italian Sixth Army along with two German Divisions (the 15th Panzer Grenadiers and the Hermann Goering Panzer Division) — more than two hundred thousand troops were stationed there. The Italian presence consisted of six divisions defending the coastline, most of whom were inexperienced or unmotivated. The Allies knew where the defensive units were stationed since Italian prisoners of war (POWs) in North Africa were receiving letters from their army buddies in Sicily — complete with unit numbers and return addresses. Inexplicably, the Italian army censors did not remove this information, and it allowed the Allies to pinpoint where the Axis troops were positioned along the coast. The German divisions were good fighters, but they were weakened and in the process of reinforcing their units after the beating that they had taken in North Africa. It was not certain how good the defence of the island was going to be, especially with the Italians defending their homeland for the first time.

The Canadian role in the Italian Campaign began on April 23, 1943. General Sir Alan Brooke (the Chief of the Imperial Staff) requested Canadian involvement from Lieutenant-General A.G.L. McNaughton (Canada's Senior Combatant Officer). The request went to Ottawa for approval, which it received. Canadians had been joining up since 1939 and finding only disappointment as they were being left out of the action. While the navy and air force were actively engaging the enemy, the majority of Canadian volunteers found themselves in limbo in Britain, waiting for a chance to fight — a chance that for years seemed like it would never come. The

The arm patch that gained respect throughout Italy. The men of Canada fought valiantly, leading the way into battle.

monotony of training and inactivity created morale problems, and to exacerbate the situation, the Americans, who didn't join the war until late 1941, immediately went into action in North Africa. Now the opportunity had come. It would be the first time Canadians would make an amphibious landing, so they went through rigorous training. For many it would also be their first time in combat, so the previously monotonous training suddenly took on a sense of urgency and meaning. The men were moved to Inveraray, Scotland, for two months of advanced training, including preparations for mountain warfare. Their destination was unknown to the men, and they wondered where they could be going — especially when one hundred mule saddles arrived.

Al Sellers (Governor General's Horse Guards)
The morale was going down because we were getting a little tired of being over there and everybody else fighting. Then time came for us.

Top right: *Al Sellers of the Governor General's Horse Guards, 2006.*

Bottom left: *Portrait of Al Sellers during the Second World War.*

Bottom right: *Al Sellers in training during the early years of the Second World War.*

The planning for Operation Husky was unprecedented. It was risky since it involved an amphibious landing on defended beaches. Nothing had ever been attempted on that scale before. The logistics of landing several divisions with support is a daunting task, requiring the precise planning of the movement and positioning of three thousand ships and naval craft, with the continual support of three thousand aircraft. It was a matter of not only congregating all of the forces in one place at the same time but also continuing a flow of men and supplies to the beachhead once it was established. To ensure a successful invasion, the navy and air force had to control the seas and skies. Various aspects of the planning were delegated to different groups, with decisions being made from Washington to London, from Cairo

Top left: *Accommodations for the men were typically tents, even during training.*

Bottom left: *Governor General's Horse Guards crew in training with a tank.*

Above: *Canadian soldiers in training.*

to Rabat. The distances between these groups created issues, and initially there was a lack of coordination of the effort. The job of pulling it all together was given to General Bernard Montgomery, fresh from his victory in North Africa.

The plan included the U.S. 7th Army (under Lieutenant-General George Patton) and the British 8th Army (under General Montgomery). The Canadian 1st Division and the 1st Canadian Army's Tank Brigade were attached to the 8th Army under British command. The landings had to occur along the southern shore of Sicily to be within the range of their supporting aircraft. The ports of Messina and Palermo were preferable since they could be used to supply the advancing armies, but both cities were out of the range of air support, so they were dropped from consideration.

The Canadian 1st Division was representative of Canada, with units from all across the nation, and was commanded by Major-General H.L. Salmon. On April 29, 1943, Major-General Salmon departed for Cairo for a briefing with some of his staff officers, and tragically the aircraft crashed, killing all on board. With planning well underway for Operation Husky, no time could be wasted in naming Salmon's replacement. At forty years of age, Major-General G.G. Simonds became the army's youngest senior commander, and within days he was making the trip that Salmon never completed.

In Cairo, Simonds was briefed on Operation Husky and informed of the Canadian role in the plan. Immediately he had to devise his plans for the 1st Division and submit them to his corps commander, General Leese. Within a day Simonds's plan was approved, and he returned to his men in Britain.

While the plans for Operation Husky were being finalized, the initial stages of the operation were launched. For the six weeks leading up to the invasion the Allied air force bombarded Sicily, Italy, and Sardinia, disrupting communications and transportation all over the country. The Royal Canadian Air Force's No. 331 Wing joined the campaign late in June, flying their Wellingtons over the targets and lambasting the enemy positions, while the No. 417 (City of Windsor) Squadron flew their Spitfires in support of the bomb runs. The air force destroyed the enemy positions, demoralized the defenders, and drove the German Air Force off of the island of Sicily. The aircrews found that anti-aircraft fire was light across Sicily, with the exception of Messina. This allowed the crews to fly low and hit their targets with greater accuracy than the crews in northern Europe were used to. The bombardment increased in the final ten days prior to the invasion, and more than five thousand sorties were flown in an effort to make the landings safer for the infantry.

One of the great feats of Operation Husky was the gathering of forces from thousands of miles apart. They came from North Africa, Britain, and the United States to rendezvous off Sicily at the same time. The Canadian 1st Division began its journey in late June, departing from Clyde, Scotland, and heading out into the Atlantic. The men were billeted in a variety of ships, with accommodations ranging from spartan merchant ships to luxurious cruise liners.

Sydney Frost (Princess Patricia's Canadian Light Infantry)
We left Gourich, Scotland, on June 23, 1943, and we didn't know where we were going. All sorts of rumours flitted around. One was this was a massive deception plan and really we were headed for Norway. Then we were issued with summer clothing and we thought, "Well, it has to be North Africa, or maybe we are going to Japan." We were very keen to go because the 1st Canadian Division had been in England for about three years and were well trained, beautifully trained troops. We were ready for it — wherever it was.

Joseph Reid (Calgary Regiment)
The convoy went out to mid-Atlantic from Scotland, two weeks on the water, and then we came in to the Mediterranean from the south and we didn't see lights until we hit Gibraltar.

While at sea, the men finally learned what their destination was. Briefings began, and the men were given information pamphlets on what to expect in Sicily and Italy.

On the night of July 4–5 they came under attack by German U-boats off the North African coast. Three freighters were sunk — the *City of Venice*, the *St. Essylt*, and the *Devis*, with the loss of fifty-two Canadian soldiers and more than five hundred vehicles and guns. This incident has a bizarre twist to it. Each day on the voyage Lieutenant-Colonel George Kitching would have Simonds select the names of three ships from a hat. Kitching's staff would calculate the impact if those three ships were sunk. One of the draws selected all three ships that had division headquarters equipment and transport. The odds were so ridiculous of that happening that another three names were drawn. Those three ships were the ones sunk off the coast of Algeria. The Canadian fleet escaped any further attacks and gathered into one unit on July 5 to make its way into the Mediterranean.

Gord Outhwaite (48th Highlanders)
God, it was quite a madhouse, it was boats all over. And we had the German submarines in there too.

Herb Pike (48th Highlanders)
They actually sunk one of our ships as well — a transport.

Gord Outhwaite (48th Highlanders)
They sunk three of them. They torpedoed the ship that had all our transport on it and we were then into Sicily.

Gord Outhwaite of the 48th Highlanders, 2006.

Meanwhile at the other end of the Mediterranean, the Royal Canadian Navy's 55th, 61st, 80th, and 81st Canadian LCA and LCM Flotillas transported British troops from Alexandria to Sicily.

Lloyd Williams (Royal Canadian Navy)
At Sicily there were four Canadian Landing Craft Flotilla. Two of them were Landing Craft Assault, LCA, and two of them were Landing Craft Mechanized, that's LCM. The LCAs carried assault troops, and LCMs carried small tanks, Jeeps, little carriers, gun carriers, and stuff like that. The LCAs were carried on troop

ships that were converted from liners, and they would be the two ships — the 61st Flotilla was on the ship Strathnaver, *and the 55th Canadian Flotilla was on the* Otranto. *These were both very large passenger ships and they carried a few thousand assault troops each. The LCMs were carried on freight ships, on the decks. The LCAs were carried in the lifeboat davits, while the LCMs were lifted by cranes onto the decks of the freighters. All four of us, we worked with British troops. They were with us probably a month or so training, and then it took us probably three to four days to sail from Port Said over to Sicily. These were big convoys, we had almost the whole of the Royal Navy supporting us, the battleships and aircraft carriers, destroyers, cruisers, the whole darn thing.*

Operation Husky was an ambitious endeavour, requiring the precise coordination of the army, the air force, and the navy in a scale that had never been attempted before in history. For Canadians, there was pride involved in every aspect of the operation.

Sydney Frost (Princess Patricia's Canadian Light Infantry)
I was called in by the ship's captain, and he said, "Look here, I want you to give a briefing to all the troops in the ship, all three thousand of them, on the operation." Well, I didn't know anything about it, and he said, "Come with me." We went into the swimming pool, and here the whole of Sicily was laid out in beautiful relief — a sand table. Our division was part of the famous 8th Army. On our right was the 51st Highland Division, and on our left was the Americans. Now this was the biggest landing of all time. There was something like 180,000 troops — American, British, Canadian. There were three thousand ships involved and they came from all over the planet and they all had to converge outside Sicily at the same time. A monstrous problem, but they pulled it off, and the Germans — they hadn't a clue where we were going to land. So we did it and the rest is history.

The following day the Canadian fleet had another close call. The convoy was ahead of schedule, so Rear Admiral Sir Philip Vian decided to circle back. During the manoeuvre a U-boat was spotted that had been following them. Immediately depth charges were dropped, destroying the German craft and averting a major loss. Danger lurked all along the route as U-boats patrolled the seas in search of prey. For the men aboard the ships, there was always the chance of being sunk before even getting the chance to fight, adding to the tension.

At noon on July 9 the Canadians arrived at the rendezvous point near Malta, then turned north to head for Sicily. They soon found themselves in a force-seven gale, with ships being tossed about in the churning sea. The weather

**Italy
1943-1945**

was so rough that the operation was in danger of being postponed, but within hours the storm abated, and the last-minute preparations for the invasion began.

The Allied armada was spotted by German aircraft on the afternoon of July 9. The Germans did not anticipate an invasion in Sicily due to the bad weather and the disinformation that they had received about an invasion of Sicily to precede an invasion of Greece. While they knew the Allies were gathering there, the Germans did not make any special preparations to defend the island.

Just after midnight the Canadian convoy moved into position off of the coast of Sicily.

Seven divisions of Allied soldiers prepared to land, including twenty-five thousand Canadian troops. More soldiers would land in this operation than on June 6, 1944, in Normandy.

They prepared to board more than 2,000 landing craft, all under the protection of 6 battleships, 2 aircraft carriers, 15 cruisers, 119 destroyers, and hundreds of other naval vessels. It was the largest amphibious invasion force ever assembled. The invasion of Sicily was about to begin.

SICILY

SICILY IS THE LARGEST ISLAND IN the Mediterranean, 250 kilometres wide and with 1,000 kilometres of coastline. Triangular in shape, Sicily is almost entirely covered in hills and mountains that are a continuation of Italy's Apennines range, while most of the coastline is lined with plains. The island is dominated by the volcanic Mount Etna, which stands more than 3,000 metres tall. In 1943 the population was approximately 4 million. For an invading force, the main challenge was Sicily's topography and climate. During the summer months the temperatures soared high enough to make any activity unbearable. On July 10, 1943, the Allies prepared to wage war on this inhospitable island, facing not only a well-armed enemy but also the natural elements.

In the early hours of that day Allied aircraft flew low over Sicily, dropping the paratroopers of the British 1st Airborne and the American 82nd Airborne. These brave young men silently floated to the ground, well back of the beaches. They would cut off the coastal defences, stop any German counterattack, and destroy any large guns that could hamper the landing. The Italians manning the coastline would face attack from in front and behind, which would quickly diminish their resolve, allowing the Allies to establish a beachhead. At 0300 the naval bombardment began, incessantly pounding the defensive positions to soften the target for the invasion.

Before daybreak the ships began to load up with the infantry units and sappers, working their way down the scramble nets and trying to negotiate a way into the bobbing landing craft. The men were loaded down with equipment and supplies, carrying everything necessary to take the beach and to move inland.

Lloyd Williams (Royal Canadian Navy)

After the Dieppe landing it was decided that any time that there's an advance by a British army, there's going to be an awful lot of bombardment going on first. Aircraft and ships bombardment. So this is what happened there. You still have to wonder what's going to happen, because all of us were either in or watched or knew all about the Dieppe landings. The British, which included us, we were night landers. We did all our landings in dark hours. It was only the Americans that landed in daylight. We left our mother ship between 2:00 and 4:00 A.M. We landed in a terrible storm. They nearly called off the whole damn

26

thing because there was a gale force winds blowing and it made the seas very rough. They dropped us seven miles off shore, so we had a long run in these heavy waves.

Gord Outhwaite (48th Highlanders)
Talk about a heavy sea, it was unreal. We were there waiting, we were supposed to go in in the dark, in the dawn. The little LCTs that took us back and forth, we were trying to get in them. The swells of the water were so high, the swells were coming right up the side of the damn boat, knocking us off the lines. See, we had grapple nets over the side of the boat, and we had to crawl down them to get into the landing craft. So this is what we were doing, and we get down there and you let go to get in the boat and the damn swell goes down and you're about ten feet above the damn boat. The boat's going down and you're going down and then it comes up and meets you.

Around the armada everyone on watch was alert as the area was teeming with submarines and enemy craft. As the landing craft were filled, they moved off and circled, lining up for the run into shore at the pre-planned time. It was deafening as the large guns pounded the Axis positions on shore. Then the landing craft began the mad dash into the beach.

Lloyd Williams (Royal Canadian Navy)
It was so rough, nobody expected anything. We're talking about ten-foot waves. One of the Royal Navy ships, it was a motor launch that was supposed to be taking us in, it didn't make it. We thought we were picked up by searchlights, they were as bright as daylight. We could see all of our boats easily, but apparently what had happened was the searchlight hit the water about a half a mile or a mile in front of us, so they couldn't see anything past where it hit the water. It was very lucky.

With so much shoreline to defend, the Germans held back their mobile units in order to react to an invasion, rather than committing to a few likely positions and being outflanked by invaders in areas on either side of them. While this plan made sense, the Germans' mobility was hampered first by the damage to the roads by the constant bombing of the air force for the previous six weeks, then by the naval bombardment, so they couldn't react. Once the infantry started to move inland, the Germans would still have to contend with the Allied air force. Overhead the Royal Air Force, along with the Royal Canadian Air Force's No. 417 Squadron's Spitfires, flew in support of the invasion. The Allies controlled the skies, as the Germans had had to withdraw most of their aircraft during the bomb runs of the previous month. As a result, the Germans were not involved for the first few days of the campaign, and it fell upon the inexperienced Italian units along the coastline to repel the invasion.

Lloyd Williams (Royal Canadian Navy)

The men were very sick. You've got to visualize, the landing craft is a flat-bottom boat between four and a half to five feet wide, it would be about four feet high from the bottom to the top. It was a flat thing on the bottom and a flat thing on top. We were protected by steel armour plating. These soldiers would be sitting on their haunches, very uncomfortable.

The sandy beaches were guarded by fifteen large coastal guns that would provide a fearsome barrage. In the shoals, as well as on shore, there were mines. Beyond the mines were obstacles: barbed wire, trenches, and twenty machine gun positions that would rake the approaches with unending gunfire. The men were facing a deadly gauntlet with little cover on the beaches and a long run in before engaging the enemy.

As the landing craft neared the beaches, a navy officer in a small boat gave directions to ensure that the landings were spread out and units went in together as planned. Some men on board the landing craft succumbed to the rough waters, still choppy from the previous day's gale, along with nerves over the impending battle and the shock of the cacophony of sound. More than a few began to get sick. Relief would come after stepping on firm ground again, only to face a savage barrage of enemy fire.

Sydney Frost (Princess Patricia's Canadian Light Infantry)

July the tenth the ships all converged together and the assault troops went in in landing craft. Different types: Landing Craft Infantry for the infantry, Landing Craft Tanks for the tanks.

The unforeseen problem that the landing craft encountered as they neared the shore was natural: sandbars. The water along the approaches was quite shallow, with numerous sandbars well off shore that were hard to see and navigate around. As a result, landing craft were running aground far from shore, with water far too deep for the men to wade across. In some places the stranded men were still able to make it to shore, albeit waterlogged. In other areas they managed to land directly on the beach. As the landing craft landed the men moved out quickly, facing machine gun fire.

Gord Outhwaite (48th Highlanders)

When we went in it was daylight. We ran aground on several sandbars. The landing craft dropped the ramp on the front and everybody out, and we're on a sandbar! We still have another hundred yards to go, and it's about ten feet deep or even more. We had some good swimmers, thank God. We put lines in to shore, and if we had a lot of resistance we would never have been able to do that, because they would have been chopping them all up to pieces. We landed in Pachino, and the navy, you got to give them a lot of credit too because they had these little landing craft and they have two guys — bosun and bosun's mate — and they would bring in a load, drop them, and then go back out to the mother ship. They were being shot at, and they had to go back and forth until they emptied out the mother ship, until they got us all on shore. That sand, you'd bog down with your equipment too. They shot ack-ack guns all across where we had landed, and that's when we went in and formed the beachhead so that they could have a place that they could bring the equipment in.

Lloyd Williams (Royal Canadian Navy)

We landed at a fishing port called Marzamemi. It was well fortified, but nobody really expected us to be coming in at that time. A number of our landing craft did get hit, but not seriously, just small arms fire. One boat went into a rocky area where nobody would think no landing craft would come, and these guys landed in these rocks and made their way up the hill to where there's a gun battery and captured it. The other two boats attacked two small islands, each with a gun emplacement. Another one was on the pier. They landed after the two islands had been taken and took it out. There were four guns aiming at us, and all four were captured before they fired a shot. Then our boats came back through between the islands on a beach landing, and nobody was lost at all.

Joseph Reid (Calgary Regiment)

I would think that there wasn't as much resistance as they would have anticipated, but you know, there was a hell of a lot of us. The landing takes place with force, and scattered in different places. They were chosen with special tasks to do, some of the units of the Calgarys were, but I wasn't. We were in Syracuse. We came in, oh, maybe twelve hours or so after the original assault had taken place.

The Allies landed along a seventy-kilometre stretch of shoreline, with the U.S. 7th Army landing in the Gela and Licata area on the south coast of Sicily. The British 8th Army landed in the southeast between Syracuse and Pachino.

The Canadians landed at Pachino, near the airfield that was an objective for the Allies. This was the Canadians' first major operation since the ill-fated raid on Dieppe almost a year before, and they were determined to exact revenge on the Axis. The Calgary Regiment of the 1st Armoured Tank Brigade had suffered greatly at Dieppe, and they were one of the three tank units who assaulted Sicily that day.

Joseph Reid (Calgary Regiment)
The tank landing craft had a ramp that dropped, and so we always had to get to a dock or a sand beach. Dieppe was a different concern because they had waterproofed the tanks to get in. Usually we could go into water about two feet deep. The tank landing craft had a sort of lid that dropped down, which is used as a ramp, and we drove off. We hoped that we were in shallow enough water that the tracks would catch a little traction, and if not, the tank craft would back up and pick another spot for that landing craft. Most of the time we just drove off onto the solid ground.

The Canadians landed with two brigades along a stretch of beach code-named Bark West. The 1st Brigade landed on the right and the 2nd Brigade on the left, with support from the Three Rivers Regiment's tanks. The 2nd Brigade arrived on shore at 0645 and raced across the beach under fire until they reached the first obstacles, where they blasted through the barbed wire with Bangalore torpedoes. The Canadians surged forward and hit the Italian positions with grenades. Quickly, the gun

The Canadian landing beaches at Pachino, Sicily.

30

positions were neutralized and the first prisoners of the campaign were taken. The landing of the 1st Brigade was delayed due to a huge sandbar blocking the way to their designated beach, and they came ashore quite late. This left the 2nd Brigade's flank wide open, but it was not exploited since the Italians had disappeared by that point. The invasion had caught the enemy by surprise, and the beachhead was established with little opposition. There were small pockets of resistance, but for the most part the landing was a lot easier than expected. There were few casualties, while the number of Italian POWs streaming in steadily increased. Less than an hour after the landing, the signal was sent to General Vokes that the beach had been taken.

Top left: *An Italian officer surrenders his garrison to Captain G.R. Coderre of the Vandoos.*

Bottom left: *Specialized landing craft allowed for quick delivery of men and* matériel *during the invasion of Sicily.*

Above: *The landing at Pachino was relatively unopposed, allowing the rest of the army to quickly disembark and advance.*

Sydney Frost (Princess Patricia's Canadian Light Infantry)
Well, we were very lucky because the Germans had been faked right out of their drawers. They hadn't a clue. There wasn't a German to be seen. There were Italian coastal divisions, but their heart wasn't in it. They didn't want to fight, because they had old brother Joe back

here in Toronto. They were very friendly in the south because, you see, we had mass immigration for years from southern Italy. They're such a poor country, before the war they immigrated in the thousands, and a lot of them came to Toronto. In fact, the Italian population in Toronto today is something like six hundred thousand. So they gave up in droves, and really there were very few casualties on that landing. Perhaps that's why we haven't really [been given our due] — because there were no casualties, it takes a second rate to D-Day in that regard, but nevertheless it was very important in the overall conduct of the war because at last we had a winner. I was in the reinforcement group D+3. It wouldn't have made any difference to my life, as there was no opposition really.

Joseph Reid (Calgary Regiment)
We didn't have any armour to contend with, or severe enemy artillery. There were a few of a lesser kind. So the landing was fairly successful, and the only thing is we had balloons flying over the ships, they were shot down and they caught fire, which lit up the whole bloody scheme. Didn't like that very much. We drove inland not very far, and we got it together to muster forces and move on.

Lloyd Williams (Royal Canadian Navy)
What sticks out in my mind in Sicily was how successful our landing was. It was really a well thought out and well executed landing. It was almost picture-perfect how it was done. We worked all day, all into the next two days getting all our troops off. Well, it was strictly ferry work. We'd go out and we would latch onto the falls that would lift the boats, lift them up to deck level, and a boatload would get in and we'd lower the boat into the water and away we'd go. It got pretty boring, but you never know what's going to happen.

Once the beaches were captured, the plan for the Allies was for the British to make an attack from their right flank into the Catania Plains and to push up the east coast towards Messina. The city of Messina was situated on the northeast coast of Sicily, and it was the primary objective of the Sicilian operation. It would give the Allies control of the island, cutting off the enemy's escape route, and it would become the launching point for an invasion of Italy. Across the Strait of Messina, Italy lay only a few kilometres away. Montgomery's plan was to have the British lead the advance and take the city. The Canadians were to take the airfield at Pachino and then protect the British 8th Army's inland flank along with the U.S. 7th Army. This would require that they move through the mountainous interior of Sicily, using the specialized training that they had received in Scotland.

Lloyd Williams (Royal Canadian Navy)
We went back to Malta and we picked up more troops, not for an assault, but to take in. Then we went back to Algiers and, being troop ships, we picked up prisoners of war from the Afrika Corps and took them back to the U.K. as prisoners. The LCMs stayed around longer than we did because they came in later carrying the mechanized parts, and they worked their way up the coast of Sicily, and then some of them went across the Strait of Messina into Italy and carried Canadian troops across that way. The assault flotillas eventually went back in to make the initial landings at Salerno.

The Canadian 1st Brigade was given the task of taking the airfield at Pachino so that it could be used by the air force; the area west of the airfield was to be taken by the 2nd Brigade. As the assault troops moved inland, wave upon wave of landings continued, delivering men and supplies to maintain the forward momentum. The units hailed from coast to coast in Canada. The 1st Brigade was made up of the Royal Canadian Regiment (RCR), the 48th Highlanders, and the Hastings and Prince Edward Regiment (Hasty Ps). The 2nd Brigade included the Seaforth Highlanders, the Princess Patricia's Canadian Light Infantry (PPCLI), and the Loyal Edmonton Regiment (Loyal Eddies). The 3rd Brigade consisted of the Royal 22nd (the Vandoos, as in "Vingt-deux"), the Carleton and York Regiment, and the West Nova Scotia Regiment (West Novas). They were supported by the 1st Armoured Tank Brigade, which included the Calgary Regiment, the Ontario Regiment, and the Three Rivers Regiment. The tank regiments were assigned to different infantry units and would often be attached to units from England, India, South Africa, Malta, New Zealand, Poland, and other nations that were supporting the Allies.

H.E. Cooper of the 48th Highlanders in Sicily.

Sydney Frost (Princess Patricia's Canadian Light Infantry)

Were we going to succeed? Oh, I think that was a given right from the start. We felt that confident. This was going to be a piece of cake, but soon the Germans stole our cake and made it a little difficult. But against the Italians — no problem. We had a tremendous superiority in air force, tremendous artillery. It was just a matter of time before we cleaned them out.

Fred Scott (Perth Regiment)

I found the Italian people very co-operative because I think they were like anybody else, they really didn't want this war. The way I understood it from a couple of books I read, Hitler wanted the strongest armies to stay in Italy to make the Italian people suffer for what they had done to him by letting him down.

Al Sellers (Governor General's Horse Guards)

They'd wave, and I never really did know them. We never quite trusted them, because they were our enemies.

Peter Routcliffe (Governor General's Horse Guards)

Well, they were very cold to begin with, most of the Italians were very cold towards us, and maybe once in a while you'd find somebody that was friendly.

Gord Outhwaite (48th Highlanders)

The one thing that a lot of people don't think about is when you're fighting, we're in a foreign country, and actually the enemy's in a foreign country, but everybody forgets about the people who live there. They die, getting wounded and shot and killed just the same as the rest of us. And they're not mad at anybody. Their land is being taken over, and they're hiding as best they can.

*Peter Routcliffe of the Governor General's
Horse Guards, 2006.*

Herb Pike (48th Highlanders)

I don't think the general populace wanted to be involved. People in our country, the hardest they had it they had food rationing, or they had gasoline rationing, but really nothing of consequence. Our country didn't know what it was to be overrun and to have a war go through your home and your home all blown to pieces. It had to be pretty traumatic for them. They were all right with us, there was no problem.

Gord Outhwaite (48th Highlanders)

As a matter of fact, I think they were glad because they could relax a heck of a lot more. When they were dominated by the German army they were having a bit of a problem there, and they had to watch their Ps and Qs so to speak, and they couldn't say anything out of order or do anything out of order. They had to do what they were told. I think they were relieved at the fact that the Germans were gone and the Canadians were there.

Beyond the beach, vineyards and orchards were scattered over the countryside, partitioned by stone walls as they had been for centuries. In many ways, for the Canadians it was like stepping back in time. They witnessed poverty and squalor — something beyond what they had experienced through the Great Depression. Hunger was rampant, as the Italian and German troops had taken whatever food they could find.

Herb Pike of the 48th Highlanders, 2006.

Herb Pike (48th Highlanders)

Italy at that time — the coastal areas were quite modern. When you got into the interior part, it was a medieval society. It was unbelievable. I mean the way they lived. A farmhouse with half that's a barn. You can imagine the conditions, but they didn't know any different. They had these caves dug where they used to go when the shelling started.

Gord Outhwaite (48th Highlanders)

It's all poverty, that's what it was really. They had nothing at all, primitive tools and God knows what. How they even managed to dig — well, the equipment they used for the plows, their horses, the mules. They used to ride around on their mules all the time.

Herb Pike (48th Highlanders)
Well, we did too! In the mountainous area to bring up supplies. We had mules, they'd carry the ammo up to us.

It was not all mechanized warfare in Sicily and Italy; with brutal terrain the Canadians had to make use of mules as a means of transport. Here the RCRs advance near Regalbuto in July 1943.

Gord Outhwaite (48th Highlanders)
It was like way back in a primitive time; it looked like the world had passed them by.

The Canadians worked around wetlands and salt lakes, and as the day progressed the temperature started to soar. For many of the men, they had never experienced temperatures like they would in Sicily. The temperature would often climb to 38° Celsius or more. To make things worse, they were weighed down with a large amount of supplies, putting a greater burden on them in the stifling heat.

Sydney Frost (Princess Patricia's Canadian Light Infantry)
First of all we had to get acclimatized to the funny country, and then the other problem of course was the intense heat, very, very hot — 110 to 115 degrees — can you imagine carrying fifty pounds of equipment, plus your Bren gun, trying to fight in that kind of hot weather? But we learned gradually.

Joseph Reid (Calgary Regiment)
It was the heat of the summer, and there were mosquitoes. Heat, mosquitoes, I guess that was the biggest enemy.

The only road in the area that could handle the Canadian vehicles was one that led to Ispica. As the Seaforths and PPCLIs advanced along this route, the RCRs and Hasty Ps landed, cleared the coastal guns, and moved inland as well. By 0900 the Canadians had reached the Pachino airfield, and by the afternoon it was in use by Allied aircraft.

The Italian Army put up little resistance, and the Germans were pinned down to the north during the landings. It wasn't until the afternoon that the Canadians faced a counterattack, but the Saskatoon Light Infantry drove off the enemy with mortar fire. The landing was a major success for the Canadians, as 25,000 of their men came ashore that day with only 7 dead and 25 wounded. Meanwhile, 700 Italian and 20 German soldiers were taken prisoner. The operation was so swift and decisive that very few of the Canadians even had to fire their weapons on the landing. As the day progressed, the beaches became clogged all along the Allied beachhead. Hundreds of tanks and thousands of guns and vehicles came ashore, along with 160,000 men. Since amphibious landings were new, traffic control of the beaches was uncharted territory, and as a result it was organized anarchy. As night fell over the thin beachhead, the men struggled for rest. The night provided a respite from the high temperatures, which cooled off somewhat in the evening.

Sydney Frost (Princess Patricia's Canadian Light Infantry)
Well, I had been in the reserve battalion, I hadn't yet joined the regiment, and they had surplus officers kicking around, waiting to go forward, but there hadn't been any casualties so we had nothing to do. Well, the AMGOT — that's the Allied Military Government of Occupied Territories — were short of people to go into all these towns that they had liberated and get them going again, because they were in terrible shape. The people were starving, they had no supplies, no food, no organization, they were fed up completely with the Fascists, and of course the Germans were cruel and brutal and took everything from them. So they needed somebody to go in there and reorganize the town and get it going again. Well, they came to me in the reserve battalion and said, "Look, go ahead to this little town called Ispica and take over as the town mayor until we find a qualified AMGOT officer." I went up and proceeded to become — this was at twenty years old — the mayor of a town of about twelve thousand people. I had to lay down the law, and I must say I rather enjoyed it! I figured that a benevolent dictatorship isn't too bad after all! As long as you're the dictator. I got the food supplies going again, and I got the mill operating to make bread — at least they existed on bread and wine — vino. I can remember people were dying left, right, and centre from malaria, from jaundice, from wounds — these poor Italians, they didn't know a grenade from a melon. And they would pick up these grenades and fool around with them and of course they'd blow them up. So they'd come into our little first aid post, hands blown off, feet blown off, and we had to try and take care of them. It was a pretty exciting time because also there were looters around from other units, particularly the air force. They would come into the town and take what they wanted — sheep, cheese, vino — and I had to stop that. I can remember one time when I was down to the beaches trying to scrounge some food from the British, and I came back and three Australians had grabbed three lambs. Well, I soon stopped that, and the baron who complained to me about it, he got his lambs back, and the Aussies got the boot. So from then on I was a very, very popular man for two to three weeks. Finally I got the call because they had casualties and needed replacements, and I went up the line.

Sicily provided a most uncomfortable environment for the Canadian soldiers, from the sweltering heat to the choking dust; they also suffered from such pests as mosquitoes, fleas, and scorpions. In such temperatures water is a necessity, but clean, drinkable water was a rare commodity in Sicily. Thirst and dehydration became a new foe on the island. As the days progressed, the units began to lose more men to dysentery, jaundice, and malaria than to the enemy. Under the harsh summer conditions, many of the men suffered from varying degrees of sunburn, further adding to their discomfort. The dust was so prevalent that it covered everything — man and machine. It proved to be difficult to clean off, and the clouds of dust that were kicked up in the wake of any vehicle made movement easy to detect by ally and enemy alike.

The Loyal Eddies march into Modica in the sweltering heat.

A column of PPCLI infantry pass by a Sherman tank in the stifling heat of Sicily.

Sydney Frost (Princess Patricia's Canadian Light Infantry)
A lot of casualties from malaria, from jaundice, from rat fever — you name it, and they had it in Sicily. It was a dirty, filthy place in those days. We were told never, ever to eat the watermelon or lovely fruits because they were fertilized with human excreta. But of course no one paid any attention to that, and we all came down with monumental doses of this and that.

Gord Outhwaite (48th Highlanders)
Well Sicily, we had a saying that it was like a dead end of the world. The roads were all chalk, there wasn't any paved roads. You're covered in white chalk, and we'd just jump into a pond or whatever and that would wash all the damn stuff off.

Advancing through Sicily was an arduous task. The vineyards and orchards were dangerous as battlegrounds. As the Canadians headed into the mountains, the terrain was so rough that the battles were mostly confined to the general vicinity of the roads. The men embarked on a two-hundred-kilometre advance that would have to be done mostly on foot. Occasionally there was transportation or a few tanks to hitch a ride with. But in the extreme heat, sitting on the metal vehicles was not always comfortable. Many of the roads in the mountains were too narrow or dangerous for vehicles to use, so the infantry had to advance on foot without support.

Providing an artillery barrage in the searing heat of Sicily.

For the first few days there was little opposition to the Canadian advance. They moved with two brigades at the front and one back in reserve. The marches in such unbearable heat became an endurance test. The greatest challenge that they faced from the enemy in those early days was how to deal with so many POWs. The Italians were giving up in droves, averaging more than one thousand every day. They became a burden on men and supplies, so they were quickly sent off to POW camps in North Africa. Three days after the invasion, the troops had to halt their advance to allow for the supply columns to catch up with them. By this time the Germans had moved into position, and the resistance began to increase.

Sydney Frost (Princess Patricia's Canadian Light Infantry)
Well, there was no real resistance until we hit the Germans. They had sensibly concentrated their troops in the centre of the island. They didn't have enough, but they were paratroops and very skilful, and it was pretty tough going.

Joseph Reid (Calgary Regiment)
There was German resistance early on of an infantry kind. There was little or no German armour there for quite some time. We met the German armour as we reached Siracusa [Syracuse] further across from Palermo. Basically, I think there was only one real armoured contest, which didn't really amount to too much.

By the time the Germans began to engage the advancing Allied troops, they had already come to the conclusion that they could not win the battle for Sicily. They could not turn and retreat either — the withdrawal across the Strait of Messina would take time. A fighting withdrawal was necessary to ensure that all troops and *matériel* could be transferred to Italy without creating anarchy at the port. A complete collapse and withdrawal would inevitably lead to many valuable troops being trapped and taken prisoner before they could be evacuated. The Germans needed every soldier possible for the defence of Italy.

The German plan of withdrawal involved a series of defensive lines that circled Messina. Like ripples in a pond emanating from a dropped stone, these fronts spread out across Sicily with Messina at their epicentre. The Germans were well acquainted with Sicily and made use of its topography to constantly position themselves on the high ground, a distinct advantage in warfare. Each defensive line would impede the Allied advance with snipers and artillery fire for as long as possible. They used minefields and barbed

Desperate for relief from the scorching sun, some Loyal Eddies use an umbrella to create some shade in their universal carrier. Pictured (L-R): C.J. Morgan, T. Lickacy, Hugh Millar, V.A. Lawrence, and S. Ptacharyk.

wire to create obstacles, funnelling the advancing troops into concentrated areas where the Germans would open fire, creating deadly killing fields. Once the Allies were able to move their artillery up in support of the lead infantry units or to launch an attack, the Germans would withdraw to the next defensive line. Typically it was the next hill or position of strategic advantage behind them. The German tactic was not intended to stop the advance, just slow it down. This stop-and-go action became a source of frustration for the Allies, as they never got the opportunity to face the Germans in a stand-up fight. Every time the Allies were ready to respond to a German attack, they were gone. So the advance would proceed again, but would quickly be halted by the next defensive line.

Herb Pike (48th Highlanders)

The advantage Jerry had was he knew his field of fire, because he had been there, and these were all set up. We're sort of in virgin territory. We've got to figure out where the positions are and how to attack that position.

Al Sellers (Governor General's Horse Guards)

They were masters. In the attack, the attacker has to find out where his enemy is. The defender, he knows exactly where you are as you advance. So they could range in on every crossroad, every building, every bit of shelter. They'd use howitzers to lob a shell over the hill. Aerial bursts were a common thing. The infantry guys, as they would attack, they would be spread out … maybe ten to fifteen feet apart. The ploy used by the enemy at that time was to use aerial bursts, and you'd have this shrapnel just raining down, so it was pretty hard to protect yourself from that. Artillery fire is not just a few hundred yards away from you, it could be a couple of miles away. They were on high ground, and they used it to their best advantage. Our artillery couldn't because they were on the bottom shooting up. Moaning Minnies — they had one particular mortar that made a terrible noise when it was coming over. It was more noise than it was dangerous, but it was dangerous too. It scared the living daylights out of me with the noise it made. Their Spandaus — they had machine guns that had such a high rate of fire, I can remember driving by a section of 1st Infantry guys that all got knocked out at once. This gun was on fixed fire, and you could see this whole section of men just lying there, they looked just like roadkill. That gun that hit them, oh, it had to be around seven hundred to eight hundred yards away.

The Canadians faced the worst of this fighting retreat by the Germans, as they had the assignment of advancing through Sicily's mountainous interior. The British and the Americans faced their battles along the flat coastal plains, where the Germans had less of an advantage. Many of the German defensive positions in the mountains were virtually impregnable, and they had an excellent view of the advancing Canadian columns; they would act as artillery observers and call down incredibly accurate fire. It would be something that the Canadians would have to contend with for the next year and a half, as the Germans continued to use the same scheme all the way up the Italian peninsula.

While the Germans used the hilltop villages and buildings as their strongholds on each defensive line, the bulk of their army and *matériel* was being loaded onto transports in Messina and shipped the eight kilometres to Italy. It was a very organized and orderly withdrawal, and in the end, the Germans left very little behind.

Sydney Frost (Princess Patricia's Canadian Light Infantry)
Well, we had artillery, and the Canadians are famous for artillery. We would just blast them out of their holes. Of course we had the air force as well. There was good co-operation between the air force and the infantry.

Early in the campaign, the Germans put up a determined defence of Catania, bringing Montgomery's advance to a standstill. To counter this, Montgomery had the Canadians move towards Enna and then turn eastward to expose the German defences at Catania by outflanking them. This decision exposed the tricky balance of politics that the Allied commander faced. Montgomery had decided to give the Canadians right-of-way along the Americans' main axis without consulting the Americans. This decision, and more importantly, Montgomery's disregard for etiquette, angered the Americans. It didn't help that Montgomery and Patton did not like each other. This flashpoint led to Patton abandoning his role as a mere flank guard, and he set off with his 7th Army along the western coast of Sicily. If Messina was the main objective in Sicily, Patton decided that he would take it his own way. Thus began the race between the British and the Americans to see who would take Messina first.

Herb Pike (48th Highlanders)
Patton was coming up the other side. He and Monty [Montgomery] were at loggerheads all the time. They're both eagles, and anyway they were vying as who was going to get to Messina first. The race was who was going to get there first, and you've probably seen movies of Patton standing there and Monty coming through with the pipes blaring and here's old Patton with his tanks already there. It was the old ego game.

Sydney Frost (Princess Patricia's Canadian Light Infantry)

We were fighting with the famous Desert Rats, the 8th Army, they'd been all through Africa — they were good! They assigned to us the most difficult thing, right through the centre of the island, through the mountainous part. So we were sort of in the centre, supported by the other troops. We also had to contend with the terrain. We had to be smart about it and adapt to the different kinds of terrain. Our favourite trick in battle was a pincer movement. You go around the object and attack it from behind. Now this wasn't in the German book of regulations, and I can remember one major, he was furious with me. He says, "You don't fight fair! You go on either side and you come from behind, how is this?" Well I said, "This is called a pincer movement." He thought this was wonderful, never heard of that. Sounds a little far-fetched, but it was true. It wasn't in the book of regulations, and Germans are very organized, everything has to be in the book. If it's not in the book, well, you don't do it. So Canadians are like that — you had to improvise. Because in the Depression nobody had any money and you learned to improvise. So a lot of things enter into it.

Harry Fox (Hastings and Prince Edward Regiment)

Infantry can go anywhere, but you can't support them unless you are on a road. So all you have to do is defend the roads, and what we did quite often, manoeuvre around, just go and walk off into country for five or ten miles and try to sneak in behind them. The Hasty Ps were good at that night marching business because a lot of them were coming from the backwoods area of Ontario. A lot of them were farmers, a lot of them were bushwhackers, a lot of them worked in lumber mills and so on — they were used to going through the woods hunting, it was second nature to them, and they weren't afraid of it. A lot of people are afraid of getting in the woods at night because they get lost. Our guys weren't.

Harry Fox of the Hastings Prince Edward Regiment, 2005.

John Richardson (Ontario Regiment)

In the summertime the roads are very dry and the old flumes of dust coming up the back of our tanks kind of give you away. They can look and just watch you as you come along and say, "Okay boys, there they are, right in the crossroads, now fire," and they could get you no matter where you were because they always had a higher elevation and they could always look down on you, and that was a difficult. If there were any mountains around, you could bet your boots that they had the highest one and they were looking down at you.

Harry Fox (Hastings and Prince Edward Regiment)
Of course, they defended it with troops, and if you were going up the hill, it's tough on you. You're puffing and going up the hill, and they can stand in their trench actually and just throw their grenade and it rolls down the hill. They don't have to take a definite aim at you.

Gord Outhwaite (48th Highlanders)
When you think of the terrain itself — it's all hills, and you don't have too much to hide behind. They can see you, they're dug in, you don't see them. You just got to hope that you could find them. If you see them take a shot at you, well, then you got to hope you know where they are.

John Richardson (Ontario Regiment)
In some places it's very close, we went through vineyards and olive groves and things like that and you couldn't see your hand in front of your face sometimes if you muddled through the vineyard. There wasn't a lot of open country.

The Canadians moved north with the 1st Brigade leading the way along the main road. Between the suffocating heat, the choking dust, and an enemy that proved elusive, it was a tough advance. On the night of July 14, the Canadians set out for Vizzini with the RCRs at the head of the column. After a while the Hasty Ps took the lead and they headed for the town of Grammichele, where the Canadians would have their first encounter with the German Army.

Grammichele sat atop a hilly area, 521 metres above sea level. The medieval town had narrow streets that all led to a central piazza. As the Canadians approached it, the town was in ruins from continual Allied bombings. The small town had been a major target since it was the headquarters of the Herman Goering Division, and little was left to occupy. Around 0900 the Canadian column advanced along National Road 124; just outside of Grammichele the five-kilometre-long column stopped due to a large crater in the road caused by a mortar. Ahead the Hasty Ps had a company scouting in the streets of the town, riding on top of the tanks of the Three Rivers Regiment. Then all hell broke loose.

Z.S. Cormier and S.A. Robbins of the Carleton and Yorks carry a wounded soldier back from the front in Sicily.

The scouts turned a tight corner in the labyrinth of narrow streets and came face to face with a German 88mm gun, which hit the first tank as it arrived. The Hasty Ps outflanked the German gun crew before they could reload and killed them all. Meanwhile, German artillery unleashed a barrage at the Canadian column on the road, making direct hits on the stationary targets. Immediately the Canadians took cover, then prepared to attack. They quickly found that the Germans had every entrance to the town covered, but the 48th Highlanders and the Three Rivers Regiment pushed the enemy back. Two companies of the Hasty Ps moved around Grammichele to cut off the town's defenders. As the units moved in, they discovered that the Germans had withdrawn, giving them no opportunity for retribution for the twenty-five Canadians that were wounded in the action.

The first clash between German and Canadian forces would represent an ongoing theme in the Italian Campaign: the cost for advancement was paid with Canadian blood. While the first engagement may have left the Canadians bewildered, both by the loss of men and the Germans' withdrawal, the continuation of this pattern would adversely affect morale over the long term.

The Canadians were in pursuit of the Germans as they withdrew to their next defensive line, chasing them all the way to Caltagirone through the night. The next day the Loyal Edmonton Regiment took the lead along with a tank squadron from the Three Rivers Regiment. They encountered the Germans at the key junction of Piazza Arminera, and the ensuing battle once again halted the Canadians' progress. At the same time, the 3rd Brigade was facing similar circumstances at Enna, where they were engaged by two German battalions. Mount Etna dominated the central part of Sicily, and the Germans were using it as a natural obstacle to hinder the Canadians while strategically positioning their units at key road junctions and other defensive positions. Once the Germans withdrew from Piazza Arminera, the Canadians moved north a few kilometres, pursuing the enemy to Valguarnera.

The advance was difficult as steep cliffs and deep ravines made travel treacherous, especially under enemy fire. The Canadians also suffered from a lack of reliable maps. Throughout the Italian Campaign the Allies would depend on maps that were incredibly inaccurate and out of date. Old tourist maps and antique charts had to be used at first, and these endangered the men's lives when the discrepancies exposed them to deadly fire. Battling through the mountains, the Canadians had to rely on their mountain warfare training and sense of initiative to overcome the drawbacks that they were facing.

Joseph Reid (Calgary Regiment)

Every time a tank made a turn, it scraped a little bit off the road. It was just like a razor. The tank would brake one track and the other one moved, and as it moved it scraped the surface, and when we were going through the hills or the mountains they were bad as it is. It scraped a little bit off the curve, and so sooner or later, depending on how many tanks went by and how much was scraped off, it ruined the roadway.

Gord Outhwaite (48th Highlanders)

I can remember meeting the first German plane. Somebody said, "There's a German plane." And I said, "Where?" And the bomb landed and I went up in the air. Heh heh. Oddly enough there was three of us, there was a piper, he had to go to the washroom, so you used a shovel, dug a hole, and he had just dropped his drawers and this plane came over. He dropped a bomb, and it wasn't very far from us. Fortunately the concussion went over him, but it blasted all the dirt and everything else right into his hide because he had just dropped his pants. Another fellow was urinating against a tree and it split the tree right down and he took a dive right out. Split the tree right down to where his head was. There was a couple of trucks there and the concussion took me over the top of the truck and the shrapnel hit the truck, so I guess that was the good Lord looking after me at that time.

Medics tend to a pair of wounded Canadian soldiers near Valguarnera.

The PPCLI advance up a hill near Valguarnera while mortar fire screams overhead.

The Canadians moved north towards Valguarnera, an ancient town that overlooked the surrounding area. The West Novas, the Carleton and Yorks, and the Royal 22nd put in the attack, under the supporting fire of the Royal Canadian Horse Artillery. German observers in the hills beyond the town called in heavy mortar and artillery fire, forcing the Hasty Ps to withdraw from the area south of the town, where they were to support the attack. As the battle for the town raged, the RCRs captured the southern entrance, and the 48th Highlanders followed up with an attack that led to the capture of the town on the night of July 18. It was a difficult battle, and the victory was not without a heavy price: 40 killed and 105 wounded.

The fighting continued and intensified in the mountains around Valguarnera, and the number of casualties started to rise. The fighting by the Canadians was soon gaining notice, especially their effectiveness in the mountains. Field Marshal Kesselring reported them to Berlin as the "mountain boys." To be mentioned in dispatches is an honour, but to be mentioned in the enemy's dispatches is another distinction altogether. The Canadians were gaining a great reputation on the battlefield, but they were about to face their greatest challenge yet.

The next engagement for the Canadians was to the northeast. Along a high ridge the towns of Assoro and Leonforte perched, overlooking the steep approaches below. Elevated nearly one thousand feet, the two towns were able to control

Members of the PPCLI in action near Valguarnera.

The mountainous terrain included dangerous switchbacks that would expose the Canadians to the enemy.

all of the roads in the area. The roads up the steep inclines were long switchbacks, which precluded an advance along them since the troops would be exposed to long periods of enfilade fire.

The Canadians faced an impossible approach to the two towns, without cover up the steep approaches, and then once they got there the towns themselves had steep streets and alleys, making them very difficult to take as well. The initial assault would be impossible for the tanks, so the infantry would have to make the ascent on their own. The towns were a few kilometres apart, with Leonforte positioned near the ruins of a Norman castle that overlooked Assoro. The German position seemed impregnable, and the enemy held it in strength with all three battalions of the 104th Panzer Grenadier Regiment dug in and prepared to repel any attempt to take the stronghold. They controlled the road to Messina, and that had Montgomery's 8th Army at a standstill. It was up to the Canadians to clear the way so the advance could continue.

The only weakness for the Germans was the position above Assoro where the Norman castle stood. From there, the Allies would be able to fire down on Assoro and then be able to turn on Leonforte to attack. But this position was on top of a sheer cliff, one that the Germans considered impossible to scale.

Sydney Frost (Princess Patricia's Canadian Light Infantry)
Sicily is a very ancient island and its history goes back to the Romans and the Normans, and they built castles on all these hills, and the Germans of course would occupy them. What we had to do was to somehow get in behind and scale these mountains, and the Germans couldn't believe it could be done, so they hadn't looked to the rear, and that's the way we attacked them.

During the first week and a half of combat in Sicily, the action had been on a small scale, with isolated engagements of platoons or companies. The assault on Assoro and Leonforte would be the Canadians' first large-scale battle in Sicily. In the early hours of July 20, the 48th Highlanders crossed the Dittaino River south of Assoro and established a bridgehead. The riverbed was dry at that time of year, but the elevated riverbanks on both sides of the river created an obstacle for tanks and vehicles. They created a basin with steep sides, tough approaches, and a low, exposed centre. The embankments were under constant observation by the Germans. The RCRs moved through with Three Rivers tanks. The advance was stopped by accurate fire from Assoro, so movement was done under the cover of darkness. The Hasty Ps then advanced through the valley towards the sheer cliff below the Norman castle. They were led by Major Lord Tweedsmuir, the son of a former Governor General of Canada. Not only did they face the task of scaling what was considered an impossible cliff, they had to do it under the cover of darkness, and they had to complete the climb before daylight — otherwise the element of surprise would be lost, and the men trapped on the face of the cliff would be easy targets for the snipers in Assoro. Under the moonlight they followed donkey and goat paths and found a way to the cliff, which towered three hundred metres high. The climb was so hard that the mule carrying the radio dropped dead, but a Hasty P picked up the equipment and carried it the rest of the way. With that radio they would be able to direct the mortar and artillery fire on Assoro. Then the men ascended into the darkness, moving silently from one rock ledge to another. They passed weapons and supplies up to one another as they made the miraculous climb. The men moved up the cliff quickly and quietly — the slightest sound would give them all away. Not one man fell, nor was anything dropped. They managed the climb in just a few hours, and for the three German sentries at the Norman castle that morning, it was a rude awakening — one was killed and the other two captured very quickly.

While the Hasty Ps made their incredible climb, the 48th Highlanders silently approached Assoro. Rather than following the long switchback roads, they took the direct route and did some climbing of their own. They crossed the road and climbed the embankment to reach the road again as it circled back at a higher elevation. And so it went that night: climb, cross the road, climb, and cross the road again. The 48th Highlanders climbed the cliffs by standing on one another's shoulders and pulling one another up. At the crest of the ridge they waited for the signal to attack.

At daybreak on July 21 the tables had been turned on the Germans. They no longer held the high ground, and they were about to pay the price. Hidden in the ruins of the Norman castle five hundred Canadians waited. As the sunlight shone on Assoro, the Hasty Ps had a good view of the German defences. They called in the fire of the 25-pounders on the Germans, who quickly realized their predicament. After retaliating with some mortar and artillery, the Germans withdrew. Their position was exposed, and the element of surprise was completely in the Canadians' favour. Once the artillery barrage ended, the 48th Highlanders took the major road junction at the entrance of Assoro and held it while the armoured units drove up the lengthy switchback in relative safety. Once reinforced by the tanks, they moved into Assoro and swiftly seized the town. The Germans eventually put in a counterattack, but it was repelled, and Assoro was secure by noon on July 22. The casualties were relatively light for the Canadians in Assoro. The same could not be said for Leonforte.

As the battle raged in Assoro, the 2nd Brigade battled the Germans for Leonforte, a small village of only twenty thousand. The town was situated on top of a hill like Assoro, but with Leonforte, there was only one approach by which to attack. The Germans made the approach to the town very difficult since they had blown up the only bridge, leaving a wide ravine between the Canadians and them. Not to be denied, the Loyal Eddies climbed into the ravine and came up on the German side. From there they assaulted Leonforte, and it deteriorated into house-to-house fighting as the Loyal Eddies battled their way into the town's centre. The Germans countered with tanks and reinforcements, quickly surrounding the Canadians in the centre of Leonforte. The fighting went on through the night. From the other side of the ravine the rest of the 2nd Brigade watched helplessly, as they thought that they were watching the massacre of the Loyal Eddies. They couldn't shell the city to help them since no one knew their exact location. It seemed the regiment was lost. Then a miracle came in the form of a young boy who delivered a message from Lieutenant-Colonel Jefferson, the commanding officer (CO) of the Loyal Eddies. The men scrambled to save their desperate comrades. The 3rd Field Company rapidly constructed a fifteen-metre Bailey bridge to traverse the ravine. As soon as it was in place, the PPCLI climbed on board the tanks of the Three Rivers Regiment and raced across the bridge while under fire. The rapid assault caught the German guards at the entrance of the city by surprise, and they surrendered immediately. The PPCLI and the Three Rivers fought their way into the town and found the remaining members of the Loyal Eddies. Just as they arrived a German tank appeared, only to be blasted by the Three Rivers tank. Through such vicious fighting, Canadian heroes emerged. Captain Rowan Coleman of the PPCLI received the Military Cross for leading the rescue of the Loyal Eddies, and S.J. Cousins, also of the PPCLI, was recommended for the Victoria Cross for his bravery, but he died a few days later in action.

The fighting continued to rage in Leonforte, and by the end of the day on July 22 the town belonged to the Canadians. It had been a bloody fight, and it signalled a new resolve in the Germans. They were no longer content to slow down the Canadian advance; they were determined to hold their ground and to engage in close-quarter combat. Most likely they were ordered to, as Messina was getting congested with evacuating troops. But there was a lesson to be learned as well: the Canadians had overcome a virtually impregnable position through sheer determination, and the Germans knew that they had a fierce foe to reckon with.

Sydney Frost (Princess Patricia's Canadian Light Infantry)

One of the big problems was supplies — food and water and ammunition too. We realized very quickly that the Italians were with us, they were very helpful. They would tell us, "Tedeschi qui, tedeschi" — German there, German there — and so on. I very quickly got on to the Italian language and I was able to use it. My first thing would be when I entered a village, I'd say, "Dove tedeschi," which means, "Where are the Germans?" And they would come out and show me where they were, and this was a great help. And so we progressed from village to village, cleaning it up and going on like that. Tough campaign, we learned a lot.

Al Sellers (Governor General's Horse Guards)

It didn't take the Canadians long to work out their own little bit of language, you know like, "Petrol per carne," that's gas for meat … "petrol per vino" … "sigaretta" … and of course the kids would come up and try and peddle their sister off … "sesso per carne" … "for sigaretta." We didn't have much to do with the general population except when they tried to steal from us. We didn't barter for wine — I didn't bother with it because I did taste it, and it was no screaming heck to me.

Peter Routcliffe (Governor General's Horse Guards)

I wouldn't want to eat their food because they'd be making pasta and there'd be a million flies over it and the old lady would swish away the flies and keep kneading the dough with flies in it.

Joseph Reid (Calgary Regiment)

Our rations were only tin rations that we'd add water to and eat. The compo boxes were lettered A, B, C, D, or whatever, to indicate the different content, like carrots, soup, beets, or rabbit or something like that, or you get a beef stew. So you'd get a variety and there were countless boxes issued. They became a regular feature for well over six weeks or so. All the while we're in Sicily we warmed up the tins with boiling water … use a can opener and pour it into your mess tin and away you went.

With the capture of Assoro and Leonforte, the main road to Messina was now safe to use for Montgomery's 8th Army, and they resumed their advance. Meanwhile, Patton's army was hurtling along Sicily's northern shore towards Messina, forcing the Germans into the northeast corner of the island. For the Canadians, the route that lay ahead of them was along the main road between Catania and Palermo, with the objective of taking Nissoria, Agira, and Regalbuto.

The advance was slow, since the Germans had damaged the roads and bridges, so the men had to proceed on foot most of the time. They constantly faced harassment from German snipers, machine guns, and artillery. Major-General Simonds believed that the Germans would be in Agira, 123 kilometres east of Leonforte, and prepared to attack it with the 1st Brigade from the west. The 48th Highlanders led the way at midnight on July 22 but were ambushed by the Germans in Nissoria. The unexpected positioning of the Germans caused the Canadians to halt operations while a new plan was devised.

A group of Hasty Ps on board a universal carrier heading for Nissoria.

Gord Outhwaite (48th Highlanders)

I can remember we were going to clean this one house out and I said, "See if you can hit that door," and we hit the door all right. We went in, and we ran up to the top and started to clear our house out, and a friend of mine kicked one door open and there was a nice mirror there, so he let fly. He pulled the trigger and he blew the mirror all to hell, he was looking at himself, and he scared the hell out of himself! I'll tell you, if it wasn't for a little humour, it would be a terrible war, you would go crazy, because you're frightened all the time. You can't sit down and say, "Well, I'm going to go to sleep and I'll worry about the war tomorrow." You're awake all the time basically, and that takes its toll. I can see where a lot of people can get fatigue or confused and even fear — it can paralyze you. I have seen that in the middle of an attack and a fellow standing there with a perfectly operating weapon, and he can't fire a shot. He's frightened so bad he's paralyzed. So then finally you knock him down or something like that, and that breaks the spell.

Herb Pike (48th Highlanders)

Of course, that's where good training comes in. If a man is trained properly, you're not only trained how to operate weapons, you're trained psychologically. Fear can kill a man by him doing something that would be absolutely ludicrous.

Jeeps move past destroyed German vehicles in the Nissoria area.

Benito Mussolini, leader of the Fascists in Italy.

On July 24 the RCRs, the Malta Brigade (attached to the Canadians), and the Three Rivers tanks set out for Agira. Simonds was a former gunner, and his plan included the use of a creeping barrage. The artillery units were to lay down a barrage that would hit the area in front of the advancing troops, and it would advance two hundred metres every two minutes. Infantry are often wary of creeping barrages since any error would put them in the middle of the shelling. The problem on that day was that the artillery advanced faster than the infantry could march, giving the Germans the opportunity to return to their positions and fire on the advancing troops as they reached Nissoria.

As the Germans opened fire on the RCRs from the dominant ridgeline in the area, two companies took cover, as they were being devastated. The tanks of the Three Rivers Regiment proceeded without support and quickly lost ten tanks. Meanwhile, the other two companies moved around Nissoria along a gully and emerged behind the enemy. One of the companies under cover eventually moved around to join them. Not knowing that the Germans were defending Nissoria instead of practising their usual delaying tactics, the RCRs had outflanked the position without realizing it. Since they were not in communication with headquarters, Simonds came to the conclusion that he had lost the three companies. The Hasty Ps were sent in to attack Nissoria, and they were repelled. After a major artillery barrage, the Germans still held on to the town, and the 48th Highlanders took a crack at them. Then the 2nd Brigade was moved in, and for the next three days they engaged the enemy in a very intense battle. On the second day of fighting, the Allies were encouraged by the news on the radio: Benito Mussolini, the Fascist leader of Italy, had been deposed, leaving many to wonder how long Italy would stay in the

A tank of the Three Rivers Regiment roars through the streets of Agira.

Members of the PPCLI patrol the main street of Agira.

war. On July 26 the PPCLI cracked the German defences, and the Seaforth Highlanders exploited it to capture Nissoria and the hills south of Agira.

The day after Mussolini was deposed, Adolf Hitler decided to withdraw his troops from Sicily. The Germans were still determined to defend Italy, for no other reason than to protect Germany by keeping their enemies as far away as possible. On Sicily, the Germans continued to fight out of necessity to protect their withdrawal. For the Italian soldiers, it became increasingly apparent how futile their fight was, and the flood of prisoners giving themselves up to the Allies continued to grow.

As the fighting in Nissoria raged, the Loyal Eddies moved around Agira to take the hills north of the town, outflanking the Germans in the process. Meanwhile, the Seaforth Highlanders were given the task of capturing the main objective: a small mountain in the area. They scaled the one-hundred-metre cliff on one side of the mountain and took the Germans completely by surprise. The PPCLI fought their way into Agira, fighting the Germans street by street in a bitter battle. By July 28 the city was securely in Canadian hands. As it turned out, the battle for Nissoria and Agira was to be the biggest battle in Sicily for the Canadians: they used two brigades and they sustained 438 casualties in only five days. At the end of the battle a late afternoon thunderstorm rumbled overhead, spelling relief from the searing heat. It was the first rainfall since they had arrived in Sicily.

The campaign for Sicily was gradually winding down, but the fighting continued as the Germans desperately held onto every last defensive position that they could. They were squeezed around the base of Mount Etna in Adrano, Catenanuova, and Regalbuto. The final task for the Canadians in Sicily was to overcome the enemy positions in these towns and neutralize what was left of the enemy in the interior of Sicily. This would not be easy, as the Canadians

Beast of burden: mules were used to carry matériel *to the front, saving the men from the arduous task of carrying heavy equipment in the scorching heat.*

The PPCLI move through a barbed wire fence while advancing on Adrano in Sicily.

faced warfare in the open country, across rough terrain, without the benefit of transportation other than mules. The three Canadian brigades spread out and focused on separate objectives as they headed east. The Herman Goering Division held Regalbuto and Centuripe as the last defence before Adrano, which was key to the Mount Etna defensive line. The 1st Brigade headed for Regalbuto, which was being heavily bombed. The 2nd Brigade advanced through the Salso River valley, and the 3rd Brigade fought in the Dittaino River valley, taking Catenanuova on July 29.

Gord Outhwaite (48th Highlanders)

The Germans still had airplanes flying, and I remember in Regalbuto we had some friendly fire. Our own Allied forces, I won't say which one, they bombed us three days in a row at Regalbuto. I remember we were trying to get through, we had to borrow trucks and transport until we could be reimbursed for the stuff we lost. I remember I was on the back of this one truck and we were being bombed and I thought, "To heck

Members of the 48th Highlanders advance through a field en route to Adrano.

with this, they're going to see these trucks and they're going to bomb them." So I fell off the darn thing. I just rolled, and I said, "Well, if they get the truck they're not going to get me." Then I suddenly realized that they're dropping the bombs all over the place. I had to run and get back on the truck. We got out of there all right.

With the Germans still in possession of two nearby mountains, entry into Regalbuto was impossible. Assaults were launched against the two mountains by the British and the Maltese. By the end of the day on July 31 the mountains were secure, as was the road. The 48th Highlanders took possession of the positions that night. That same evening the RCRs were moved into position to launch an attack on Tower Hill just east of Regalbuto, as it was of strategic importance for any assault on the town. Tower Hill rose above the town and would provide an advantage to whoever held the position. The RCRs had just arrived in the area and were not given time to do an adequate reconnaissance of the situation when they were ordered to put in an attack. The attack was delayed; then, when the men went into the deep ravine, they were pinned down by heavy fire. They were trapped there throughout the day without water in the merciless sun, able to withdraw only once darkness enshrouded them. The next night the Hasty Ps were sent in on the same mission, but they had been given time for a proper reconnaissance, and the results were successful. There was one last mountain to seize before an assault on Regalbuto could take place. On August 2 the Hasty Ps took Mount Tiglio while the 48th Highlanders simultaneously entered Regalbuto. Mount Tiglio was cleared within a half-hour, whereas Regalbuto was found deserted by the Germans. All that was left was a demolished town.

Gord Outhwaite (48th Highlanders)
Well, we had some resistance and it got less and less, and by the time we got up to the straits, they had gone, they had withdrawn. Once we took the airport and Regalbuto the fight was pretty well over. Well, any battle is severe because those bullets hurt, but there wasn't that much really.

The Canadians had not seen such devastation in the war. Not a single building was undamaged, and rubble blocked the streets. The once lovely town in the shadow of Mount Etna lay in a shambles, and there was an eerie silence. No one was around: the inhabitants had left to escape the incessant bombing and were hidden in the hills. The people would return, but not much was left of their town.

Early in August the Canadians continued to move east, clearing the Troina Valley along with a few of the German positions left in the area. On August 6 the Canadian troops were put in reserve and transferred to the Lentini area on Sicily's east coast for a well-deserved rest. Since the landing on July 10, they had marched two hundred kilometres in

Sherman tanks of the Three Rivers Regiment roll through the ruins of Regalbuto.

A Canadian Sherman tank crosses a ditch and moves into action.

sweltering heat, enduring unsanitary conditions that led to various diseases. Thousands were hospitalized due to the horrible conditions in Sicily, not just due to wounds inflicted by their enemy. In a period of four weeks they had forged a new identity for the Canadian military through great victories while battling through the most challenging terrain in Sicily. In their first combat experience since Dieppe, they had done themselves proud. It was not without a painful price. In that time, they had suffered 2,310 casualties, including 562 killed.

Joseph Reid (Calgary Regiment)
We had two or three weeks of doing nothing, so we organized a field day. The three armoured units had a ball team, and they rode donkey races and all that stuff.

For the next eleven days the Americans and British continued their race to Messina, with Patton arriving just hours before Montgomery on August 17. The invasion of Sicily was complete, and it was a great success for the Allies.

Sydney Frost (Princess Patricia's Canadian Light Infantry)
Sicily was occupied in thirty-five days. Phenomenal! That was the original launch of the attack against Europe, without that we could never have put on D-Day in Europe without horrendous casualties. It is very doubtful that they would have succeeded because the Germans would have had all these extra reinforcements from Sicily facing us in Normandy. Then, of course, we had a toehold from which we could get air bases to bomb southern Germany and southern Italy. It was a very significant operation.

For the Allies, the first stage was complete. They were now ready for the next stage: the invasion of Italy.

THE INVASION OF ITALY

THE INVASION OF ITALY WAS NOT always a part of the plan for the Allies. The Americans had not agreed to move beyond Sicily until just before the invasion (during the Trident Conference in May 1943), and it wasn't until the Quebec Conference in August that the Allies finally decided on specific objectives in Italy. They eyed the airfields in Foggia as the launching site of an aerial assault on Austria and central Europe. They also wanted to maintain the momentum that they had gained in Sicily. With 1 million soldiers stationed just eight kilometres away from Italy, the Allies were poised to overrun one of the Axis powers. The debate over fighting the war in Italy stemmed from the conflicting goals of the campaign. While the intention of the operation was to keep the German forces in Italy, the ultimate goal was to run them out of the country. Some military leaders felt that this paradox made the overall plan unclear and subject to failure.

To confuse the situation even more, the Italian government had representatives approach the Allies to discuss switching sides. The debate was over the timing of the Italian announcement, which dragged on for some time. Whether it was official or not, the Italians were clearly through with the Germans, and they would not pose a threat to the invading Allied armies.

Sydney Frost (Princess Patricia's Canadian Light Infantry)
I ended up in hospital with malaria. I started to feel very weak, with temperatures ranging from 105 degrees down to 98, and I refused to be evacuated. At last I had a wonderful job with the battalion as the scout officer and I wanted to hold onto it. But the CO said, "No, you go down and get metracine and you'll be back." But I didn't get back to the regiment for about four or five weeks. I had an awful dose of malaria and they took me to a hospital in Catania. I must say that was pretty nice because it was staffed by Canadian nursing sisters, our angels of mercy. So I missed the Sicily invasion, now I miss the invasion of Italy, and I was pretty downhole about the whole thing. But I soon got over it. The tender loving care from the sisters took care of that!

On September 3, 1943, the invasion of Italy began with the Canadian 1st Division, the British 5th Division, and the 1st Canadian Army Tank Brigade crossing the Strait of Messina to the toe of Italy. The American 5th Army would land in the Gulf of Salerno on September 9, and the 1st British Airborne Division would land in the Taranto area. The plan was for the three groups to link up and then advance north to seize Naples before moving on to Rome.

The 1st Division was to land near Reggio di Calabria, with the West Novas and the Carleton and Yorks leading the way. In the early hours of September 3 the men loaded onto the landing craft of the Royal Canadian Navy's 80th Canadian LSM Flotilla, and the craft moved out to sea, lining up for the run into shore. As the craft

Above: *Members of the 3rd Canadian Infantry Brigade on board a landing craft, ready to invade Italy at Reggio di Calabria.*

Top left: *Canadian troops make an amphibious landing at Reggio di Calabria.*

Bottom left: *The landing at Reggio di Calabria in the early hours of September 3, 1943, faced minimal opposition.*

Left: *Landing craft and amphibious vehicles on the beach in Italy.*

Above: *Members of the PPCLI land at Reggio di Calabria.*

quietly traversed the strait, the silence was shattered as the Allied guns unleashed a massive artillery barrage. Under this deafening rain of destruction they moved in towards the shoreline. The craft ran up onto the beaches and the ramps were quickly lowered, exposing the Canadians to … empty beaches. They found that the Italian soldiers had left their defensive positions and hidden in the countryside. Even the German division in the area had been withdrawn to a defensive line in the mountains a few days earlier, so the Canadians had an easy start to the invasion. The Canadian battalions formed up and began to move inland while more and more craft landed, delivering the rest of the 1st Division. The West Novas, the Carleton and Yorks, and the Vandoos expanded the beachhead, and so began several days of advancement through the Aspromonte region.

Gord Outhwaite (48th Highlanders)

The farther up we went, the tougher it got. Of course, by that time we had the opportunity to experience good times and bad times and really hard times. You'd say, "Well, okay, it's getting a little worse here so we have to do a little bit more, and if we're going to stay alive we've got to do something more," which we did. You're only a kid and you can run up and down these hills like you wouldn't believe, and you don't realize it, but this is fear. When you're scared you run and you'll be surprised at what you can do. The adrenaline always comes up, and you run like hell, and you get to where you're going. When you get there you can actually fight because you conserved all this energy, you're healthy. We were well trained.

An early casualty in Italy. Initially losses in Italy were light, but that soon changed as the Canadians moved north.

On the day of the invasion, Marshal Pietro Badoglio signed the documents for Italy's unconditional surrender to the Allies. Hitler had anticipated this turn of events, and his men were ordered to take over the country and to defend the airfields and Rome. The fact that Italy surrendered only made things more difficult for the Allied soldiers, as they were going to face highly disciplined professional German soldiers in every engagement from that point on.

The first few days found the Canadians advancing fairly quickly, despite pockets of resistance and the Germans' frustrating technique of a fighting withdrawal. Sabotaging roads and bridges, they left a trail of mines and booby traps to hinder and harm the Canadians. Try as they might, the Germans could not stop the Canadian pursuit as it wound along the Calabrian coast towards the Gulf of Taranto. The men trudged on, negotiating the treacherous roads through the mountains.

Gord Outhwaite (48th Highlanders)

We had the battle at Montesoro. We came into a little copse, a dozen or so trees, and they had this radio equipment. It was quite a set — big — but it was on. So naturally we were saying, "Don't anybody touch this radio — don't touch anything. That's left on there for a reason." So somebody got inquisitive and went over and picked up the mic, and right off the bat the Germans knew we were there. They left it there just so that we would tamper with it and give them a clear message, and the shells came in like rain! I'll tell you, it was something else. They hit some carriers, and we didn't even have time to dig a slit trench, and you'd be surprised how your fingers can work, I'll tell you! The smoke was so thick, the cordite and everything. And there was this one fellow said, I could hear him, he said, "I'm hurt, I'm hit." I said, "Okay, where are you hit?" and I reached out to touch him and I put my hand right in where he got hit and all that warm blood, and I thought, "Oh God." So I wrapped him up and said, "Well, I've got to get him out of here." Fortunately there was a bit of a tunnel, so I got him into that. There was another guy that was hit. We finally got out of there. They had a runner, this was hilarious, his name was Gordie Lake, and he picked up this bicycle — now we're on a mountainside, for Pete's sake! He said he'll make time on this bicycle, and he started to come down and the chain comes off and he couldn't stop the damn thing. So he was going down this hill and he was going, "Holy hell, where [am I] going?" And of course he almost kills himself on this darn bicycle.

He said, "There's thousands of them, there's thousands of them up there!" By the time we fought our way up, well, they started to withdraw. We were very fortunate. There was a huge house at the top of the hill where we had a little bit of a party afterwards. There was this Italian fellow and he was speaking in broken English and we're speaking in broken Italian and how we understood each other, I'll never know. We did.

As the Canadians advanced, the American 5th Army landed in Salerno, where it faced a determined German division. In complete contrast to the Canadian landing, the American and British division attached to the 5th Army had a terrible time getting ashore.

Lloyd Williams (Royal Canadian Navy)
The Salerno landing was much more difficult than the Sicily landing in that when we were sailing from North Africa with troops up to Salerno, Italy capitulated, and a lot of the troops and their officers — we were carrying Americans there — they thought the war was over. Looking around, the best beach where they could do any help was Salerno, and it was well fortified by German troops. So when we were going in there we got quite a pasting — there were quite a few troops shot on the beach. I remember quite vividly one of the commanding officers leaving my boat was shot two steps off the boat, and killed. Just stopped right there. So we knew we were in a war, in an opposed landing there. It took quite a bit of time for the Allied troops to move off the beachhead because of the firepower from the Germans. People say, "Were you scared?" and I don't think we were. I think we were too bloody interested in protecting ourselves and getting the job done and get[ting] the hell out of there. We knew we had to come back in, so we were back and forth all day and we were under fire. They were really working on the army on the beach by this time, they weren't after us. In fact, I don't think they would because we had a fleet of cruisers and destroyers that were throwing a lot of stuff at them. So if they started to bombard the landing craft coming in they would have been picked up pretty quickly. So we were pretty well looked after.

The battle around Salerno would go on for six days, with elements of the 8th Army becoming involved as well.

Lloyd Williams (Royal Canadian Navy)
We went back to Algiers and we picked up the 1st United States Army Medical Corps, with all the doctors and nurses and their hospitals and all this stuff. We took them into Naples. That was not too onerous,

that one. That was more of a cruise. Then from there we went back to the U.K. and went into training for LCILs — the landing craft infantry large. The ships are quite big, they're sea-going ships, landing craft. They can carry up to three hundred fully armed troops. We trained on them from January '44 until June, when we made the assault on Normandy.

By September 10 the Canadians had reached Catanzaro, covering 120 kilometres in just one week. They then turned north to head towards the Americans at Salerno in order to link the beachhead together. On September 12, it was announced that Mussolini had been rescued from his prison in Gran Sasso d'Italia by German troops, and soon after he was installed as the leader of Italy once again. With two governments in place, Italy fell into a civil war that pitted Fascists against Partisans. Italian Fascism had been born in the north, where the wealthy landowners lived. The concept was not embraced in the south, whose inhabitants were looked down upon by their northern countrymen. The arrival of the Allies allowed the south to battle the north in a virtual class war. The result was two simultaneous wars being waged in Italy — separate, for the most part, but with some crossover of activities.

Ready for action: the Vandoos prepare to land at Villapiana.

Herb Pike (48th Highlanders)

As you gradually get up the boot, things start to improve and the language — the dialect — changes. People become a little more European, and as a matter of fact the northern Italian looks upon the southern Italian as Mediterranean. The northern Italian is a European. Actually the whole thing is Europe, of course, but that's the chain of thought as far as the Italian populace was concerned. But as you got further up your conditions that you fight under are different because your terrain becomes a little more built-up. The towns would become modern, and things are vastly different than it was in the south of Italy.

As the 5th Army took control of Salerno, it needed to expand its beachhead. Again they met stiff German resistance, so the Canadians sent a brigade to capture Potenza, just east of Salerno. This strategic town controlled the roads in the area and would give the 5th Army the assistance that it needed to break out. The West Novas and the Calgary Regiment set out on an arduous trek through minefields and around demolished bridges. Once at Potenza they battled the German paratroopers that held the town, taking it on September 20. The next day the Allies linked up to form a front line that spanned the peninsula from Bari to Salerno, giving them control of southern Italy.

The Canadians continued to suffer from the harsh conditions and the endemic diseases. Major-General Simonds was incapacitated by jaundice while in Potenza, leading to Brigadier Vokes being put in command of the Canadian contingent in Italy.

Members of the Saskatoon Light Infantry (MG) man their position near Potenza with their machine gun ready.

The rolling terrain of Italy created breathtaking vistas and strategic strongholds all the way up the peninsula. A Calgary Regiment crewmember observes Potenza from a hill during the advance.

A group of West Novas enjoy a ride on a Calgary Regiment tank while advancing from Villapiana to Potenza.

Sydney Frost (Princess Patricia's Canadian Light Infantry)

You know Italy has a central range of mountains and all the rivers run across laterally, and there's dozens of them. So they had to cross one river after another, and the Germans would blow all the bridges and so it was very difficult to advance, and it took them a long time to go from the toe of Sicily up to the place where I finally caught up with them at Potenza. That was about five hundred miles away, but I commandeered a truck, and our Italian driver — his name was Joe — well, he wasn't a very good driver. We're going through the mountain passes — now these are snaky — and he wasn't paying much attention and all of a sudden he pulls around a bend and there's a donkey and a cart in the middle of the road. There was only two choices: either hit the donkey or you headed off the mountain into the air — well, he tried a third course. He swung to the right and then back to the left, and it was no use — he cleaned out the donkey and the cart — although the cart driver escaped. "Sorry boss," he said. So the cart driver of course was very upset. I paid him a few hundred lire and that seemed to help. We tore off the bumper and the fender of the truck that were badly damaged, and I took over and I was the driver for the rest of the day and we finally got safely to our objective.

Medics and stretcher-bearers showed great bravery tending the wounded, often becoming casualties themselves. Captain A.W. Hardy (Medical Officer, West Nova Scotia Regiment) is tended to by Private W.E. Dexter (stretcher-bearer), who was also wounded in the head, near Santa-Cristina D'Aspromonte.

Late in September the Germans decided on their plan for defending Italy. Hitler was concerned about keeping northern Italy under his control due to its industrial assets and its strategic thoroughfare to Greece and the Balkans. Field Marshal Erwin Rommel was given the responsibility of safeguarding it for the Reich. The south was under Kesselring's command, and it was up to him to hold back the Allied advance as best as possible. He was determined not to give up an inch without a fight, and so the Italian Campaign slowed down to a crawl. The Germans began to prepare defensive lines throughout Italy, spanning the peninsula from coast to coast. The Allies were facing a difficult task: each time they breached a line, there would be another one just beyond it.

Early in October the Allies broke out from their positions in the south, with the Americans taking Naples and the British seizing the key objective of the Foggia airfield.

The advance north by the Allies was divided by the Apennine mountain range, with the Americans on the west pushing towards Rome and the British on the east heading for Pescara before moving west to surround the Italian capital.

The Canadians moved across the Foggia plains and headed west

V.C. Northey of the RCA loading shells near Campobasso.

Calling back directions for the artillery, members of the 1st Field Regiment stationed in a Forward Observation Post zero in on the German positions near Potenza.

for their objective, Campobasso. They advanced through the Apennines facing the Germans, who were in their familiar position on the high ground. Just like in Sicily, the men faced obstacles, shelling, and deadly fields of fire. When they prepared to assault the German position, the enemy was gone, having moved on to the next defensive position.

D.B. MacDonald of the RCRs carrying a Bren gun into battle near Campobasso.

Sydney Frost (Princess Patricia's Canadian Light Infantry)

We weren't really given any objective, just to get on with it. So I was given the wonderful job of scout and sniper officer. Now this was something new, dreamt up by that headhunting guy, General Chris Vokes. His one idea was to "get the bastards," get forward quick and don't waste any time — just get moving. I was the first scout officer of the Princess Patricias and I'm very proud of that. I had thirty desperadoes, they were wonderful in action, these men, but very poor in discipline. So you had to keep them active and they just loved to be out in front, running around trying to find where the Germans were. We would go out before the battalion made any attack and scout the routes. We did that for three or four hundred miles. Good fun, if you survived.

Joseph Reid (Calgary Regiment)

Across the whole foot we had to go from the toe and then to the heel. The first military tank battle was on the Plains of Foggia. It was a wide open plain and there we ran into the German tanks, and going up the Adriatic side was a rough job. We weren't involved in too many battles as such in very early days of the Italian Campaign. The Ontario and Three Rivers were more of the lead units through that time period. But once we got into the Campobasso area we did.

On October 1 the Canadians fought their first battle in Italy at Motta. The mobile nature of the campaign in Italy began to disappear as the Germans began to resist. The RCRs and Calgary Regiment fought a fierce battle to clear the town, which needed to be secured before the division could progress towards Camposbasso.

Sydney Frost (Princess Patricia's Canadian Light Infantry)

En route we passed places like Foggia, Troia, Castelfranco, Alberona, San Bartolomeo — quite a battle there. Cercemaggiore, la Rocca — immense mountains on top of which was a castle — and finally

E.H. Pruner of the Hasty Ps carries both a PIAT and a Thompson machine gun while advancing near Motta.

The Hasty Ps advance through the town of Motta.

Irene Roy of the Vandoos distributes the men's ration of rum while they man their positions along the main road between Gildone and Campobasso.

Campobasso, and that was the route we took. It took about a month, maybe three weeks for us to travel this, because there were firefights all the way along. The Germans would blow the bridge, we'd approach it and then we'd charge them off, and then we had to build a bridge so we could cross over it. It was strenuous work, and dangerous.

The fighting moved from one ridge to another, with very little cover available for the Canadians. The Germans had the major advantage of being well acquainted with the terrain, while the Canadians faced a possible ambush at every turn. From their mountaintop vantage points, the Germans could deny the advance of any force within their

line of sight. With few roads available and fortresses that were difficult to attack, the Germans made the most of their advantages. Five days and thirty kilometres later, the 1st Brigade arrived at the Fortore River. They battled the Germans at Monte San Marco and Carlantino, clearing those strongholds before they continued their advance. It would take another week to reach Campobasso. It was a frustrating way to fight a war.

Adding to the problems of the men was the fact that the radios they were issued were not dependable, and they were practically useless in the Apennines. These factors left units isolated and in fear of being cut off or outflanked. It led to units fighting more by using individual initiative rather than as a part of a grander plan. Canadians proved time and again that their determination and ability to improvise was a valuable asset in such a war.

Top left: *As the advance slowed down, combat was small in scale. J.E. McPhee of the Seaforth Highlanders works as a sniper to dislodge the enemy while facing mortar fire.*

Bottom left: *RCA members prepare to fire their 17-pounder at a German position near Campobasso.*

Right: *A Regimental Aid Party bravely moves a wounded soldier from the battlefield while under fire.*

Holding their ears while firing a mortar, three Canadians blast Germans in the Sangro area.

Herb Pike (48th Highlanders)

I joined the 48th Highlanders just around the Campobasso campaign. It was the start of the hot and heavy stuff, and from there on it really got heavy.

Early on October 13, the 48th Highlanders were within a couple of kilometres of Campobasso when some of the men ran into a few Germans in a nearby town. The ensuing battle alerted the Germans at Campobasso to the close proximity of the Allies, and they responded with heavy shellfire.

Joseph Reid (Calgary Regiment)

It was a military combined forces operation with infantry involved to a great degree. Campobasso was in the hills, which didn't lend itself to movement, and we were sort of a secondary influence there, but it was good for the Canadians — they finally took it. The tanks, rather than filling a tank role, they were used as a close-up artillery role. Usually the observation posts were church spires or some damn thing like that, and we'd always shoot the thing out.

The RCRs and the Hasty Ps soon arrived, and the 1st Brigade prepared to attack the town on the morning of October 14. The RCRs led the attack, only to find that the Germans had already left. Before long Campobasso became a recreation centre for Canadian soldiers on leave; it was soon dubbed Maple Leaf City by some, and Canada Town by others.

Three Canadians move in on a German sniper's hideout in the Matese Mountains, ready to blast him with a grenade.

Top left: *Not all the river crossings were difficult, as some were quite shallow until the rains came. Here a tank from the Ontario Regiment's A Squadron makes a crossing near Colle d'Anchise.*

Centre left: *A group of Canadian soldiers help push a vehicle through some deep mud during the advance near Torella.*

Bottom left: *Canadian soldiers carry Ronnie Leather of the Three Rivers Regiment on a stretcher after being hit in a tank that he commanded near Termoli.*

Right: *The narrow streets of Italy were a death trap that the Canadians had to battle through. Here the men of the Carlton and York Regiment advance slowly through Campochiaro while facing sniper fire.*

The next day the 2nd Brigade finished a tough march through the Italian countryside and captured Vinchiatura, which was located near Campobasso. The Germans were in retreat, and the Canadians continued to pursue them to the Biferno River. Meanwhile, Canadian tank units assisted the British in their assault on Termoli and participated in the push to the Sangro River. The next step for the Canadians was to dislodge the Germans from their positions on the far side of the Biferno River. On October 19 the RCRs took Busso, while the Carleton and Yorks worked they way across rugged terrain for six days before attacking Boiano and capturing it on October 24 after an exhausting ordeal. At Colle d'Anchise and Spinete there was a pitched battle as the Loyal Eddies and the PPCLI launched an assault and took the two towns. Further along the river the 1st Brigade faced a daunting task: the villages of Roccaspromonte and Castropignano, situated on top of a steep incline overlooking a nearby river and the towns of Molise and Torella. On October 24 the RCRs attacked Roccaspromonte and Castropignano, finding the first deserted by the Germans, and then taking the second after a small skirmish. On October 26 the 48th Highlanders and the Ontario Regiment advanced on Torella and faced stiff resistance from the Germans, who then withdrew that night. The Canadians entered Torella on October 27. Meanwhile, the Hasty Ps made a tough advance and arrived in Molise.

Smoke rising in the hills where the PPCLI advance near Spinete.

The Canadians faced many river crossings during the Italian Campaign. Here a vehicle uses a temporary bridge to advance over the Biferno River.

Royal Canadian Artillery personnel firing a 25-pounder near Torella.

L.G. Kenny of the RCRs providing cover from a balcony in Castropignano.

Sydney Frost (Princess Patricia's Canadian Light Infantry)

We were to have a very nice leave at Campobasso, but just before we arrived there my luck finally ran out. I was told to take a patrol to a little town called Frosolone about eight miles in front of the battalion and report back what the enemy's situation was. So I had done this hundreds of times before without any trouble, but I didn't like this one because number one, it was in daylight; number two, there was no cover and we didn't know really where the Germans were. So of course you accept orders and you carry on. As I approached this little hamlet with my thirty men, I had a funny feeling, and my sergeant — Sergeant Slimkowitch, a real character, he had been in the Spanish Civil War — and he says, "Sir, I can smell Germans all around, but I can't see them." And I said, "I'm inclined to agree with you." So we held a little O group [an orders group] and I split my little command up into three sections. One would go into this town on the right, one on the left, and I would go in the centre. There in front was the first outlying building about sixty yards away. I stood up to attack and wham! I'm on my back, and I can't believe it. And another wham, and then I realized that I'd been hit. There was actually a company of Germans — they were very cute about this. They didn't let us know anything about it until we were right there, and I could just see them smirking to this day — we're going to get those guys, all thirty of them — but they didn't, they only got me. I was badly wounded in the face. My men put up a terrific fight and they helped me get out. I could walk, but I was very tired from losing all this blood. I marched back eight miles with my face in that condition, and then they took me by ambulance to the nearest hospital. It was called a maxilla-facial wound, and the problem was I lost a considerable part of my jaw. The Canadians didn't have hospitals in those days to cope with that sort of thing — plastic surgery, it was almost unknown. So they transferred me

M.D. White of the Loyal Eddies views the valley below through a hole that was blasted through a wall. Below, Canadian troops advanced near Colle d'Anchise.

to a British hospital in Bari, Italy, and they did some preliminary work — for instance they put the teeth together and bound them up with wire and that sort of thing to hold the jaw in place. They shipped me down to a hospital in Algeria. Well, that was very nice to get out of the war zone, I suppose, but it was a filthy, dirty place. This was an old rundown shack, really. There were window frames but no windowpanes, they were open, and so the flies came in and the Arabs came in and grabbed your stuff. I was there for about two months waiting to get a ship back to England where I could get some surgery done. The Lady Nelson, a Canadian ship, finally came around and picked me and other Canadians up and took us back to England. Then I got into Basingstoke, a plastic surgery hospital in England. Wonderful, talented doctors — and they did a great job on me, fixed me up. What they had to do was to take a bone out of my hip and put it in my jaw. Years later my wife would kid me that I had the jawbone of an ass! So I was out of it, I didn't get back for six months. It wasn't until October or November that I got back into action again.

By the end of the month the Germans had withdrawn to the Sangro River, and on November 1 the Canadians were relieved by the British and moved to the rear to reinforce the units that had been thinned out by the sixty-three days of continual fighting.

Albert Wade of the Royal Canadian Dragoons, 2006.

Albert Wade (Royal Canadian Dragoons)

I was a member of the Royal Canadian Dragoons. I was an NCO [non-commissioned officer], and we were detailed to go into reconnaissance work. Eventually we ended up going to Sicily. It was in the latter part of November, the weather had got a little cool. We had attacks from the German Air Force during our crossing of the Mediterranean to our destination, and one of our ships got hit. We lost quite a few Canadian hospital staff and nurses. We landed and we were immediately taken by truck to Siracusa. We set up a camp there and a headquarters at an Italian college, and we were there through Christmas of 1943.

While the men of the 1st Division enjoyed their break, they would soon find out that their ranks were about to grow. Canada decided to expand its commitment to the Italian Campaign, and on November 5, Lieutenant-General H.D.G. Crerar arrived along with the headquarters of the 1st Canadian Corps, the 5th Armoured Division, and the corps' support staff.

Fred Scott (Perth Regiment)

I went on the J.C. Fredericton and we went out into the middle of the Atlantic Ocean. Well, we were given the understanding that we were going for further training in Northern Ireland, but we went down into the middle of the Atlantic and we set there for two or three days. They were building up a convoy, and then all of a sudden we sailed for Italy. Our first attack came as we were going through the Strait of Gibraltar. This convoy had to break down into twos to go through the Strait of Gibraltar, and that's when the German dive-bombers attacked us. The ship ahead of me had a friend of mine from the town

The Italian stone houses were particularly solid, but the odd blast hole would create a sheltered position to fight from. J.A. Robb of the Loyal Eddies holds his position at Colle d'Anchise.

81

of Mitchell, just west of Stratford, that was on that ship. It was sunk that night, and it carried a lot of our medical supplies. But anyway, we ended up going right straight in through Naples.

Al Sellers (Governor General's Horse Guards)
We're finally going to go to war. We were told that the enemy's going to be putting up a stiff resistance, and how to handle the local population and so on. Not to upset them and whatnot.

H.W. Allen, J.H. Carmoey, A. Budd, A.J. Webster, and C. Johnston of the 7th Light Anti-Aircraft Regiment prepare to disembark at Catania.

Peter Routcliffe (Governor General's Horse Guards)
Everybody was frustrated a long, long time waiting for the word to come for action, when they sent us to Algiers. They put us in the boat, sent us to Camp Ferdinand in Algiers. The advance guard had already gone off to Italy to get everything ready for us. The main body of troops was left in Camp Ferdinand, and there was the Lord Strathcona's Horse, the BCDs [British Columbia Dragoons], and [Governor General's] Horse Guards were all in one big area. From Camp Ferdinand we went up to Naples.

Thousands of Canadians arrived in various ports in southern Italy, ready to play their part in the campaign. The armoured brigade included the Lord Strathcona's Horse, the 8th New Brunswick Hussars, and the British Columbia Dragoons. The 11th and 12th Brigades were motorized infantry units from all across Canada. They included the Cape Breton Highlanders, the Perth Regiment, the Irish Regiment, the Princess Louise Dragoon Guards, and the Westminster Regiment. The Governor General's Horse Guard (Sherman tanks) and the Royal Canadian Dragoons (armoured car unit) were also part of the 5th Division. With such a large contingent committed to the Mediterranean theatre, most Canadians back home had either a family member or a neighbour involved in the Italian Campaign. For now, the eyes of the nation were on this pivotal battleground.

Al Sellers (Governor General's Horse Guards)

When the boats docked there was so much sunk — cranes and boats — that they had made sort of a dock out of all this stuff, it was like a bridge, that's how you get to the mainland. We got off the Cameronian *and we marched up through Naples and it was filth! Disgusting to me. The smells. And the little kids, they were such a shame to see them — ragged clothes, dirty. So we got out of Naples and we got into a camp and we stayed there a couple of weeks. Then the equipment started to trickle in, and it was a letdown because the fighting regiments had to have theirs first. All the fighting regiments in our division, like the British Columbia Dragoons, the Lord Strathcona Horse, and the New Brunswick Hussars — they would naturally have the first choice of the tanks.*

Top left: *All forms of sea-going vessels were used as troop transports during the war.*

Bottom left: *Berthing card for the* Cameronian, *1943. This was one Canadian's ticket from England to Italy to become a part of Canadian military history.*

Peter Routcliffe (Governor General's Horse Guards)

Our second or third night down there everybody had a pup tent given to them and they were two men to a pup tent. Dug a hole about two feet deep and then put the pup tent over it, and they were just like a room. There were a lot of guys that used to get intoxicated with the charcoal burners because they used to heat their tents with it.

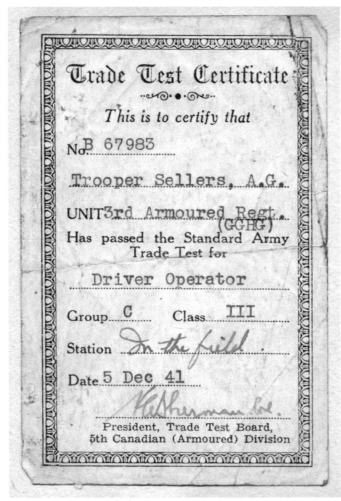

Certification card for operating a tank for the 5th Division.

Al Sellers (Governor General's Horse Guards)

The range of a Sherman tank was only 100 to 150 miles. Well, that's in top gear. But you get these damn things crawling around at about five miles an hour and zigzagging and getting stuck and you go through a lot of gas. Those things would hold a couple of hundred gallons of eighty-octane gas, but you go through a lot of gas. I can always remember the truck pulling up alongside my tank. We used to have these four- or five-gallon cans and it would be nothing to unload a whole twenty-five or thirty of these cans and we'd have to load the tanks up again.

Up to early November the Germans had been willing to concede territory to the Allies, but only after inflicting losses on them. For more than seven hundred kilometres the Germans had conducted a fighting retreat that allowed for a certain amount of mobility to the campaign. That was to change, as the Germans had prepared the Winter Line across Italy, reaching from Gaeta to Ortona. The line was a series of obstacles, minefields, and machine gun posts strung together in mutually supporting positions. The Germans exploited the advantages that the high ground provided them and meant to deny the Allies access to Rome and beyond. As the Americans pushed up the west side of Italy towards Rome and stalled at the line, Montgomery conceived a plan that would capture all of the glory for himself. His plan would have the British race up the east side of the peninsula to Pescara and turn west to cut in behind the German defences facing the Americans, and then Montgomery would lead the troops into Rome, liberating the Eternal City. Ahead lay the Sangro River, and beyond that was terrain that would allow for a rapid advance. There was only one thing that Montgomery could not plan for: the weather. The rains began to fall in Italy, and they did not stop. It was heavy, it was unceasing, and it created two new obstacles for the Allies: flooding and mud.

Albert Wade (Royal Canadian Dragoons)
The roads mostly were unpaved, except for some of the main highways. When you got in the centre of Italy where the mountains are, very few roads were paved. Some of the roads leading in and out of the hills were paved, but not very many. They were just clay roads. Moving in and out of the different areas was all right as long as it stayed dry. When you got rain, snow, or anything like that, moving about was rather hard.

Al Sellers (Governor General's Horse Guards)
Italy was very, very poor tank country. When it rained, we mired down. It's not as if the 8th Army was repeating the war with the desert. They had flat and mostly undulating ground, but not wet stuff. When we were bogged down, we turned into infantry.

In advance of the assault across the Sangro River, the Canadians were to clear the area along the front all the way up to the river's edge. The 3rd Brigade made the ninety-six-kilometre advance constantly facing obstacles as the Germans left a path of destruction in their wake. After great effort the Canadians cleared the way for the British to cross the Sangro River on the night of November 19. It was a miserable night, and the British 78th Division was driven back by a determined German counterattack. A successful crossing and development of a bridgehead on the far shore would take a week.

The Sangro River became the first of a series of major river crossings in Italy. The countryside was a series of one river after another, all flowing from the central mountain range into the sea. In the summer these rivers were dry, but they still presented a problem. The riverbanks were steep and provided the Germans with natural defensive positions: they would fire from the high ground and could have a clear shot at all of the advancing Allied troops. The Allies would have to face fire going over the crest of the near riverbank, then cross the flat riverbed without any cover, only to face the steep riverbank on the far side while Germans were simply dropping hand grenades over the edge onto them. Tanks could not support these assaults, as they could not handle the steep grade of the banks. In the winter the problem was of a completely different nature. The rains fell heavily in the mountains, turning the rivers into dangerous torrents that would often flood over the banks. Once again the tanks could not help, this time due to the mud that turned the banks into a quagmire. Crossing the river was dangerous, as the swift current would sweep the men away or make the landings inaccurate. Getting bridges across was risky, and sometimes a bridge would become engulfed by the flood water. The water would also be ice cold in the winter, adding even greater risk to anyone who tried to wade across or who might fall in. Men were lost in river crossings not only to enemy bullets but also to drowning. River crossings were a dangerous operation at any time of the year, and along the Adriatic coast the Allies faced a series of deep river valleys. After each difficult crossing they would advance a couple of kilometres and then have to repeat the process all over again.

Sergeant Jimmy Walker gets help from W.J. Black in getting his motorcycle out of the thick mud that hampered all movement in Italy during the fall and winter.

The mud in Italy would bog down the Canadian vehicles, eliminating vital support for the infantry at the front and virtually stalling the advance.

Sydney Frost (Princess Patricia's Canadian Light Infantry)
Can you imagine coming to a river — all the forests have been cleaned into what they call the killing ground, and the Germans are very good at that. They cleaned out all the bush, all the houses to create the perfect fields of fire. How would you like to attack in that situation: in the rain, in the mud, with no

support — suicide. It was cold and it was miserable, and of course another factor was the rains. The rivers swelled up and became almost impossible and yet you can imagine these men — Canadian soldiers — swam across, with their equipment, holding their rifles up. That's guts. A lot of people can't swim with fifty pounds on your back, but they did. Or wade across. The [Royal Canadian] Engineers were most important in these things, and they were a wonderful, brave bunch. They would proceed first and try to throw across a Bailey bridge. This was a preformed bridge that was fitted together, and they would carry it down and launch it across the river and hopefully the Germans wouldn't blow it up. That way we would get across, or we would go across in assault boats. One or the other, both manned and directed by the Engineers. Both were highly dangerous, of course.

At the Sangro River the flooding made the crossing particularly difficult, washing away bridges and hindering the operation. The Italian Campaign seemed to be one hardship after another for the Canadians. They were outnumbered by the Germans, yet were on the offensive. They fought from disadvantageous positions. They struggled against an inhospitable terrain and a less than healthy environment. Now it seemed that the weather was conspiring against them as well. Eventually the flooding subsided and the Allies were able to establish a foothold on the far side of the river. Amphibious DUKWs ferried men and *matériel* across the rapidly moving Sangro, and they were soon in a position to continue the offensive.

Harry Fox (Hastings and Prince Edward Regiment)
The mud kept the tanks on the road, they couldn't go through the fields, they'd just get mudded in, so it was just a battle to capture the roads. The tanks would go forward, the leading tank gets knocked out, and the infantry spread around and crawl forward and knock out the anti-tank gun, and then they'd advance again.

Albert Wade (Royal Canadian Dragoons)
The roadways became inaccessible sometimes. We'd get stuck. Luckily our cars were all four-wheel drive. We used to have a big eight-wheel transport type of a vehicle. They were big buggers, and if things got really bad and if you had to get pulled out, they'd come and get you. So you kept on the road. If the road didn't look right, we didn't bother with it unless we had to. But we did get stuck a few times. It always seemed to happen at the bad times too, when you're under attack or something. You had to be careful.

Al Sellers (Governor General's Horse Guards)

In the tanks we always wore gloves simply because the winter was cold in Italy — if you had bare hands and you tried to climb aboard, you were stuck to it. In the summertime it was so hot you'd burn your hands, so we always wore gloves. There was no air conditioning and [the tanks] were pretty hot, and in the wintertime they were darn cold. The only people who got any heat was the driver and the ball gunner because their feet and their thighs were against the differential and the transmission. The crew commander, the gunner, the loader — they were cool, if not cold. It was terrible because we actually had summer dress, and somebody invented a tank uniform, which was the worst creation I ever saw. It was all zippers, and you'd stand there and you'd try and zip each leg up, and then you'd try and zip the arms closed, and then you'd try and do the body. We finally said "To hell with it" and just threw them on the back of the tank. Everything we carried, everything we owned was on the back deck. A lot of times when somebody was unlucky, all their rations, their bedrolls, and kit bags would be shredded by either machine guns or there was an aerial explosion. You'd lose water, because the cans were strapped on the turret, and they'd get holes.

Herb Pike (48th Highlanders)

You know, we'd take rations and carry them on the back of our belt rolled up in a gas cape — it was handy at night because they were warm and could keep the heat of the body in. When you're in a slit it can get damn cold and damp, and they'd fill up with water occasionally so you'd wake up you'd be half under water. But these things kept you warm. We rolled them up in the back, and we used to put a couple of tins of bully beef or rations, in case you needed to have a bite and you didn't have time. I remember one time we were under fire and I was crawling along on my belly and I got a burst of machine gun across my back. They actually took the gas cape right off my back and the rations. What are you? Inches away from getting a burst? You know, things like that, just luck!

Albert Wade (Royal Canadian Dragoons)

When it rained, it rained consistently maybe for a couple of days at a time. When it snowed, it would snow and then it would melt and turn into sleet. So there you were sleeping in a cotton type of a mattress similar to what they use in tents now. You'd roll it up and you had a blanket, maybe two blankets. You usually had that wrapped in either one of these gas-protection coats — it was made of some kind of like an oilcloth, and you could wrap your bedroll in that — plus what we had was a ground sheet, and that was a rubberized sheet with a cotton sheathing on the inside, and you carried that. You threw that over you. So that was your so-called protection from the weather.

On November 19 another group of Canadians landed in Italy — members of the elite commando unit called the First Special Service Force. It was a specialized unit made up of Americans and Canadians, noted by the unique shoulder patch that represented both countries. They were a gregarious group, trained in parachuting and mountain climbing, prepared for battle in any conditions. Originally they were slated to be a parachute unit, but in the end they were used for special missions due to the diverse collection of skills possessed by the men. The force quickly gained an excellent reputation, even being dubbed the Devil's Brigade by the Germans. One of the most famous members of the force was Tommy Prince, Canada's most decorated Native Canadian soldier.

The First Special Service Force was attached to the U.S. 5th Army, and they landed on the west coast of Italy to participate in operations in that area. They had their first taste of action at Monte la Difensa. For two nights they climbed the mountain, scaling its nine-hundred-metre height with full gear. Appearing out of a blanket of fog that covered the mountaintop, they assaulted on the German positions and caught them by surprise. Swiftly the men of the First Special Service Force took the position, then went on to attack the village of Monte la Remetanea. For six days they battled, finally forcing the Germans from their stronghold and opening the path to Monte Cassino for the Americans. This first taste of the Italian Campaign for the men of the First Special Service Force cost them 511 casualties, including 73 dead.

The Germans left a path of devastation in their wake as they attempted to slow the Canadian advance. F.H.J. Ricketts ponders the devastated railway ties at Carovilli.

Al Sellers (Governor General's Horse Guards)

When I think of our naval service — we got what equipment we could get and the supplies that we could get, they did a good job of getting that down there. Mail — you know there were times when we'd get that thing in a couple of weeks. I have a picture Marie sent me, and I thought, "Heck, this thing had been on fire" — there was an explanatory note that came with it that the ship that it was on had been torpedoed and the mail was salvaged. I think all of the services did a good job. When you talk about the services, I think about the WRENS, and the WAVES — and the nursing sisters. This field general hospital in Italy, and those nursing sisters did a good job. I had to go back when I blew up — you just have to experience an explosion like I did — a great big WHAM! It goes off and the mud turns into dust and I couldn't hear for a couple of weeks, just this constant ringing, and you feel like you're spitting out dust all the time and your eyes are full and you've got a headache. I was just sent back for examination. Waited two days, and I watched those dames working, they did a good job.

On November 28 the British battled the Germans to take control of the ridge overlooking the Sangro River valley. Two days later it was secured, making the Allied advance beyond it possible. The 8th Indian Division and the 1st Canadian Armoured Brigade set up a base along the ridge while two divisions began the advance. The New Zealanders pursued the Germans along the interior while 1st Canadian Division pushed north along the coast. In early December they reached the Moro River, where a deadly German force lay in wait on the other side. Few could have guessed the hell that they were about to face.

BLOODY DECEMBER

Herb Pike (48th Highlanders)
Ortona was the first real defensive line per se.

Gord Outhwaite (48th Highlanders)
Oh yeah, that was a bloody December.

Herb Pike (48th Highlanders)
Bloody December, that's what they called it.

THE PLAN WAS SIMPLE: CROSS THE Moro River, advance to Ortona, and clear the town. It was anticipated to take only a few days. The area was extremely muddy due to the recent rain, making any advance difficult for vehicles. While the Canadians held the high ground overlooking the valley, on the other side of the Moro was a steep cliff where the Germans were well entrenched. A big issue for the Canadian infantry was the complete lack of intelligence on the German strength and positions. Little did they know that the Germans had decided to make a major stand at this location, with some of their best troops assigned the task of stopping the Canadians. The Germans had established a formidable defensive line across Italy, stretching from Monte Cassino in the west to the Moro River in the east, calling it the Gustav Line. The Americans and the British were going to attack the line in the west,

Top right: *Smoke rises in the distance as Canadian tanks advance under German shellfire during the attack on San Leonardo.*

Bottom right: *R.J. Garcon snipes from behind a stone wall at San Leonardo di Ortona as the Germans counterattack.*

Left: *The Hasty Ps on the move near San Leonardo with a destroyed German S.P. gun in the foreground.*

while the Canadians were given the task of clearing the Adriatic Coast. The New Zealanders were already in the area paying a heavy toll during their attempt to take Orsogna, near the Canadians' objective of Ortona.

Along a three-kilometre front, the Canadians found three possible places to cross the Moro River. One was just south of San Leonardo, one was near Villa Rogatti, and the last was where the Via Adriatica crossed the river. It would be the first time that the Canadians would attack as a full division in Italy. The rain had let up and the conditions were favourable for a river crossing — albeit a very muddy one — and so it was that on the night of December 5 the men made their way down to the Moro River under the cover of darkness. They descended the steep approach to the river with the element of surprise on their side, as they attacked without a preliminary artillery barrage. The 2nd Brigade assaulted San Leonardo and Villa Rogatti in the main thrust of the attack, while the 1st Brigade moved along the Via Adriatica towards the Cider Crossroads.

R.W. Hansen of the Loyal Eddies cautiously advances through San Leonardo di Ortona.

The PPCLI crossed near Villa Rogatti and caught the German sentries asleep at their posts. The Canadians quickly captured the town, enjoyed the breakfast that the German cooks had been preparing for their own men, then prepared for the inevitable German counterattack. The Seaforth Highlanders crossed the river near San Leonardo and established a bridgehead. The Hasty Ps crossed along the coastal road, facing fierce resistance. With the support of the 2nd Field Regiment and the Saskatoon Light Infantry, the Hasty Ps were able to prevail and to establish a foothold on the far side of the Moro. The Germans were fighting with more ferocity than the Canadians had seen in the previous five months.

The Germans counterattacked early in the morning, driving a number of Canadian units back across the river. At Villa Rogatti the PPCLI were able to hang onto their bridgehead after repelling two German counterattacks. Along the coast the Hasty Ps faced a major German counterattack. In one area they let a German company move in close before opening up on them and wiping them out. Another German company was caught in a ravine and destroyed by enfilade fire from the Hasty Ps' machine guns. The Germans withdrew after suffering heavy losses to the determined Canadian unit.

The effectiveness of the German counterattack in areas along the river forced a change of plans for the Canadians. Vokes decided to make the Hasty Ps' bridgehead the focus of the attack, so the 1st Brigade was moved in to

Helping a wounded Loyal Edmonton soldier at San Leonardo di Ortona.

enlarge the territory. The Indian 8th Division was sent to relieve the PPCLI in the Villa Rogatti area. The Indians would take the left flank while the PPCLI would join the rest of the Canadians in the coastal area. The change in plan was to launch a more powerful attack along a narrower front. This meant that the Canadians would have to advance through an area of ridges, streams, and other natural obstacles. The mud bogged down the tanks and armoured units, forcing them to take the few good roads in the area.

The Seaforth Highlanders began to advance on San Leonardo along with the tanks of the Calgary Regiment. The approach to the town was intimidating: a narrow road snaked up the hill to the elevated village, from which the Germans could fire down on them. One long stretch of 350

Above: *The terrain around the Moro River created additional hazards for the Canadian tanks.*

Left: *Members of the 48th Highlanders prepare to attack in the vicinity of San Leonardo di Ortona: Lieutenant I. Macdonald (with binoculars) and (L-R) J.T. Cooney, A.R. Downie, O.E. Bernier, G.R. Young, T. Fereday, and S.L. Hart.*

metres was completely exposed to machine gun fire and made for a dangerous advance. As the Canadians descended into the valley to make the treacherous approach, the Germans began shelling them. Two tanks were lost over the edge of a mountainside road, falling ten metres into a ravine after failing to negotiate a tight corner. The advance quickly turned into a series of smaller objectives where gains were measured in yards instead of miles. The fighting was bitter as they battled their way across the valley to the town. Mines did damage as well, taking out the lead tank when they were about to make the climb towards the town. With the road blocked, the rest of the tanks moved out into the olive groves to advance.

Gord Outhwaite (48th Highlanders)
There was not too much foliage in the trees, not too much to hide behind, not too much cover other than the terrain itself, which was rolling hills and the odd valley. The whole thing was rough.

Jim Holman of the 48th Highlanders, 2006.

Jim Holman (48th Highlanders)
The east side of Italy was quite hilly and mountainous. I remember one time when it was so bad we had to get mules to take stuff up, to get us up, and of course the tracks were only wide enough to walk in, you couldn't get a vehicle up anyway.

Meanwhile, the RCRs and the 48th Highlanders moved out from the Hasty Ps' bridgehead towards San Leonardo to participate in the assault. It was December 8, and at this time the Germans had just moved their elite paratroopers into the area to launch an attack on the Hasty Ps in an effort to drive them back across the Moro River. The RCRs were caught in a vulnerable position while moving out and came under attack. One platoon became isolated in a solid stone farmhouse, where they withstood the German onslaught. The bravery of these men became legendary, and the farmhouse became known as Sterlin Castle. The skirmish diverted the intensity of the German attack on the Hasty Ps, who then punished the enemy when they did reach the line. The men hid in their positions and allowed the Germans to penetrate their defences before opening up on them at point-blank range. The Germans lost two hundred men before retreating. The bridgehead was secure, and the 48th Highlanders, along with the RCRs, continued on their trek to San Leonardo. The Germans made their way to the nearby ridge to prepare to defend against the Canadian advance there.

Harry Fox (Hastings and Prince Edward Regiment)

It was safe to get into a house because their houses had thick stone walls. Most of them had their roofs knocked off, but you weren't in the top floor anyway. So it was a big area and you can get maybe twenty or thirty men in there.

Gord Outhwaite (48th Highlanders)

You're under all kinds of stress. I remember digging a slit trench, so you're there and the weather was bad and the next thing you know your slit trench fills up with water, so you've got to find another one. I'll tell you in the wintertime it really slows you down a little, but how everybody didn't die of pneumonia or something like that I'll never know.

Soldiers carry a dead comrade who was killed by shellfire. The German prisoners that he was escorting escaped injury.

Jim Holman (48th Highlanders)

When you had to dig in for any length of time, it was neat how some of the guys would make their slit trenches. They have a name for these things where it was rocky. You couldn't dig so you piled the rocks up around. Some of the guys would make openings so they could look through the windows.

Transporting two wounded soldiers from the Moro River, south of San Leonardo di Ortona.

The advance on San Leonardo was taking its toll on the tanks of the Calgary Regiment. They were vital in support of the Seaforth infantrymen, and they paid a heavy price. The advance across the valley and up to San Leonardo cost the regiment twenty-seven of its fifty-one tanks, and of those assigned to support the Seaforths, only four survived to enter the town. The infantry stormed the town, clearing the gun nests and defensive positions. Soon a dozen German tanks counterattacked, and the four remaining tanks of the Calgary Regiment bravely held their ground, eliminating the German armour at close range. Those German tanks that were not destroyed were driven back, and by 1740 on December 9, San Leonardo was secure.

The Germans withdrew to their next defensive line, which was along a ridge with a ravine below that made any assault on the position extraordinarily difficult. On the near side was another ridge, which would become known as Vino Ridge, while the whole battleground would become known as the Gully. The ravine was impossible for tanks to traverse, and with its steep slopes, the infantry faced a near impossible task to assault the German positions. The 90th

Above: *Men of the 48th Highlanders run for cover during a German counterattack near San Leonardo di Ortona. Pictured (L-R): L.N. Welbanks, G.D. Adams, and L.G. Thompson.*

Left: *Burial of a comrade who was killed by shellfire. These temporary graves would later be replaced by proper war cemeteries.*

Panzer Division was dug in along the top of the ridge. The positioning of the dugouts and the angle of the slope made it impossible to drop artillery on the Germans. The only way to take it was with an infantry assault.

For the Canadians it was a dreadful situation. They could not get armoured support, and the approach to the ridge was thick with mud, making any advance slow. The overwhelming firepower along the ridge would cut down many of the men, leaving precious few to scale the slope and attempt to dislodge the Germans.

On December 10, the Loyal Eddies set out for the Orsogna road when they were attacked alongside the ridge and pinned down. The PPCLI then moved in, believing that the Loyal Eddies had reached the road, only to face the same fate. The German position and strength became clear, and after a heated debate with some of the COs, Vokes decided to launch a frontal attack. On December 11 the men faced machine gun fire from close range, and there was no possible way to succeed. It turned into a bloodbath. The PPCLI advanced close to the German line and dug in on Vino Ridge. The Seaforths and Ontario Regiment put

A pair of Perth infantrymen race for cover while on a daytime patrol near Orsogna, with Mount Maiella in the distance.

Sniper in action: Jack Bailey of the Perth Regiment takes aim on the enemy near Orsogna.

up a valiant effort, but their battle ended in a standoff. Nothing was gained and a lot of men were lost that first day of fighting at the Gully. That did not stop Vokes from ordering a second attack on December 12. That afternoon the Canadians launched a creeping barrage with the Carleton and Yorks advancing warily behind it. Once again the result was a brutal loss of men with no ground gained.

Fred Scott (Perth Regiment)

I can remember being in the three-inch mortars — they sent us up in the place where the 1st Canadian Corps had a heck of a problem with what they called the Gully. They sent us up into the Gully to set up our mortars because they thought the way the battle was going, that the Canadians might lose, but a few days later things started to turn around.

The majority of the Canadian battalions were positioned along the front but were below fighting strength. Most were at half strength but were still expected to fulfill the tasks of a full-strength unit. During the second day of fighting at the Gully a reconnaissance patrol came across a route that tanks could use at one end of the depression, although a few German tanks guarded the access. On December 13 the West Novas and three Ontario Regiment tanks exploited this weakness by taking out the German tanks and moving behind the Gully to the Orsogna road. Unfortunately they ran short on supplies and had to withdraw, losing the opportunity to outflank the Germans. That same day the Canadian artillery unleashed their fury on the German positions as the Carleton and Yorks along with the Calgary Regiment's tanks put in an attack. What they didn't know was that the elite German Parachute Regiment had just been moved into position there. The Canadians were stopped, although one company did get across, only to become surrounded and taken prisoner.

The Royal 22nd Regiment and tanks from the Ontario Regiment set out to breach the Germans' line again on December 14, but quickly found that the gap used by the West Novas had been filled with crack paratroopers. The fighting was furious, with half of the men becoming casualties. As the battle raged, Major Paul Triquet of the Vandoos found that the few surviving men of his company were surrounded by Germans. Heroically he rallied them to make a charge in the only direction possible: forward. Incredibly, fifteen Vandoos and four Ontario tanks made the incredible assault on the village of Casa Berardi, capturing it. No sooner had they taken the position than they faced a counterattack. They repelled the Germans, including several tanks, and held on desperately. Most fought while wounded, some with multiple wounds. Throughout the battle Triquet led his men bravely, encouraging them and exhorting them on to great feats against all odds. That night a small group of reinforcements arrived, and that band of brave men withstood the worst that the Germans could throw at them. With ammunition quickly running out, they waited for help. When it came, their brave action had opened the way for a Canadian assault on the strategic crossroad near Casa Berardi. For this display of gallantry Paul Triquet was awarded the Victoria Cross, the highest honour for any member of the British Commonwealth; he was the first Canadian to win it in the Italian Campaign. Snuffy Smith of the Ontario Regiment was awarded the Military Cross for his bravery and leadership.

Paul Triquet of the Vandoos proudly holds up his Victoria Cross medal.

A group of Canadian soldiers man their positions in the Moro Valley.

Royal Canadian Engineers built this vital bridge over the Moro River overnight while facing German shelling.

Montgomery was perturbed by the Canadians' lack of progress. He made a personal visit to the battlefield to survey the situation. He originally thought that the Canadians weren't "pulling their weight," but the reality of the battlefield soon changed his mind. The Canadians were facing a formidable task against some of the best units that the Germans had in all of Italy. His view of the Canadian participation in the campaign changed greatly that day.

The breach in the Germans' line created by the Vandoos and the Ontario tanks created the wedge through which the Canadians could overcome the Gully. The 48th Highlanders and a squadron of the Three Rivers Regiment assaulted the Gully on December 18, preceded by a powerful and accurate artillery barrage that made the advance quite successful. They moved past the Gully to protect Casa Berardi to the west, outflanking the Germans along the ridge.

Royal Canadian Engineers performing the dangerous task of clearing a minefield.

That same morning the RCRs launched an attack on the pivotal Cider Crossroads, and like the 48th Highlanders, they had artillery support. But tragically the shellfire was not accurate and the regiment came under friendly fire. Once this was signalled back to the artillery, it immediately stopped its barrage, which left the RCRs vulnerable to two unscathed German units nearby. The resulting bloodbath left less than two hundred men able to fight, well under strength for a proper assault. They dug in that night and tended to their casualties. The next day the RCRs were given orders to complete their mission, and the survivors attacked the Cider Crossroads. This time the artillery support was on the mark, and they were able to take the strategic junction while suffering only three casualties. The Germans had withdrawn from their positions along the ridge, and the battle for the Gully was over. It had been eight terrible days in December for the Canadians, with more than one thousand casualties. But the worst was yet to come.

Allied intelligence felt that the next obvious defensive line for the Germans was the Arielli River, and that the local area would be a minor task of clearing small pockets of resistance. The Germans in fact had moved to Ortona to set up their defences. The small coastal town had been a major command centre for the Germans. It was heavily fortified,

and they were determined to defend it. Two battalions of Germany's elite paratrooper units were holed up in the city, ready to stop the Canadians at all costs. These German soldiers were experienced professionals, and they were prepared to fight to the bitter end. Hitler wanted Italy held at all costs. Ortona was chosen as the place that they would make their stand.

Street fighting in Ortona: Lance Corporal E.A. Harris of the Loyal Eddies fires on a German position.

Sydney Frost (Princess Patricia's Canadian Light Infantry)
The regiment had terrible casualties there crossing the river and on the other side of it. Names like the Gully and the Ridge and San Leonardo and San Vito were all places where the regiment suffered grievously. They didn't get into Ortona because by that time the regiment was exhausted, we had no men left to speak of.

A Three Rivers Regiment tank advances through Ortona amidst the terrible street fighting.

On December 20 the Loyal Eddies and the tanks of the Three Rivers Regiment encountered resistance just outside of Ortona. The medieval town was perched on a cliff by the sea, with a deep ravine along the side facing inland, leaving the only possible approach along Route 16, the road that the Canadians had fought for at the Cider Crossroads. The town was a maze of stone buildings with narrow streets and irregular intersections. In these streets and buildings the Canadians were about to face a litmus test of bravery and endurance. It would become known as Little Stalingrad, and it would be one of the greatest battles in Canadian history.

The Germans positioned themselves in the buildings with the thick stone walls that would protect them. They took up locations at windows to fire down into the streets, waiting for the Canadians to advance into these narrow thoroughfares, where they could massacre them because there was nowhere to take cover. To force the Canadians into these killing zones, the Germans had blown up buildings to block access to side roads with rubble. The clear route was in the crosshairs of the German machine gun posts and mortars. Houses were booby-trapped with mines, and snipers silently plied their trade. Danger and death lurked around every corner. The Battle for Ortona was a major contrast to the spread-

The men of the Seaforth Highlanders' B Company carefully advance along a mined path. Ortona is visible in the distance.

December 21, 1943: moving up with an anti-tank gun during the brutal street fighting in Ortona.

out advances in the countryside. Here the Canadians faced claustrophobic conditions with narrow alleyways and tight corners. The fighting was at extremely close quarters.

The Canadians quickly assessed that one battalion would not be able to take the town alone, so the Seaforth Highlanders were sent in as well. Quickly the men adapted to street warfare, and the fighting turned into a house-to-house affair. The Germans were strictly by the book in their conduct of war, and improvisation was not their strong suit, as it was for the Canadians. As the fight for Ortona progressed, this factor would turn the battle in the Canadians' favour.

On December 21 at 0700 the Loyal Eddies and the Seaforth Highlanders, along with a half squadron of Three Rivers tanks, moved cautiously along the main street. Both companies were under strength, and the narrow streets did not allow them to spread out. Each company stayed to one side of the road as they made their way towards the first piazza (the town had three). Immediately the quiet town erupted into a raging storm of smoke, bullets, and shrapnel. The Germans fired from their barricades and windows. Mines immobilized tanks, but they continued to provide as much support as possible. They were limited in their mobility due to the narrow streets and impassable rubble obstacles.

As the Canadians slowly progressed up the street, they began to clear houses one by one. Without any experience in this form of warfare, the men began to improvise tactics for safely eradicating the enemy from each building. It became a matter of trial and error, with errors having deadly consequences. The dangers of moving from house to house while bullets were flying up and down the street led to a Canadian invention: mouse holing.

The Loyal Eddies maintain communications in the tight streets while on the move in the battle of Ortona. Carrying the radio is W.D. Smith, while W.L. Waske talks to HQ.

Firing on three Germans in a slit trench only one hundred metres away, members of the Loyal Eddies use a wall for cover during the deadly firefight in Ortona.

Herb Pike (48th Highlanders)

That's where mouse holing was invented. Remember, it's an ancient town and the streets weren't boulevards such as we're used to here and the homes were all joined together. And you couldn't get out on the streets, snipers would get you, so the fellas would blow a hole. When you cleared a house you always cleared the top first and worked your way down. So they'd run in and get upstairs. They'd clear that and clear the bottom, then they'd blow a hole in the wall to the next one, so that way they wouldn't have to go out to the street. And that's where it was invented — mouse holing.

The street fighting dragged on throughout the day as the Canadians slowly advanced to the first piazza. The battle took on a surreal atmosphere as the battleground became filled with smoke and dust, and advances became confusing, with fighting taking place in closer proximity than any of the soldiers had experienced before. The tight streets also

A dangerous advance through Ortona by B Company of the Loyal Eddies.

The battle of Ortona: firing an anti-tank gun at a German position down the street.

reduced the range of observation for the soldiers, and the conditions made communications nearly impossible. As night fell on December 21, the Canadians were securing their hold on the first piazza, and patrols became essential. The progress was extraordinarily slow and dangerous.

John Richardson (Ontario Regiment)

In Ortona they slugged it out with the house-to-house with the toughest troops in the German Army. It was rated the first best division in the German Army. They went from house-to-house blasting from one wall to the next, that's how they made their way up the street. That's how bad it was.

While the battle in Ortona raged that day, the 1st Brigade advanced around the town and moved towards the villages of Villa Grande and San Tommaso. The move would protect the flank of the Canadians fighting in Ortona and cut off the Germans' supply route.

Herb Pike (48th Highlanders)

We had to go to the left to cut off the main road that came from Rome into Ortona and Pescara. If you cut that road off, Jerry couldn't bring any more reinforcements in to Ortona, because it was a key place to take at that time. So we were told to go to the left through these small towns and clear that out and cut the road off.

Herb Pike (48th Highlanders)

There was a place we were in called Villa Grande. We were dug in and Jerry was about a hundred yards over the hill from us, and right at the point of the hill there was a position we had to man. We used to put a patrol in there every night to stop Jerry from infiltrating. I was up there this one night with a section of my platoon. This was an old ancient farmhouse, and one half was living quarters, the other half was where the stock was kept. There were two big dead cattle in there and they had been dead for some time. You know what happens, they bloat up with the gas in them. Anyway, Jerry's coming in with a patrol, and it's a fighting patrol. I grabbed a Bren and I jump up to this window on the front that they're coming in, and I land on top of this cow and he just went phhhhht! The gas — well you never in your life smelled anything like this. Even Jerry called the attack off! It was terrible!

George Netherwood, W.L. Soderberg, and Earl Israel hold a position in Ortona.

A West Nova firing a PIAT gun near Ortona.

Some Loyal Eddies prepare their hand grenades while taking shelter in a damaged building in Ortona.

Men of the Loyal Edmonton Regiment move through the streets of Ortona under the protective watch of the tanks of the Three Rivers Regiment.

Gord Outhwaite (48th Highlanders)

Ha ha ha. There's no way to fight under those circumstances.

December 22 saw the resumption of street fighting along Ortona's main street. Since the secondary streets were blocked by rubble, the Canadians decided to make the main push along the major thoroughfare so that they could use their tanks for support. The Canadians divided Ortona into sectors, with each infantry battalion assigned to clear one. The house-to-house fighting expanded throughout Ortona. Street by street the town was torn apart by warfare, block by block it was destroyed. It took another day to seize the second piazza, while the Canadians had to contend with German snipers all over the town. Slowly, painfully, the Loyal Eddies and the Seaforth Highlanders cleared buildings and secured blocks. As they mopped up, their tank support hammered German positions. Targets were windows, rooms, and entire floors of buildings as the battle was reduced to small-scale objectives.

Joseph Reid (Calgary Regiment)

We knocked down every house you could see. The enemy tanks or infantry would be lodged behind the corners of the houses. So the first task was to shoot out the corners of the buildings so they couldn't be hidden. In time we ruined every Italian building along the way just by shooting out the corners.

The Canadian infantry units were suffering horrific numbers of casualties while their fighting strength continued to fall to dangerous levels. The companies adapted to the situation and continued the fight with determination. As vicious as the fighting was, strange things did happen in the heat of battle. At one point on December 23 two Canadians were seriously wounded crossing one of Ortona's squares. The Germans waved a white flag and called a ceasefire, at which point a pair of their medics crossed no man's land to look after their fallen enemies. Once first aid had been administered, the medics signalled for Canadian stretcher-bearers to come and retrieve their wounded. Once the square had been cleared, the flag was taken down and the fighting resumed.

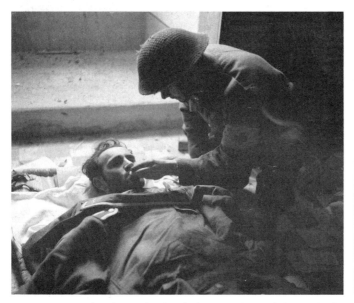

Compassion in battle: medical orderly B.D. Flynn of the Seaforth Regimental Aid Party gives a badly wounded German soldier a drink of water.

A group of Loyal Eddies receive mail from home only two days before Christmas, raising morale in the unit.

Joseph Reid (Calgary Regiment)

Are you wanting me to say how badly was I scared? Many times, many times. Unfortunately in a tank you had to ride with your head out so you could see where you are going, and you can give proper directions. More than once I sure as hell hated to shove my head up there outside of the tank opening. We were in that, the Calgarys were in that. Three Rivers were charged with the task of Ortona, and they did a marvellous job. They brought down houses on the tanks, got the building to collapse. Rode the tanks over piles of rubble, loose rubble that gave way sometimes and fall into a basement. Another tank would tow them out and this kind of thing — all under fire. Small arms fire, mind you, but Ortona was terrible.

A group of Loyal Eddies dig out a comrade who was buried alive by debris at Ortona.

Heroic rescue of Roy Boyd of the Loyal Eddies, who was trapped under rubble for three and a half days.

On Christmas Eve the battle for Ortona intensified as the Germans got a new life from fresh troops that had just arrived. The Germans at one point blasted the Loyal Eddies with a flamethrower, one of the most feared weapons in the battlefield. A response by the Canadian artillery soon put an end to that. The artillery was a powerful ally as the Canadians continued to apply pressure on the German strongholds. With the infantry units at only half strength or less, the Loyal Eddies welcomed an early Christmas present: seventy-five Cape Breton Highlanders joined them. The Canadians continued their relentless assault on the Germans, and with a large portion of the town under their control, it was apparent that they would soon prevail. The Germans knew it too, and Kesselring ordered a withdrawal, albeit a fighting withdrawal. They had to evacuate the town before their escape route was cut off, as the Canadian 1st Brigade was pushing towards the Riccio and Arielli Rivers at their rear, while the 3rd Brigade was applying pressure towards the coastal road that was their only means of escape.

Christmas Day provided a small respite for the men as they were rotated back to enjoy a hot Christmas meal. As welcome as the break was, the process of moving back was highly dangerous. Some had their meal in nearby buildings. The cooks worked under the most trying of circumstances to prepare the meals for the men, but nothing was spared for the brave souls who had spent almost a week in hell. At the church of Santa Maria di Constantinopoli, the men had linen covered tables, a hot meal, and were entertained with carols being played on the organ. The only thing missing was a roof over their heads, as the church had suffered in the early stages of the battle. The break from fighting was all too brief, and the men stoically returned to Ortona, carefully winding their way through the streets and taking safe passages to their forward positions.

Top left: *Christmas dinner at Brigade HQ, 1943. The horrors of war were forgotten for a brief few hours while the men enjoyed a warm dinner.*

Bottom left: *View from RAF aircraft of the beach by Ortona.*

Above: *A Canadian truck burns in Ortona after being hit by a German mortar.*

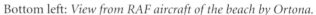

The fighting reached fever pitch on December 25, and one group of Seaforths faced a strange situation. No sooner had they returned from their Christmas dinner than they were overrun by a German unit and taken prisoner. The situation was precarious for the small group of Germans, and they were in no position to deal with prisoners. A gentlemen's agreement was then made: the Germans freed the Canadians on the condition that they promised not to fight again. The bargain was honoured by their CO, and the men were sent to the rear to finish the war in a support role. It was very fortunate for them that they were facing paratroopers and not the SS Waffen; otherwise their fate would have been a tragic one.

The Canadians spent the day clearing more houses and apartments, and as night fell the Canadians had control of the entrances to the last piazza in Ortona. Two-thirds of Ortona was controlled by the Canadians on December 26, with much of the town in ruins. The Canadian soldiers fought with little opportunity to sleep at night. Exhaustion became as great an enemy as the Germans. With fatigue men became less alert, and their decision-making capabilities suffered dramatically. Added to that was the dwindling morale of the men who had spent much of the month witnessing their friends and acquaintances being killed and maimed, and the situation was becoming increasingly dangerous. Some of the Canadian senior officers risked a visit to the front to bolster the sagging spirits of the troops.

Above: *Tanks and men advance through the ruins of Ortona during the last stages of the battle.*

Left: *A dead German soldier who was killed fighting the Loyal Eddies in Ortona.*

The next day the Germans had a scant few buildings left to make their stand. Desperately they made a few attacks, blowing up one building filled with Loyal Eddies and burying them. Canadian retribution was swift, and the Germans were pummelled by shellfire. With the Canadian 1st Brigade attacking their escape route to the northwest, the Germans hastily retreated. By 0945 on December 28 the city had been cleared. The eight-day battle for Ortona was over. The damage to the town was appalling, with no building left unscathed and many either reduced to rubble or in the process of collapsing. It had been a monumental struggle, and the bravery of the men was unparalleled: they overcame exhaustion with incredible endurance and mental toughness. The success of the battle was due to the superb leadership of the NCOs and junior officers, since so much of Ortona was fought in isolation. No prouder accomplishment could have been achieved as the victory at Ortona. It is one of Canada's greatest military achievements.

The Loyal Eddies take German prisoners at Ortona.

The devastation of Ortona was unlike anything the Canadians had seen, leaving no building unscathed.

Left: *Some civilians remained in Ortona throughout the hellish fighting, only to come out of hiding once the battle had ended.*

Above: *The town of Ortona was utterly destroyed during the fierce battle there.*

Gord Outhwaite (48th Highlanders)
We were fortunate, we had a lot of good officers, and that makes the difference. We were very lucky and we had some good officers, and our own common sense of course.

Joseph Reid (Calgary Regiment)
I had the opportunity to go back to Ortona. There was hardly a building there. Imagine a whole town — all rubble. We weren't able to get past the road in it without a diesel.

The month of fighting at the Moro River and beyond had a staggering impact on the Canadian Army. The 1st Division suffered 695 dead and 1,738 wounded. During the week at Ortona one company of the Loyal Eddies was reduced from 90 men to a mere 18. The loss of officers was acute. The RCRs, for example, had only 9 officers remaining of the 41 that had landed in Sicily only five and a half months earlier. Their battalion as a whole was reduced to 206 originals from the 756 that had started the campaign. The rest of the division had suffered in a similar fashion, leaving it vastly under strength.

Graves of the Loyal Edmonton Regiment soldiers who were killed in the battle of Ortona.

The Canadians had developed a solid reputation as an army in the early part of the Italian Campaign, but after the Moro River and Ortona, they were a force to be feared. As the Italian Campaign progressed, the Germans would be very aware of where the Canadians were stationed, knowing that they would spearhead the attack. It became a matter of course that they would face the elite German paratroopers whenever they went into battle. The best would have to face the best.

Fred Scott (Perth Regiment)
When the Germans got to know the Canadians had moved into this front, they started to prepare for an attack, because the Canadians always seemed to be in the attack. Wherever we were, there's going to be an attack, and the Germans got to know this.

Herb Pike (48th Highlanders)
We were the sharp end of the spear.

Gord Outhwaite (48th Highlanders)
Well, they had the crack troops against us all the time.

Herb Pike (48th Highlanders)
Crack troops. The Herman Goering Division, they were fantastic troops.

Gord Outhwaite (48th Highlanders)
Wherever we went, they moved their army the same way. You got to understand, these were professional people. These Germans were well trained and they were really good soldiers. Unfortunately, they were on the wrong side. That's what we were up against.

Harry Fox (Hastings and Prince Edward Regiment)
In the long run we didn't mind because we knew we could beat the best of the German army. So if we could beat the best, we were pretty good.

So hasty was the German departure from Ortona that they left nearly one hundred of their dead behind, which was unusual for them. They were in a race to escape the 3rd Brigade's advance on the coastal route north. On December 29 the objective of the Carleton and Yorks was Point 59, a hill that dominated the coastal plain and was

G.C. Butcher of the 48th Highlanders looks over the wreckage of a German PzKpfW III tank that was destroyed by the Calgary Regiment.

heavily fortified. Several attacks failed to drive the Germans out, even during a storm on New Year's Eve. After the Canadian artillery hit Point 59 with airbursts, the Germans finally relinquished the position on January 4. By that time the Canadians had cleared San Nicola, San Tommaso, and Torre-Mucchia.

Gord Outhwaite (48th Highlanders)

I was in a gun pit with one of our Bren gunners. Everything was sort of quiet, we could hear the Bren guns popping off, because they were not that quick at firing. Then all of a sudden this cheese cutter opened up, which is an MG 42. Jerry fires fifteen hundred rounds a minute, and it waves like this [up and down]. If you happened to be in the wave you're all right, but if it comes back down, you've had it. I shook for ten minutes after that, and I wasn't even near it. Well, I heard it, it just echoed right in your head.

Meanwhile, on the west coast of Italy near Monte Cassino, the First Special Service Force continued to make a name for themselves by enduring horrible conditions while capturing Monte Majo. They continued to clear ridges in the area, particularly those that overlooked the Via Caslina. This strategic road led right to Rome, and it had to be secured for the advance on the capital, once Monte Cassino had been taken. The Germans put up fierce resistance, but eventually they had to withdraw across the Rapido River to the Gustav Line. The Devil's Brigade suffered terrible losses, including sixty-seven Canadian casualties. They were taken out of the line in mid-January and prepared for a special mission that would take them to the shores of Anzio.

Bill Park, Andy Jannock, Joe Armstrong, and Alex Buchanan of the Saskatoon Light Infantry fire a 3-inch mortar near Ortona.

THE LONG, COLD WINTER

THE CANADIAN ARMY WAS DEVASTATED BY the huge losses of December. The divisions were particularly hard hit in their ranks of officers. This created a weakness that had to be addressed immediately, as all future success would depend on the leadership of those ranks. General Vokes put in a request for the Canadians to go out of the line to be reinforced, refitted, and retrained. It was turned down as there were no divisions available to relieve them, and so the advance halted near the Arielli River. The weather was horrendous, so both sides dug in and prepared to hold their positions through the winter. The push to Pescara stalled, and Rome remained in German hands.

Albert Wade (Royal Canadian Dragoons)
Our equipment arrived from England — we were equipped with Staghound armoured cars, they were new vehicles, a new fighting vehicle at that time. We were quite proud to be the regiment to be selected to receive it. We also had Daimler scout cars, which were later christened Dingoes. We were just south of Ortona, so our job was to go up this roadway, which was the coastal road, and check out the little villages along the way and report any suspicious looking movements of any of the citizens, and of course be on the

Reconnaissance car and Honey tank of the Royal Canadian Dragoons (taken in Leeuwarden Holland). Bill Maitland and Albert Wade are shown in the car.

lookout for Germans. We ended up in a town, a little place called San Vito, which was on the south bank of the Arielli River. There was a canal adjacent, and the Germans had drained it, of course, because that was the supply of water for the villages around there and also for the farmers' crops. Well, they did their usual thing, you know. They make sure nobody is going to have anything when they left. Suddenly out of nowhere came the storms, and the place became mired. We dug slit trenches on the north bank of this river. We were in a static position and there was a field kitchen set up by the squadron in the shade of this high embankment, and so we had to go there for some of our meals. Which meant rest because the Germans had these positions under fire all the time we were there.

Herb Pike (48th Highlanders)

I remember one seventeen-man patrol, I was the sergeant at the time, and I had to do a recce across the Arielli — as you get up across the river the terrain lifted. Jerry was dug in across the top of the ridge and I remember very distinctly this group of homes. The officer at that time was a fella by the name of Hunter, and he was a fellow from South Carolina and he had a real southern accent, and anyway, after the recce patrol we knew exactly where we were going, we did the fighting patrol two nights later. We encountered Jerry once we got up there and we shot up the place a little bit with small arms and Bren gun fire. I carried a Thompson sub. The officer said to me, "Do you know the way out of here?" and I said, "All you have to do is give the word and we'll be out of there." It took us about an hour and a half to make the crossing, to infiltrate where we wanted to go, and once he said go, we come back in about three-quarters of an hour. We got out of there in a real hurry.

Winter in Italy was a blend of snow and rain, accentuated by frigid temperatures, and characterized by thick mud everywhere. The Canadians were suffering in the cold as the dampness soaked into their clothing and the temperatures froze them. It had become a static line, with both sides huddling in their trenches trying to find warmth. The men were in desperate need of a break from the front, but it was not possible. To bolster their numbers, units from the 5th Division were moved up to join them on the line.

Fred Scott (Perth Regiment)
The weather was really dirty — the tanks were having trouble with the mud and everything seemed to be against us.

Gord Outhwaite (48th Highlanders)
Going through the Seaforth regiment — Padre East was there, and they carried a Seaforth guy out on a mattress, and when we saw him, Christ, he was all chewed up to rat shit. Gee, I tell you, I didn't think he'd survive. He had about ninety-five pieces of shrapnel in him.

Three members of the 17th Field Regiment run to their 25-pounder to bombard the enemy in the Castel Frentano area.

Herb Pike (48th Highlanders)
He's talking about Padre East, he was one of the most decorated padres in the Canadian Army, other than Foote who got the VC. Padre East was six foot six and a half. Marvellous man.

Gord Outhwaite (48th Highlanders)
Great man.

Herb Pike (48th Highlanders)
It was funny when he came up to the regiment, the colonel at that time was Ian Johnson. When he met East he said, "Well,

Chaplain S.B. East with members of the 48th Highlanders near Regalbuto.

119

you won't be here that long," because he was United Church and Johnson was the old Scots Presbyterian. When we were on the static front there and the 5th Div had come in and they made the attack through us, heading for Pescara. They said, "We'll have Pescara for you in three days," and we just said, "That's good so long as you come out with the same smile on your face as you're going in with." Well, they got riddled, Jerry just kicked the hell out of them. We were bogged down with mud, you just couldn't move. Their dead was left all over the valley there, and Padre East would come along every night and ask for volunteers to go out and pick up the guys. Well, he'd come down and the guys in the slit trenches would call out, "The padre's on his way" and all the guys would duck and try to stay down so you wouldn't have to volunteer. They'd go out and pick up the dead, well, you know, that may sound a little cruel, but you know if a guy's dead, he's dead …

Gord Outhwaite (48th Highlanders)
There's no sense in having another one dead alongside of him.

Herb Pike (48th Highlanders)
That's right. But anyway, that's the type of man he was. Guys used to go out and bring the boys back. Amazing.

Gord Outhwaite (48th Highlanders)
Oh yeah, and he was wounded himself and they shipped him out, and hell, he beat us back to the lines.

Herb Pike (48th Highlanders)
He went AWOL from the hospital.

Gord Outhwaite (48th Highlanders)
"I just wanted to make sure that everybody knew I was okay." Oh, he was a great man, he really was.

During this time, the U.S. 5th Army was continuing its push up the west coast of Italy in an attempt to capture Rome. Just 130 kilometres south of the capital, the Germans were holding out at Monte Cassino, blocking any advance to the north. Monte Cassino was a virtually impregnable village perched atop a 520-metre-high mountain, anchoring the Gustav Line. The position was protected on either side by mountain ranges, while the village itself controlled the passage through the Liri Valley, which was the route to Rome. The approach was forbidding, and the Germans refused to leave the historic sixth-century monastery that the Allies did not want to damage. So the monumental battle began, with one futile attempt after another to storm the village and take the monastery at the summit. The battle would drag on for months.

N.L. Shauer of the Devil's Brigade escorts a German prisoner to the rear near Vanafro.

25-pound gun mired in the mud during the brutal winter in Italy.

To stop the Germans from reinforcing their troops against the Americans, the Canadians and British were to keep them occupied by whatever means were at their disposal. The mud left by the heavy rains made mobility very difficult, so action was reduced to small-scale activities all along the line. This meant constant patrols to harass the enemy and to create the impression that a major attack was impending. The very nature of patrolling was dangerous: crossing into no man's land, infiltrating behind enemy lines, and sneaking around in the dark when trigger fingers were always itchy on both sides. Stealth was the key. Noise would give away one's presence, and a wrong turn could lead to capture or death. Patrols were not a popular pastime for the men during January 1944, after all that they had been through.

Al Sellers (Governor General's Horse Guards)

During the muddy season everybody stopped. The enemy was in their positions and we couldn't move. The tanks would just bog right down. So we were turned into infantry and we helped on their flanks, and of course those flanks had to be protected and this was done by patrols. There would be a set number of buildings, blown-out tanks, or something that somebody could use as an observation post or as a sniper site, and they had to check these out all the time to make sure nobody was in them, so that was called a policing patrol. The enemy did the same thing. So there'd be ambush patrols, I was on a couple of those where you have about five or six guys, and you took your guns at different points and you'd just lie in wait.

Herb Pike (48th Highlanders)

Actually a lot of our time [was] spent on patrolling, ferreting out where resistance was going to be and to patrol there. It was like needling all of the time back and forth. Again, there was never any sustained group of guys lining up and crossing over en masse, that just didn't happen there. It was more of a section and a platoon operation.

Edmund Arsenault of the West Novas mans a slit trench, ready to defend the hard-fought-for land just north of Ortona.

Al Sellers (Governor General's Horse Guards)

Well, I was on a policing patrol one night and we had gone through our checkpoints, but I was crawling up to this barn, and I had grenades on my Bren pouches, and how one got off I'll never know, but I heard it clattering and oh my God the pin's loose — I'm going to get blown up. It didn't happen but the Germans heard it and they sent flares up and they didn't bother investigating. So we carried on and at the end we had to reach the Westminster outfit. Well, my lead guy, Joe Basking, he made a wrong turn and walked through their alarm system, which was a bunch of empty three-inch mortar casings strung up so that when somebody walks through there, there's going to be a clatter. Well, he walks through and there's a clatter, and I thought, "We're dead," but the Westies held off their fire and we got through and we were so relieved.

Gord Outhwaite (48th Highlanders)

This is the hard thing with a patrol, you're going out and you don't know where the heck you're going. Your

Members of the Perth Regiment moving into the line.

Dangerous duty: the Forward Observation Officer would be positioned at the front to call in adjustments to the artillery fire, putting him at great risk. FOO P.F. Evans runs for cover north of Ortona, where A Company of the PPCLI was positioned.

officer says, "Okay, you take your section out there and come back here and tell me where the enemy is." So out you go and you got to find the enemy. Oh, and pick up a prisoner or two if you can. I can remember one time we got a couple of prisoners and in this area there was some haystacks and a house there. Inside the farmhouse kitchen looking out the window was a tank. It had come in the back of the house and he's sitting there. And so you've got two prisoners and you're trying to get back, and the next thing you know you see a haystack move. They got a tank under the cotton-picking haystack! There were three of them. You got to head for the river, and you get down there and the tank is shooting at you, and he can't get you, but he's hitting the other side. So you can't get across the river. So needless to say sometimes the prisoner gets away. When the shells come in it's hard to hang onto them.

Gradually the 5th Division was moved up to the front, and the men were able to get their first taste of combat. On January 17 two regiments were ordered to launch an assault across the Riccio River, where they were to push the Germans back to the Arielli River. The Perth Regiment and the Cape Breton Highlanders were assigned the task. They were to take a ridge that overlooked the Arielli and that was defended by the battle-hardened paratroopers who had been fighting the Canadians at the Moro River and Ortona. The assault went in during daylight, giving the Germans a huge advantage firing from the high ground. Soon the open ground leading to the ridge was strewn with almost two hundred Canadian casualties. This baptism of fire left forty-seven dead in each of the two regiments. With this unfortunate turn of events, the fighting along the Gustav Line ended, only to be interrupted sporadically by patrols and shellfire.

Al Sellers (Governor General's Horse Guards)

The Westminster, it was a mortar regiment, and those things would be working all night long. Just harassing attacks or target attacks, and I've seen those mortars after using them all night, they'd be buried so deep that the fellows had to dig them out. It would just keep on driving even farther down into the ground.

Peter Routcliffe (Governor General's Horse Guards)

It was continuous fighting night and day, and night and day. Quite often you fell asleep afterwards so it didn't matter. I mean, they always had a good guard on there and we always woke when they were around.

Above: *F.V. MacDougal and J.H. Ferguson of the Royal Canadian Artillery's 2nd Field Regiment move out of their dugout and along a trench just north of Ortona.*

Right: *A member of the Saskatoon Light Infantry (MG) fires his Vickers machine gun at the Germans north of Ortona.*

Al Sellers (Governor General's Horse Guards)

In Italy at that time our challenge word was "Delhi" and the password was "Agra," Delhi-Agra in India, and the reason they used that because the 8th Army had these Indian troops, the Gurkhas. I do recall one night in our position we heard this group of Gurkhas going through us and they had attacked a German position on the other side of the valley, and that night they had a real firefight.

Joseph Reid (Calgary Regiment)

Another thing was the digging of slit trenches. Just a little so you sat on the one side of the bank, put your feet down, and you ate on the other side. Many of the tanks were supportive of the troops. You joined up with the infantry and you made a plan. We didn't only support Canadians, we were oftentimes assigned to Indian troops, could be Punjabi, could be Gurkhas, could be something else. Oftentimes they would have us out for dinner, and we'd build a trench in a circle, put our feet down, and you'd have a place to eat off. And the Gurkhas would come along and fill our bowls with curried foods. We'd have great meals. They were great fighters too. The Indian army very seldom had a commander of Indian background, their commanders were mostly British or American. Oftentimes American, we got one in the Calgarys too. Americans seeking adventure. A lot of them were in the Indian army. For some reason or another the Indians didn't want to have an Indian, a Punjabi or a different, higher caste Indian, as their officers.

John Richardson (Ontario Regiment)

We were very friendly with the Gurkhas and they had tremendous officers too. They were a fine bunch of little fellas. Our guys got along fine with them. They used to sit around there and eating their chipattis and playing their little games. Our guys would go down there and join them, they really liked our guys. One time we had the Gurkhas with us and we were going over to relieve the French Corps. We took them up in our tanks, we had a lot of them in the back and some guys inside and the damn driver of mine, he was feeding them rum. They had this can of Moroccan rum, and by the time we got to where we were going the Gurks were a pretty happy bunch of guys. I thought their major was as mad as hell but he just laughed his head off. He thought it was the funniest thing. They didn't drink beer but they drank rum. So every time you went to the Gurkhas for a party there was all kinds of beer. The army had beer for all the regiments, you know, but none of the Gurkhas drank the beer, so they had all that beer. Oh dear. They could have a bit of fun, you know. Couldn't be all bad, couldn't be all fighting all the time.

Gord Outhwaite (48th Highlanders)

The Gurkhas. They are the greatest night fighters in the world. You don't get them better than that. They relieved us at Ortona and they come up and they brought 6-pounders and everything else, and nobody heard them. All you feel is they feel your shoes and now all you hear is "Okay Johnnie" and you know you're all right.

Herb Pike (48th Highlanders)

Canadians laced their shoes this way [straight across], Jerry did it in crosses. You'd literally be out on a post and all of a sudden you'd feel somebody feeling your boots. Just don't have your laces crossed. Heh heh. Great troops, little guys. Fantastic.

Harry Fox (Hastings and Prince Edward Regiment)

It was about the fourteenth of January when I got up to Ortona, at that time the Canadian regiments were down to skeletons, and all these men on pooch draft were just the type of men they needed. No battle experience, but experienced NCOs and so on, and that's what they needed. The regiment that I went to, the Hasty Ps, was actually in the front line at that time. Well, it was very exciting to begin with because the first night that I was up there, the village was stonked by Jerries, and we had casualties and a lot of confusion, so it was quite exciting that first night. After that it just eased down, and all the regiments were patrolling at night.

During this lull, Kesselring moved his elite 1st Parachute Division from the area, repositioning them at Liri Valley to hold the Americans back. They joined the German 10th Army, with six battalions entrenched along the Gustav Line at the entrance to the Liri Valley. Once past that, the Allies would have to contend with the heavily fortified Hitler Line. It was twelve kilometres west of the Gustav Line, and between the two lines was a series of

Charles Lord and Richard Greaves of the PPCLI's A Company observe action near the front, just north of Ortona.

minefields that would hamper any advance. Hitler ordered his troops to stop the Allies here at all costs. In late January the Americans were still bogged down at Monte Cassino, while the war had come to a standstill along the Adriatic coast. It was determined that a decisive blow was needed to cause a breakthrough.

On January 22 a joint American-British force launched an amphibious landing on the beaches of Anzio, fifty-six kilometres south of Rome and just north of the Liri Valley. The objective of the attack was to outflank the German defenders in the Liri Valley by cutting them off from behind. On February 1 the First Special Service Force landed at Anzio, including its large contingent of Canadian servicemen. The unit proceeded to distinguish itself by seizing a quarter of the forty-eight-kilometre front, well out of proportion to the unit's size. The Germans withdrew to the Mussolini Canal, and the opportunity for a quick victory evaporated. During this time the Canadian casualties amounted to 117 at Anzio.

John Richardson (Ontario Regiment)

That was a real mess-up really with the Americans, to be perfectly frank they had a pretty stupid general. They landed and it was a complete surprise. They could have walked to Rome. Nobody around at all, no Germans, no nothing, and he waited around there for about two days. Trying to land supplies instead of going full blast to cut the 6th Highway and forced the pull back of all the Germans from the Hitler Line. Of course he lost his job, and they were stuck then because the Germans very quickly put enough guns and tanks in there to stop them and they stayed there until we broke the Hitler Line and forced the Germans out.

During the fighting in the Anzio area, Tommy Prince was stationed near Littoria. On February 8 he stationed himself in an empty farmhouse to observe the German positions from close range. While only two hundred metres from the Germans, Prince reported their artillery and gun positions over a telephone that was wired back to the Allied position fourteen hundred metres away. He reported amid shell bursts and constant gunfire, until finally the line went dead due to an errant bomb. Prince then donned some

A lineup of Sherman tanks from the 8th Princess Louise's (New Brunswick) Hussars prepare to fire on a crossroad position held by the Germans.

A machine gun crew holds their position on the front.

The RCA's 17th Field Regiment fire on a German position near Castel Frentano with their 25-pound gun.

civilian garb and went out to the field to fix the telephone line. With a hoe in hand, he pretended to work the fields until he found the line. While under German observation, he pretended to tie up his shoelace while he was actually repairing the line. Prince then returned to the house and continued to report on the German positions for the next twenty four hours until all of them were knocked out. For his bravery Tommy Prince was awarded the Military Medal by King George VI. He was one of only three Canadians to win both the Silver Star from the United States and the Military Medal.

John Richardson (Ontario Regiment)

I was a sergeant — I was sent on to OCTU British to become an officer. Canadian OCTU, British pre-OCTU, then Sandhurst Military College where I graduated. I got back to Italy in February '44 and I was pretty good at signals. I was asked to set up the signals unit in Avellino, which is where all the new officers and new men were feeding back up into the lines, that's where they were stationed. That was about fifty miles south of Naples, nice little town. From there when they were getting ready for Cassino, I was called up to the line.

Facing Page:

Top left: *Canadians on ski patrol near Colledimezzo, led by Regimental Sergeant-Major Prevost.*

Top right: *A Sherman tank crosses a bridge through a cloud of smoke in the Castel Frentano area.*

Bottom: *The blast of a mortar lights up the night in Italy.*

Jim Holman (48th Highlanders)
I landed down in Italy about the first part of February, and I was in Italy the last time Mount Vesuvius erupted.

In February the Americans found that infantry assaults were not making any headway against the Germans at Monte Cassino, so they proceeded to bomb the monastery to force the enemy out. For the Canadians along the front on the Adriatic coast, the winter was brutally long, as they had to suffer through flooded slit trenches and unbearably cold weather. The constant patrols only produced more wounded, and morale was suffering from being on the front for so long. In March units were being sent to the rear for some much needed rest and relaxation. That same month Major-General E.L.M. Burns took command of the 1st Canadian Corps, while Lieutenant-General Crerar and Major-General Simonds returned to England to prepare for the invasion of Normandy in June. March also marked the shift in bombings at Monte Cassino from the monastery to the town below it. The entire city was being decimated in an attempt to clear it of Germans.

Monte Cassino was totally destroyed during the months of fighting and bombing for the key strategic position.

A 75mm halftrack gun carrier being used in the advance near Larino by members of the Royal Canadian Dragoons.

Joseph Reid (Calgary Regiment)

The Americans had tried to take it about three times … and they used restraint with respect to methods of taking Monte Cassino, but by the time we got there all exercise of restraint was lost and instructions came to blow the thing off the map.

The stalemate was not to last as both sides built up their forces at the entrance of the Liri Valley, preparing for a major showdown. The Allies believed that the only way to break through the German defence was to overwhelm them. The plan called for the U.S. 5th Army and the British 8th Army to break through the Gustav and Hitler Lines in massive numbers. The Germans would be forced to counter with all of their reserves in the valley. This would leave them vulnerable, as the seven divisions at Anzio would surge forward and crush the German 10th Army from behind. With the German defences vanquished, the road to Rome would be wide open.

To facilitate the plan, several operations were launched simultaneously. The Allied air force began a bombing campaign that would disrupt the Germans' transportation and communication in the area. The bulk of the British 8th Army, including the Canadians, would have to move across Italy and into position for the attack. To maintain the element of surprise, this massive undertaking was done with the utmost secrecy. The men had to remove their patches and all identifying insignias were removed from the vehicles when they were transported across the Apennines. The Allies knew that movement of such a large number of soldiers would come to the attention of the Germans, so instead of trying to completely hide it, they developed a subterfuge. The Allies took advantage of the fact that Canadians were always used to lead the attack, and as such, the Germans always monitored their whereabouts. The Allies had I Canadian Corps set up a fake headquarters in Salerno to deceive the Germans into thinking that was the location of the next attack. In reality, the Canadians were supposed to be in reserve for the first part of the battle in the Liri Valley.

Herb Pike (48th Highlanders)

We were notified that we were going to go somewhere, we weren't told where, and we pulled all our flashes. The red patches come down, regimental insignias, numbers off the trucks, everything — and we take off. First thing we know, we're on the other side of Italy and in the Cassino area. They figured we could be an asset to break through the Hitler Line, because there was a stalemate.

Jim Holman (48th Highlanders)

They put us in this little tiny train, and it was really slow going and it had to stop at the bottom of every hill to pick up steam to go over it. To see the people along the track begging for food, some of them with arms off, some of them with legs off. When I saw this, this is when it really hit me. I went, "Geez, this is war, this is not playing like we did in Camp Borden or in England, this is war, this is just awful." I got there in the spring and I don't think I was there more than a week when they went into the Gustav Line.

Fred Scott (Perth Regiment)
We were getting ready for the battle of Cassino, which had already been going for pretty near two or three months. The Americans had quite a battle there. I think everyone in the Italian Campaign had a crack at the mountains and Cassino. Battle after battle was lost, and I think the biggest push was getting ready. No matter where you turned, they were building up supplies because you knew this battle of Cassino was going to take place, as soon as the weather cleared.

THE LIRI VALLEY

MAY 11, 1944, FOUND FOUR ALLIED ARMY CORPS concentrated on the front in western Italy, ready to strike. The signal to the troops came via a coded message over the BBC at 2300, and immediately two thousand guns rained death and destruction on the Germans in the Liri Valley. The II Polish Corps launched their attack in the middle of the night. Their target: Monte Cassino, the stronghold that had eluded capture for four months. Simultaneously, the 13th British Corps crossed the Garigliano River to assault the Gustav Line head-on. The 1st Canadian Armoured Brigade supported the 8th Indian Division during their crossing of the Rapido River. In the well-coordinated attack the French Expeditionary Corps ascended the Aurunci Mountains to outflank the Germans in the valley, while the 2nd U.S. Corps pushed up the coast in an attempt to link up with the attacking forces from Anzio.

One of the highlights of the action was the successful deployment of the Kingsmill bridge. Prior to the attack, Captain H. Kingsmill conceived of a way to install a bridge across a river while under attack, and proceeded to modify one of his tanks to accomplish it.

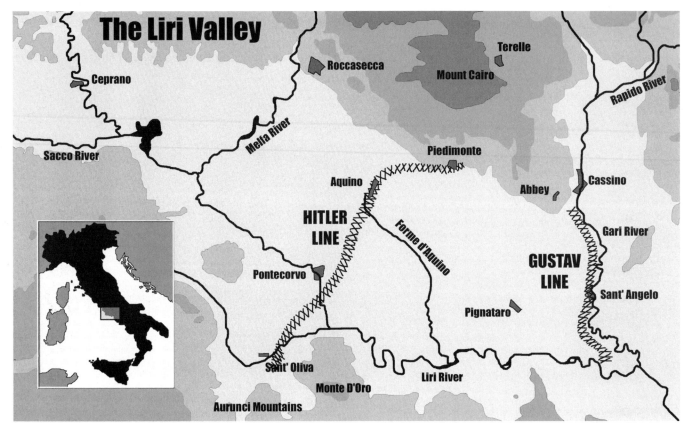

Joseph Reid (Calgary Regiment)

Tony Kingsmill was our LAE officer — that's Light Armour Engineer — and he devised a track to roll a Bailey bridge down. He put a set of rollers on the deck of tank, and they shoved the bridge across the river. A tank would shove this Bailey bridge to the other bank, and it worked. The Kingsmill bridge they called it, and the tanks were able to get across the river and in effect control the development on the other side. It ended up by us being able to take Monte Cassino. The Poles actually took it, the infantrymen were the ones that took Monte Cassino, and I have highest regard for the Poles. Men without a country, the greatest fighters you ever saw. Except for the Canadians, of course.

John Richardson (Ontario Regiment)

We got in there with the 8th Div and we had some dirty fighting for a couple of days, but we pretty well wiped out the Gustav Line.

A camouflaged tank of the Ontario Regiment prepares for the advance towards Rome through the Liri Valley.

View from Highway No. 6 of what was left of the town of Cassino, destroyed after months of bitter fighting.

A column of Canadian soldiers march beyond Pignataro on May 16.

Canadian tanks played a big role in the assault on the Gustav Line, with squadrons of the Three Rivers Regiment, the Ontario Regiment, and the Calgary Regiment partaking in the crossing of the Gari River. It was a difficult encounter, and the Germans made every inch gained a painful experience. For four days the bitter fighting continued. Eventually, several bridges were built across the river and the Allied forces surged ahead and broke through the Gustav Line. On May 15 the Canadian 1st Division entered the fray, crossing the river and moving into position along the 8th Army's flank to relieve the 8th Indian Division. The next day, the RCRs and Hasty Ps led the way across the Liri Valley, heading for the Hitler Line.

Harry Fox (Hastings and Prince Edward Regiment)

Well, to be quite honest with you, 1st Canadian Division did no fighting on the Gustav Line. It was the 8th Indian Division that broke through. It was after we passed through the Gustav Line into the Liri Valley that we went into action.

Al Sellers (Governor General's Horse Guards)

We were in the valley and there was high land on each side. The valleys were quite wide, they could be a couple of miles wide, but it was still controlled by the enemy on this high ground, and Monte Cassino was a stronghold.

Top left: *The ruins of Monte Cassino.*

Top right: *The fierce fighting at Monte Cassino left very little intact.*

Left: *The devastation of Monte Cassino.*

Harry Fox (Hastings and Prince Edward Regiment)

Well, it was open country. Hills, valleys, patches of wood, the odd farmhouse, and you never knew where you were going to get ambushed. So you had to be very careful about moving forward. We suffered casualties, but we pushed them back, just a steady push. They had observers in the mountains actually behind us. So the observers in front could see us and fire on us, and the observers in the back could see us and fire on us, so it was a tricky time.

Jim Holman (48th Highlanders)

Where we were we could actually see the action at the Cassino. You could see aircraft going in and you could see smoke over the mountain from the shelling. There was a lot of talk among the guys about how stupid it was. They wasted so many men when they could have went around it and just left it there. So many guys were killed there at Cassino. I can mostly remember being tired and hungry.

Peter Routcliffe (Governor General's Horse Guards)

The first time we went in there we went up the side of a hill and everything was sort of like a conglomerate of bodies and men. That was where I saw my first casualty — at the base of Cassino, going up the hill. This poor guy had been fighting and all of a sudden he had no chin. A shell had blown off the whole bottom of his face. So I was going to give him a shot of morphine and the doctor says, "No, don't do it" he says, "He'll be dead in a minute," and he was. He was just off like that. He was dead.

Albert Wade (Royal Canadian Dragoons)

Well, the role of a reconnaissance unit is to go forth and seek out information regarding the position of an enemy, regarding obstacles that would hinder a regiment, especially an infantry regiment or an artillery regiment, in their advance towards a battle area. And, if possible, have contact with the enemy, but nothing serious. If the worst came to the worst, we were trained to try to fight our way out. We had a troop consisting of two scout cars and two armoured cars, they were both armed — both scout cars were equipped with a Bren gun, also a .38-calibre Browning machine gun, automatic belt-fed, and we used various smoke bombs. We removed the seating and we sat on sandbags. The floors were sandbagged. The biggest enemy we had was road mines. That's where I received all these wounds on my leg. I think it's been fourteen operations on my legs, and most of the time they're taking shrapnel out. I'm still being treated for that.

Throughout the day the Canadians clashed with the German defenders and the advance was torturously slow. The 48th Highlanders were moved forward to lead the way towards the Forme d'Aquino River, where they were to capture a bridge. As they approached, they came under fire, but one company was able to get through and seize the bridge before the Germans could blow it up. That night the 48th Highlanders repelled a counterattack and destroyed two German 88mm guns in the process.

John Richardson (Ontario Regiment)
The 88 was our nemesis. They used it for artillery, they used it for ack-ack, they used it for anti-tank, they used it for everything. It was a marvellous gun.

Jim Holman (48th Highlanders)
They just knocked tanks out like crazy. I know one tank that I ran past and one guy was lying out of the turret on fire, and the other guy was lying on the ground on fire.

Gord Outhwaite (48th Highlanders)
You heard the explosion and then you heard the shell.

Herb Pike (48th Highlanders)
Yeah — phsssssst!

Gord Outhwaite (48th Highlanders)
And you'd hear a bang, so you know it's an 88, and they were deadly.

Al Sellers (Governor General's Horse Guards)
They used to call them whiz-bangs. You'd hear the whiz first and then bang! *In a Sherman tank the frontal armour used to be about seven inches thick, and the sides were maybe about two to three inches, and an 88 would go through everything. They were good gunners, and I remember one of our tanks getting hit. The gun was stuck over top of the driver's hatch, and the tank brewed, or it caught on fire. So when he*

The advance of the Canadians from the Gustav Line to the Hitler Line.

was stuck under there and we could hear him hollering but we couldn't help him. He just burned to death. So anybody trapped in their tank and it was on fire, they were goners. We had the Shermans. Sometimes we'd put on tractor wheels and so on for bits of armour — so that would increase the weight, and that thing's top weight would be around forty tons. Our infantry guys would be knocking out tanks, they would have the PIAT gun, which was pretty good, but wouldn't do anything to a Tiger tank, and we had what they called the sticky bomb. They go up and they'd ram this thing about a foot in circumference and it was sticky. Exactly as the name implies, it would stick to the hull of the tank, turret, whatever it was, and it did a good job of knocking them out.

Joseph Reid (Calgary Regiment)

Armour-piercing shells have a hard iron steel inner core, and if it hits a tank and doesn't glance off, it goes through. It starts off in the shell, but the shell is pointed and it's armour-piercing, and so the hot steel core of that shell goes through and it inevitably starts the fire, igniting the gas fumes inside the tank. So that's what happens most of the time. Crews have to bail out in a hurry and take a chance from there on.

Jim Holman (48th Highlanders)

They had broken through the Gustav Line and I couldn't see much fortification. The Germans had these things like anti-tank guns that were low to the ground, and you couldn't see them and they were just lethal things for our tanks.

Gord Outhwaite (48th Highlanders)

I rode a motorcycle a lot, and a buddy and I were going right up to the line and we came across a tank battle. So we said, "Oh, can't go through there, to heck with that." You don't have too much armour on a motorcycle you know. So we stopped and we got over to a gun pit. We thought, "Well we'll see" — there's always a lull for maybe about a minute, it could even be two minutes, and that's the time you got to get going. All of a sudden we heard this damn thing wind up, and you wouldn't believe the screech, and we say, "What in the devil is that?" Then all of a sudden you could hear the bombs and they have the tail fins pierced to create a screaming noise on its way down. There's six of them — so as soon as that sixth one goes, you have a minute to get the hell out of there.

On May 17 they were over halfway to the Hitler Line, with battles raging on either side of them. To the right the Poles threw everything that they had at the Germans in Monte Cassino, gradually prying their way into the ruins of the town. To the left the French were advancing towards Pontecorvo. The next day Monte Cassino fell and a Polish flag was raised over the ruins of the monastery, ending one of the most severe conflicts of the Italian Campaign.

Artillery played a major role in the Italian Campaign. Here shellfire wreaks havoc near Pontecorvo.

The devastation of Monte Cassino. The Germans held the monastery at the summit, and the entire town suffered through the Allied bombing. The position was key to the entry into the Liri Valley.

John Richardson (Ontario Regiment)

The Poles had quite a job getting the Germans out of the cathedral at Monte Cassino. They bombed it but all they did was pile up rubble that the Germans could just hide in. I remember heading up to Cassino and there was a great monstrous hole in the ground, a bomb hole, and it was at least three miles from Cassino. There was a big sign there, the Brits put it up: "American precision bombing of Cassino." But Cassino was sure a mess, they sure messed up that town, it was just rubble. There was hardly anything standing at all.

Al Sellers (Governor General's Horse Guards)

We were stuck in the valley for a long time, we couldn't get by because they were up on the high ground and they could just play hob with anybody who tried to get through. What got them was the Polish — gone in from the back. The Germans in there — there was so much rock over top of them a plane could come along and bomb it, it didn't bother those fellows, they were maybe twenty feet below it. It was a greater sight to see the Polish tanks come up along the ridge and to take Monte Cassino. When they capitulated we were able to move through.

John Richardson (Ontario Regiment)

Now behind the Gustav Line, further north, they had the Hitler Line erected. That was prepared with big heavy pillboxes with the tanks — if you know anything about the tanks the Germans had, they had wonderful tanks. They didn't have as many as we had, but they had far better tanks than we had, far better guns too. We were outgunned something awful, but we had more tanks and they travelled pretty fast too. Those Sherman tanks weren't a bad tank, mechanically.

Peter Routcliffe (Governor General's Horse Guards)

We had good regiments with us, there was the Toronto Irish, and the Westminster Regiment, and we had the Lord Strathcona Horse, the British Columbia Dragoons, the 8th New Brunswick Hussars, and the Perths — all their infantry regiments and they were going in and clearing out

A tank of the Governor General's Horse Guards roars across a field.

the houses. We had quite a deal with them through the actions, different ones wherever we went. Well we had heavy guns on the tanks, and they would call for a certain area to have it fired on and they would go down and do it.

Jim Holman (48th Highlanders)

We had a little short guy called Menzies, and he was the PIAT man. He got a tank one day. Hit it in the back door, in the smoke too. He was scared to death, and he fired it, and those things are very inaccurate, you don't know if they are going to hit where you aim or not. All of a sudden there was an explosion and then this door came flying out of the smoke. There was this big explosion and then you could see the fire inside the smoke, and then the smoke cleared and there was one body lying on the ground. We were so excited we were jumping up and down that he had got it.

As Monte Cassino fell on May 18, the lead units of the Canadian Army reached the Hitler Line. The Germans had established strongpoints at Aquino and Piedimonte, while the line itself was one kilometre deep, where concrete gun emplacements, artillery, tanks, and mortar were mutually supporting and well positioned. Just to get at the strong defensive positions, the Allies would have to find a way through minefields and barbed wire. There were no weaknesses, and it was going to be a brutal job to breach the Hitler Line.

Jim Holman (48th Highlanders)

They had a lot of time to work on the Adolf Hitler Line. It was really, really well made. They had big tank ditches built, and of course they had barbed wire. The barbed wire seemed to be the first thing that we ran into. The noise was just deafening, and they just shoot everything at you, like Moaning Minnies, and there was like these Spandau machine guns that would sound like somebody ripped a piece of cloth. They were really good with their mortars, and of course they all had whistles on them, which didn't help. When I still hear a whistle it bothers me, I can't go where there's fireworks, the whistles just drive me crazy.

Harry Fox (Hastings and Prince Edward Regiment)

On the Hitler Line they had anti-tank guns mounted on concrete pillboxes, and they were difficult to get around because a tank couldn't get close enough to them to knock them out. Infantry had to go in first, so it was a combination of infantry and tank.

On May 19 the 78th British Division attacked the strong point of the line at Aquino with support from the Ontario Regiment. They moved forward early in the morning, as a fog hung over the valley, hiding the men and tanks from view. Unfortunately it obscured their observation of the German positions as well.

John Richardson (Ontario Regiment)

The British supposedly did a recce of Aquino, and they reported that it was lightly held by the Germans. You couldn't see your hand in front of your face for fog. We had to talk to one another, because we couldn't see a damn thing, it was that dense! Afterwards I wished it had stayed on us all day long. We wandered up through this fog and they had these great big pillboxes that we didn't know about. They had been dug in,

waiting for us. So the sun came out and the fog lifted and all hell broke loose. I was supposed to be following my buddy, he had more experience. He went over the railway tracks and then he stopped there. I turned and we got into a nice low spot, we were behind the hangars, and the infantry unfortunately was knocked right out. They lost their colonel, their adjutant, the whole headquarters. They dropped a mortar right into the carrier and blew the whole thing apart. The infantry pulled back because they were completely disorganized and we were left out there on the airport. The airport's pretty flat and these guns were right on the edge of the airport, and they had a field day. We lost about thirteen tanks that day. Fortunately I went in this little lowland, and the gun was just placed right

Soldiers run for cover during shelling between the Gari River valley and the Aquino airport.

up the track I'd say about five hundred yards ahead of me. The railway track was quite an embankment there, and he potted at me all day long, but he couldn't get down low enough to get me. I got my first two tanks in a little further into that depression and I stayed there. We called for smoke, so they smoked out the airport and we were fine then, everything had quieted down. It was nice until the smoke started lifting, then all hell broke loose again with shelling. I bet you I could have caught these shells going over my head, they were coming that low. I had a headache for three days afterwards, I remember that. So that was the way we spent the day at Aquino, we were just stuck there. We lost our major, Harry Melon, he got hit in the head with a shell. We got him out of there and into hospital, he survived but he was never the same again. Well, we survived that day, and when night came on we got some more smoke and we got off. We all scooted out and we stayed more or less on the perimeter, back in the trees.

The Canadians lost quite a few tanks that day, while the British suffered heavy casualties. A few kilometres away the tragedy was being repeated as the advancing troops of the Vandoos and the Carleton and Yorks left the bridgehead at the Forme d'Aquino and moved ahead in the fog. When it cleared, they found themselves surrounded by German pillboxes in a maze of barbed wire. There was no way to extricate themselves easily, and the Germans opened fire, inflicting fifty casualties.

Peter Routcliffe (Governor General's Horse Guards)
I saw the battle as it went on and it seemed to me that there was an awful lot of fires that were caused by APHE shells, that's armour-piercing high-explosive shells. The shells were going off and landing in hay and would set fire to them, and set fire to the houses. There were all sorts of firing going on back and forth. So we'd take a position and keep protected for a while and then advance.

Moving supplies to the front near the Rapido and Liri Rivers.

To overcome the German defences the Allies planned to launch a full-scale attack. The main thrust would occur between Aquino and Pontecorvo, along a two-kilometre stretch of the Hitler Line. The responsibility for Operation Chesterfield was given to the Canadians, who would send the PPCLI, the Seaforths, and the Carleton and Yorks in to get the job done. The Loyal Eddies, the Vandoos, and the West Novas were to be in reserve. While rain delayed the launch of the operation, the 48th Highlanders moved through the French position near Pontecorvo on May 22 in an attempt to exploit a perceived German weakness there. They hoped to get behind the Germans and outflank them, but the weakness in the line was merely an illusion, and by noon the 48th Highlanders' advance was brought to a halt by the Germans.

John Richardson (Ontario Regiment)

The Canadian 1st Div attacked Pontecorvo and they ran into the same thing, the same fog. We went in afterwards — they must have knocked out twenty-five of the tanks, all within a very short distance. They practically wandered on top of this pillbox. It was pitiful, really, they just got banged off and one of the things that struck me was the FOO, which is the artillery forward officer, he was observing for the artillery. They gave him a Sherman tank with a wooden gun, so that he had room inside with his wireless and everything. There was this broken gun and that poor damn tank was within forty feet of that gun. He was knocked out too and was killed. I never saw such a mess in all my life.

On May 23 the quiet morning was suddenly shattered by the thunder of more than eight hundred guns unleashing all of their fury on the German positions in that small stretch of the Hitler Line.

Peter Routcliffe (Governor General's Horse Guards)

Artillery and aircraft was the main thing there, and the guns that we had were big 75s and 17-pounders, and when they blasted away with them things, well, sooner or later they got blown out of there, and we kept on going up.

Herb Pike (48th Highlanders)

A good gun crew with 25-pounders, they can run over twenty rounds a minute through, you know. Jerry used to call the 25-pounders the automatic artillery. They couldn't believe the number of rounds that could come through one gun.

A fog hung over the valley, and the men and tanks moved forward. They were slowed down by barbed wire and couldn't keep up with the creeping barrage that was supposed to cover their advance. As the shellfire moved on, the Germans in the forward defensive positions returned to their guns and started to fire on the advancing Canadians. The situation began to degenerate quickly. Some tanks ran into a minefield and couldn't advance, leaving the infantry to move forward on their own. For the PPCLI it got worse. Several German paratroopers who had escaped from Monte Cassino were holed up near the Forme d'Aquino and began raking the PPCLI with enfilade fire. It was a deadly trap, and tragically, due to a failure in communications, the Loyal Eddies fell victim to the same crossfire. All across the front Canadians were being torn apart by the German firepower.

Harry Fox (Hastings and Prince Edward Regiment)
First of all there'd be a belt of barbed wire about a good twenty-five feet wide and eighteen inches high. Then of course there were mines — anti-tank mines, anti-personnel mines — and they were spread all over. Some of them were on this side of the wire, and some of them were behind the wire. It was tricky work for the Engineers to get them out. Then there were machine gun pits, just a hole in the ground with two men and a machine gun. Other places they had the steel turret about three or four feet high for one man and a machine gun, and he could sweep an area, and of course the bloody thing was two-inches-thick metal — he was almost impossible to get. You had to crawl around him and get him from behind. There were a lot of those there.

Sydney Frost (Princess Patricia's Canadian Light Infantry)
They attacked the famous Hitler Line in the Liri Valley and were severely repulsed. It was the strongest of all the fortifications in Italy, and the Germans had years to prepare this thing. It was supposed to be impregnable because they called it the Hitler Line. It wasn't, not to the Canadians. They went in and after the battle was over, I think there was only sixty-seven, or sixty-nine, or seventy troops reported back to the regimental headquarters. Only one man succeeded in getting to the objective, and that was the famous Bucko Watson. He was awarded the Military Cross for that operation. I was fortunate not to be there. A lot of my friends were killed and today reside in the Cassino War Cemetery. I missed that battle and I was very unhappy about it, almost a feeling of guilt — being in England, lying in the lap of luxury, and my friends are all being killed.

It was a disastrous day for the Seaforths and the PPCLI, with massive losses in all ranks. Despite the dire circumstances, the brave young men continued their advance. Either they would reach their objective or die trying. As the westerners struggled, it was a different story for the Carleton and Yorks. Their reconnaissance had established routes through the minefield in front of them, and they rapidly took their objectives in a little over an hour. The German emplacements at the Forme d'Aquino posed a great threat to the Canadians, so at noon the artillery turned its attention on the town and delivered seventy-four tons of explosives within a minute. The infantry swiftly moved in to secure the town. At this point only a few of the objectives had been achieved. It was clear that they would have to exploit the success of the Carleton and Yorks to drive a wedge through the Hitler Line.

Harry Fox (Hastings and Prince Edward Regiment)

Well, I would say the artillery did a very good job. The 1st Brigade area knocked out a lot of mortars with our concentration of artillery fire. But it still boiled down to the infantry getting in close. The initial attack by the 2nd Brigade — they were enfiladed from a town on the flank — Piedimonte. That had to be knocked out by artillery fire before the second attack went in. The second attack was done by the Carleton and Yorks — they were the first regiment to actually penetrate the line, and then the 1st Brigade on the left, and the 3rd Brigade on the right — they began to push in. The Hasty Ps made three attacks that day, each one was successful. Each one overcame a little pop of opposition there, and the next one, and the next one. The first attack went in at 7 or maybe 7:30 in the morning after a two-hour barrage, and the last Hasty P attack went in at 1700. So it took all day. And of course you kept pushing forward, even though it was night, you still kept going forward. Jerry knew he lost the line and he was retiring.

The West Novas quickly advanced through the Carleton and Yorks' position late that afternoon, despite the massive losses inflicted on their supporting tanks. The West Novas found themselves virtually surrounded and under intense fire, but their held their position until help arrived. Two platoons were taken prisoner by the Germans as they were digging in, only to be freed later on

A German POW is searched by a member of the Vandoos.

when their captors had the tables turned on them and they were taken as POWs. The Vandoos followed with support from the Three Rivers tanks, and together they expanded on the breach that the Carleton and Yorks had established. The Vandoos advanced so quickly that the Germans' barrage against them actually fell behind them.

Jim Holman (48th Highlanders)

I had the daylights scared out of me at the Adolf Hitler Line. I'd been told to run across this flat field, it was just full of guys running across the field and you wouldn't believe it — in your mind you're thinking, "They're just lying down," but they're falling down and they don't get back up. I just have to try to put it out of my mind. I can see people going out of their mind in a place like that if you were a little bit inclined that way. You're tired and hungry and then this thing happens to you, you kind of go into a bit of a trance.

> **Courage!**
> There's the courage that nerves you
>   in starting to climb
> The mount of success rising sheer;
> And when you've slipped back,
>   there's the courage sublime
> That keeps you from shedding a
>   tear.
> These two kinds of courage—more
>   strength to the word!—
> Are worthy of tribute, but then
> You'll not reach the summit un-
>   less you've the third—
> The courage to try it again.
>
> —o—

Right: *Newspaper portrait of the infantry in the Italian Campaign.*

Above: *A poem about courage, clipped from a Canadian newspaper, 1944.*

> **Infantry Gives Force to War Machine**
>
> WITH CANADIANS IN ITALY (CP).—The most magnificent sight of them all is unfolding in the dust below. The infantryman is moving up.
>
> He comes up the road in endless, plodding, silent columns. His helmet is heavy on his head and he has pushed it back with the camouflage net and shell dressing that burden it further. His face is tanned and tired and impassive. His eyes squint in the dust.
>
> He seldom speaks and when he does he doesn't say much. There isn't much to be said. His shirt is open and his brown chest sweats in the sun and the dust. His rifle is slung over his shoulder, his water-bottle and mess-tin and gas cape hang from the web belt buckled about his waist. In his hand he carries a small shovel. It will soon be time to use it on the Italian soil.
>
> They call a halt and somebody pulls out the cigarets and he has a smoke. He lays aside his helmet, takes his rifle off his shoulder and leans it against a wall.
>
> He looks back down the road with vacant eye at the convoys of trucks and jeeps and carriers and ambulances that have been slogging along this narrow Italian road for three solid days. Great and relentless and powerful is the machine that backs him up. Invaluable are the tanks that coat him now with dust, indispensable the guns in the fields beside the road that draw his hollow gaze.
>
> But they are only spokes in a wheel and he is the hub. He is the spearhead, the key, the backbone of it all. He knows that and feels it and is too tired to care.
>
> **A Silent Column**
>
> He picks up his rifle with the rag knotted over the muzzle and rejoins the endless, plodding, silent column. He doesn't swagger, doesn't wisecrack, doesn't whistle. He seldom speaks and when he does he doesn't say much. There isn't much to be said.
>
> His shoulders slouch, his eyes look down and stare for minutes on end at nothing but the baggy pants of the man in front of him, and doesn't see a thing. He puts one boot in front of another and does it again again until he has covered yards and miles in his dogged, measured tread.
>
> He hears the guns and sees their flashes in the fields. He is in shelling range and the enemy lurks ahead. The front is fluid, and near. The front is hell. He'd like to be home, in England, anywhere but here on the road near the front, but he puts one boot in front of another and goes on and on and on.
>
> The trucks roll by and push him to the side of the road and cover him with dust. He hears the guns and hears the planes and senses the atmosphere of the front. He knows them all, accepts them all with dead disinterest. The thrill they might once have brought has long since passed away, and there is just one
>
> boot pushing itself ahead of another until they seem to do it automatically.
>
> Finally, he is lost in the dust and the distance, he and his baggy, weary, earthy magnificence. He is the king in his domain, the master of the scene and too damned tired to care. He is the infantryman moving up.

MAY 23 FOREVER IS SEAFORTH DAY FOR HEROIC FIGHT

By DOUG. HOW

With the Canadian Corps in Italy, June 22—(CP)—It raged for 12 hours and more, this violence which wrested from the German those few hundred yards of death he had strung across the peaceful Liri valley. They called it the Hitler line.

Men died with a courage that was magnificent, advanced when advance seemed impossible, held for hours on the objective that hundreds started for and dozens reached. There was more than one Canadian battalion involved that May 23, but this is the story of the Seaforth Highlanders of Canada.

Their advance began at 6 o'clock through fields that stood waist-high in wet grain, that hid the enemy in the fog and mist of an Italian morning and the smoke of action; that held mines and wire that went back for 20 feet, that bristled with anti-tank guns and pillboxes; whose trees gave a leafy cover to snipers, and whose soil was broken for hours by hundreds of German mortar and artillery shells.

The violence of this day may be told best with the statement that this battalion suffered as many casualties in those four hours as it had in the six days of the Ortona fighting. The British tanks that supported them had more casualties than in all their Tunisian campaign.

Helpless Before Tanks

By 8.45 Major James Allen, MacLeod, Alta., reported that he was organizing his 100 men and two officers who had fought through to the objective, the Aquino-Pontecorvo road. Behind them lay the dead and wounded of two companies. Ahead of them were hours of shelling, machine-gunning, mortaring and finally a tank attack that found them helpless to oppose it.

The tanks came about 4.30 p.m. It had been impossible to get anti-tank guns up to them. Their only anti-tank weapon, the Piat, had exhausted its ammunition. Wireless communication was broken.

Some men dived into a ditch beside the road. The tanks rode unmolested along the road, machine-gunning those figures in the ditch. Then they turned and ordered those who still lived to surrender. Major Allen, with a flesh wound in his thigh, feigned death and eventually walked back for medical aid.

Will Live Forever

May 23 was a day that will live forever in Canadian history. Courageous actions became commonplace. These are only a few that may tell some of the story of those 12 hours:

For five hours C.S.M. W. G. Coffey, Vancouver, and a little group of men sheltered in a house where their every move brought enemy fire. They had six wounded men there.

When dusk came they crept out past a German machine-gun without being spotted. When they reached their battalion headquarters kept leading and encouraging his men on. Finally the objective was reached and Cromb ordered his men to dig in. But when he looked around there was no one else to dig in. Officer after officer was wounded or killed, and more than one had to be ordered back. Finally there were no officers left and few N.C.O.'s. Privates found themselves commanding privates.

Cpl. C. M. Anderson was pinned down by a sniper. He stood up, let the German shoot at him, spotted him, then killed him.

C.S.M. Joe Duddle, of Vernon, B.C., rescued a wounded tankman, rescued an officer and took him to shelter under his tank; later took him back for medical attention. When Maj. Allen was forced to go back, C.S.M. Duddle took over.

Pte. L. B. Poppel, Vancouver, attacked and destroyed two machine-gun posts, rescued four wounded men, then went on to the objective.

The battalion sanitary corporal, Lewis Greig, of Vancouver, carried out wounded all day long. Capt. Don Colquhoun, Vancouver, organized a shuttle of Bren-gun carriers as mobile stretchers.

The bodies of six Seaforth privates were found 300 yards beyond their objective. There had been Germans to kill. They kept on going until they themselves were killed.

That was May 23 in the Liri valley. Canada's Seaforth Highlanders have known no finer day.

Paint Swastikas
By DOUGLAS AMARON

With the Canadian Corps in Italy, June 22—(CP)—A Canadian self-propelled field regiment, in close contact with the enemy for the first time, supported the infantry and tanks in the Hitler line attack, blasting out gun emplacements and wiping out machine-gun nests.

One of the first successes earned the crew permission from Maj.-Gen. Chris Vokes to paint a Swastika on their gun, was the destruction of a gun emplacement in the Hitler line. It had a 75-millimetre gun in a Panther tank turret mounted in concrete.

The crew, which included Gnr. Lloyd Colborne, Sarnia, hit the target with their second shot and set it on fire.

Other crews cleared three houses of Germans, rooting 15 enemy from one house, and shot up five machine-gun emplacements.

One crew on this job included Sgt. J. L. Spurgeon, Hamilton, and Gnr. D. C. C. McLeod, Listowel. In the other crew were D. Wood, Kingston; R. J. Mills, Owen Sound, and A. E. Clymer, Toronto.

WOULD CALL ON DRAFTEES

Kingston, June 22—Speaking in the country of his boyhood John Bracken, national leader of the Progressive Conservative party, yesterday declared that if the government needed men overseas, as it said it did, it should call on the 70,000 men now "sheltered" in the home defence army.

This should be done before it made any more demands on the boys now in industry or on farms, he added. Speaking of the peace to come, he advocated an international police force. The League of Nations was given the power only to talk following the last war, he said. This time it should be given the power to do more than talk.

Harry Fox (Hastings and Prince Edward Regiment)

In the first place you didn't think too much about danger to yourself. The guy on either side might get knocked off, but you're all right, you keep on going. You weren't really frightened of getting killed. And it's just as dangerous to keep on going as it is to sit on your ass because there were mortars coming down. So you might as well keep moving forward, and your men, your pals are moving forward — well, you can't let them go, you've got to go with your pals. So it was just a matter of well, there's a hill, for Christ's sake get up there! Which they did. All infantry soldiers are brave, they got to be.

Jim Holman (48th Highlanders)

It took a lot of fighting to get them out of there. The problem with us footsloggers is we don't know what we're doing. We're told to do something, and you just go and do it. They say we're going to spread out and we're going to run attack across that field. You don't know why, you don't know what the end of it's going to be, nobody tells you anything, and when it's finished you don't know what you've done. You just know that you dig in and you stay here for the night. I think the sergeant might be the most knowledgeable, but from there up they'd know why they were doing it. I know lots of places you just did it and come out, you're tired and you don't know why you did it. It was really an experience.

Down the line the Hasty Ps cleared the area around Pontecorvo along with the 48th Highlanders and the RCRs, and by 1900 they captured the town. Sergeant Jack Loshaw of the Hasty Ps exhibited great bravery in capturing nineteen prisoners, and he later received the Military Medal for his actions. As the sun set on May 23, the Vandoos had captured their objective as well. The Canadians had succeeded in shattering the best defensive line that the Germans could create, and

Newspaper article about the heroics of the Seaforth Highlanders in the Liri Valley.

they had done it in one day. The cost was devastating, though. They had battled through a gauntlet of fire, and in the process the Canadian 1st Division suffered 879 casualties, with many dead. A lot of fine young soldiers were taken prisoner as well, leaving the regiments under strength once again. The 2nd Brigade was particularly hard hit, with 162 killed, 306 wounded, and 75 taken prisoner — the worst losses in a single day by any Canadian brigade in the Italian Campaign.

Albert Wade (Royal Canadian Dragoons)

In the head car was a chap I knew very well, and his name was Moore. When we were approaching one of the bridge sites there, he went ahead to investigate and he discovered mines. On a bridge that had already fallen flat, it left a passageway up, so he was looking that over while I was looking at another spot. Anyway, he decided that this mine was sitting there, it seemed to be above ground, and he made a mistake of taking it by the handle and pulling it and as a result he was blown up. His car wasn't badly damaged, and the driver was in shock. We regrouped and went towards the town called Pontecorvo. When we got to Pontecorvo it had been liberated by the Hasty P regiment. We took up positions on the southern part of the town, amongst some buildings.

Herb Pike (48th Highlanders)

As a matter of fact, one section of Baker Company of the 48th was the first through the Hitler Line. They were the first to make a dent through the actual line itself, and we chased Jerry once we got through, we chased them up Route 6, which was the main highway into Rome. We chased him ninety miles in three days. He's fighting a rearguard action and we're digging in — then you'd just get the hole dug and away you'd go again. We were about twenty-five miles south of Rome and we were told to halt.

It was quite an extensive line, the Hitler Line. They had tank turret tops embedded in concrete with fellows inside working the guns, 88s. I went in to inspect one of these things and there was two Jerries still sitting at the controls of the gun, burnt, I guess if you touched them they'd disintegrate, but they were still sitting there. Just burnt to a crisp where an AP shell had gone through and set a fire with the high …

Gord Outhwaite (48th Highlanders)

…or the concussion …

Herb Pike (48th Highlanders)
…the concussion would kill them, yeah.

Jim Holman (48th Highlanders)
One of the things I don't remember too much is aircraft. There was a lot of aircraft, but we were so busy we never watched, you had to look after yourself. There was mostly our aircraft, the Germans were too busy with Europe, going into Holland and the other places with their aircraft. One time we were walking down the road and the Italian people were going the opposite direction because they were getting away from the fighting. There were mules and horses and people pulling carts, and way off to our left, you could see this aircraft and it was flying alone. It went out of sight and all of a sudden he was coming back up the road, and it was shooting. The Italian people were in the ditch off to the side of the road, and it just happened to be that this road was raised up through a fairly flat area, where most of the roads in Italy were sunken. If it had have been in one of them sunken roads, we would have been stuck there, you couldn't get away. They just shot right up the road. You know, we were trained so that everybody was to shoot at the aircraft, at a twelve-degree angle. It ended up there was nobody standing up shooting at the aircraft. Heh heh. There was nobody going to stand there with this thing just popping off up the road.

Harry Fox (Hastings and Prince Edward Regiment)
We only had one attack by the Jerry Air Force all the time I was in Italy. It was just after morning stand-to. They went in to have breakfast and this Jerry airplane came down and fired at them and hit the mortar, and put a gouge in it as thick as your thumb. Now if he had been five minutes sooner, he'd have caught them standing around that mortar in their stand-to positions. But they were all in the house by that time, so they were very lucky. That's the only time the aircraft bothered us when I was in Italy. Our air force had complete air control of Italy, but it didn't mean a great deal to us. We had the fighter-bombers who would drop a bomb, but you were very careful to make sure it was aimed a mile away from you. You didn't want any big bombs coming down on you. So we did have support, but we didn't use it all the time, and half the time with the weather — rain and smog and that sort of stuff — you couldn't use it.

With the breakthrough the Canadians had opened the route to Rome. The tanks of the Canadian 5th Division roared ahead in pursuit of the retreating German army, heading for the next major obstacle in their path: the Melfa River.

The Italian Campaign left a path of destruction through Italy, such as these ruins created near the Melfa River.

Albert Wade (Royal Canadian Dragoons)

Around four-thirty in the afternoon we were told to advance up a roadway leading north to the Melfa River. I was put in the lead car and the sergeant of my troop was a chap by the name of Spike Malone. So away we went up this road, and it was being heavily mortared. The Hasty Ps were on our right as we went up. We noticed that there were quite a few abandoned German soldiers that had been given up for dead. We bypassed them, reporting the fact that they were there, and went on up to the crossroad, and for some reason or another the Moaning Minnies stopped. We got up to the tributary of the Melfa, and there was a roadway along the south bank, and you had to go through a little bit of an inundation in the embankment, because that particular part of the waterway had been made into a canal. My job was to take a look down both sides of that road. As I made the turn onto the roadway, about four or five hundred yards ahead I spotted one of these tollgate houses and it was very well fortified. So we stopped the car and parked it by this pillbox. There were two or three dead officers in there and a lot of machine gun equipment and small mortars. In the meantime we came under fire from another Canadian regiment, which was dead ahead on our right. They were firing at us with their 75mm anti-tank guns, and it got pretty hot. So we stayed there until they called in to headquarters and had them quit the shelling. In the meantime there

The war left Italy destroyed, the likes of which the Canadians had never seen before. Pontecorvo lies in ruins.

A Cape Breton Highlander passes a dead German soldier while advancing towards the Melfa River.

153

was a continuous flow of German troops coming across that canal on the low water — they were actually walking across the creek towards us. So we just waved them on and in the meantime the other elements of my troop and some of the follow-up troops had come up the same road that we had travelled and they had taken positions along this embankment. They were receiving these troops, these surrenders. There were quite a few of them. So that was that for that day. We pulled back and spent the night in and around Pontecorvo and got some rest.

Harry Fox (Hastings and Prince Edward Regiment)

Exhaustion? Well, of course it hits different men in different ways. Some of the men just get so tired that they don't want to do anything. You couldn't send a man like that on a patrol because as soon as he got far enough away that you couldn't see him, he'd just sit down. You couldn't blame him because he was done. Other men got angry and were a menace to their friends because they'd get up and start swearing and making noise. You had to get rid of them, they were dangerous. Mostly it was just you were so bloody tired you didn't care what went on, and you weren't sharp enough on the job anymore. Things that six months previous you'd have done without thinking of it, now it becomes a task, and you figure "Well, to heck with it!"

Jim Holman (48th Highlanders)

I think it was just adrenaline that kept me going. Many times I fell asleep in a position. It was my turn to be on guard, and we'd all be in slit trenches and Al was a little guy with me. Somebody gave me this aluminum-faced pocket watch, it belonged to the sergeant, and I was to keep my two hours on watch and then hand him the watch. They were expecting a German counterattack, so everybody was on edge. Al was still digging, and then the next thing I knew I heard this guy screaming and hollering. Here was an officer and it was getting daylight and I had fallen asleep at midnight, and I had slept all night on my knees with my rifle against my shoulder in the slit trench. I woke up with a shock when I heard this screaming and I thought, "Boy, I'm in trouble, I've fallen asleep." He's coming along there just screaming and hollering, "There's nobody on watch!" and when he got to where Al was he said, "This little guy is the only one that's awake," so everybody else had fallen asleep. He just walked right past me. I was so relieved that he didn't pick me out, and when I went to hand the sergeant back the watch, I had squeezed it so tight that I bent it. I actually bent the pocket watch like almost a U.

The Melfa River was situated ten kilometres beyond the Hitler Line, and was the next German defensive line protecting Rome. Like so many other river crossings in Italy, it posed a number of problems: the banks of the river were steep, making it impossible for the Canadian tanks to manoeuvre across it. The Germans held advantageous positions along the high ground of the far bank, and there were few obvious places to cross, so the Germans concentrated their defences at those points. The task of crossing the Melfa and securing a bridgehead was given to the 5th Division, with support from the 5th Armoured Brigade.

The advance was led by the B.C. Dragoons and the Irish Regiment. They were under the command of Fred Vokes, brother of General Chris Vokes. On May 24 they clashed with elements of the 1st Panzer Regiment, knocking out one of their new fifty-ton Mark V Panzers. The tanks of the Governor General's Horse Guards covered the flanks. The Germans were pushed back to the river, and the Lord Strathcona's Horse and the Westminster Regiment took the

Above: *Canadians marching towards the Melfa River.*

Right: *Searching for a German sniper amidst the rubble of a destroyed Italian village.*

lead in the advance. The Strathconas scouted for a suitable site for a crossing. They sped ahead of the advancing column in their light Honey tanks, getting to the river and winding their way parallel to it. Not far from one obvious spot that was well defended by the Germans there was another possibility, although it would require some improvisation. The spot was not defended, and the Royal Canadian Engineers eliminated the obstacle that the steep riverbanks presented by simply digging an opening on each side for the tanks and vehicles to pass through.

Al Sellers (Governor General's Horse Guards)

Well, our tanks, the Sherman tanks, had a five-man crew — driver, ball gunner, the gunner, the loader, and the crew commander. They were cramped. The big gun would be between the loader and the gunner. When the loader loaded it and the gunner pressed a switch and it fired, there was a deflector shield behind the breach. Every time it was fired it would expel a casing and hit this deflector, drop in a bag, which would cause a tremendous clatter. When we fired the machine guns your spent casings would drop in a bag, and at the first opportunity you just take the bag and dump it. So most of the machine-gunning in a tank was what we called "hose piping." Every so many rounds there would be a tracer, and the gunner would follow the line of the tracers onto his target. So we were firing at maybe five hundred or one thousand yards away. Now the infantry — these poor guys, they were around the corner from their opponent.

John Richardson (Ontario Regiment)

We didn't bring tanks up into the mountains to any great extent. I tried to do that one day and the damn road gave way and I [was] just left balancing. The infantry asked me if I would try and get my tank up this blinking vineyard, and climb this hill. Down below there was this strong point of Germans and he wanted me to get across this little stone bridge. The tank was rubbing both sides — it was that narrow. I should never have tried it anyway because it's a wonder that bridge held a tank. The whole thing caved away and there I was, just teetering. So we gingerly got out of the tank and the tank recovery came along and put cables on it and pulled it out. When somebody asks you to do something and you say, "No we can't do it," that's a no-no. If you can do it at all, you should do it. There would be several tanks with a company of infantry — we were in support of, not under command of — thank God for that because some of the infantry companies weren't used to fighting with tanks. There was one case there my tank broke down, so they put a reserve officer in charge and promptly lost all three tanks because the infantry commander asked them to attack this hill ahead of them. It was kind of a flat land and was set up beautifully to have an SP up the top where the Germans were. Anyway, one of the officers, he refused to do it. He could see the danger, but this other officer hadn't been in action before. He said he would do it, and he lost the tanks and lost a very good friend of mine. When we went up to Trasimeno the colonel told me that we had four British divisions wanting us to work with them. That's the kind of demand we had on our time, that's why we were engaged because we no sooner finished with one division, there was always some other division getting into dirty spots and wanted our help. So they moved us from one to the other, we did this all the time. I don't think there was any other formation that got accolades anywhere close to ours. I know Montgomery said, "If you want a job done, get the 1st Canadian Armoured Brigade." Sir Oliver Leese, who took over from Montgomery commanding the 8th Army, he said we were the finest army formation in the Mediterranean theatre. We had a lot of accolades like that, so they kept us busy and that was all right, that's what we're there for.

The Germans occupied a house a short distance up the river on the far side, but their observation was entirely focused on the obvious crossing point, and so when the Strathconas made their crossing of the Melfa River that afternoon, it went uncontested. They descended on the house and quickly took the position. Immediately, A Company of the Westminsters crossed the Melfa to reinforce the small number of Strathconas defending the key position. It was vital to hold the bridgehead once it was established. If the Germans succeeded in retaking the position, they would reinforce their defences and eliminate the site for a possible future crossing. The Canadians had to hold on, come hell or high water.

When the inevitable German counterattack came, it was relentless. The small band of Canadian soldiers faced a constant barrage for five hours. They clung tenaciously to that small piece of land, surrounded on three sides by a deadly array of weaponry: several tanks, 88mm guns, anti-aircraft guns, Spandau machine guns, and an entire company of infantry with their machine guns and mortars. The Canadians were greatly outnumbered, and they had to defend against this formidable attack with what they had: a few PIATs, their machine guns, and hand grenades. It was a fearsome position to be in, but the men were inspired by Major John Mahony. Despite suffering wounds to his head and leg early in the battle, Mahony continued to bravely

Deadly fire: the Germans mounted 88mm guns at ground level to repel Canadian advances along the Hitler Line.

lead his men with complete disregard for his own safety. An hour later, down to sixty men, and with almost all of his platoon officers wounded, he faced a terrible sight: German tanks preparing for an attack along with a company of German infantry. Mahony directed the fire of his men there and stopped the advance. A small group of Westminsters attacked, throwing grenades in the tank's turrets and firing on them with their PIATs.

The Canadians were in a difficult position defensively. Not only were they surrounded by a larger force on three sides, but the ground was not easy to dig into, so the trenches were shallow and did little to protect the men. As Major Mahony continued his heroics, the Germans began focusing their fire on him, believing that to stop him was key to the collapse of the Canadian defences. Despite being wounded, Mahony painfully moved from position to position, maintaining his men's fighting spirit. The Canadians simply would not relinquish their bridgehead, and at 2030 reinforcement troops were able to get across the Melfa to join the defenders. The bold crossing of the Melfa River and the fierce defence of the bridgehead undermined the German plans for defence in the Liri Valley, and the battle for the strategic region was complete. For his key role in defending the bridgehead over the Melfa, John Mahony was awarded the Victoria Cross.

The Strathconas had had a tough day, losing seventeen Sherman tanks. So on May 25 the regiment was moved into reserve, and the job of expanding the bridgehead was given to the 11th Brigade.

Al Sellers (Governor General's Horse Guards)

At the Melfa River I was driving this HQ tank and we suddenly realized that we were in a minefield. I made a turn, the right track went over a Teller mine and it split the differential and the transmission, and of course that meant oil was going all over the place. The gunner — he got burned very badly, he thought he was bleeding but it was just hot oil. They evacuated the crew and I was left with the tank because they wanted to recover it. Well, about a day and a half later this big truck comes along and the guys hook on and he drags it. While I was waiting, the action was going through and the peasants and the property owners were

Major J.K. Mahony of the Westminster Regiment, winner of the Victoria Cross.

Left: *T. Hallam and A.H. Wharf of the Royal Canadian Artillery get a close look at the German Mark IV tank that had been knocked out.*

Below: *J.A. Thrasher of the Westminster Regiment poses on the German self-propelled 88mm gun he knocked out with the PIAT gun slung over his shoulder.*

coming back and they were clamouring for gas. Well, I had a lot of gas in this tank, so I traded gasoline for pigs and chickens and some wine. Well, at the time it was hot, and I can always remember that the tank was stinking like heck with the rotting food, and of course nobody knew about the gas because we had just siphoned it off.

Harry Fox (Hastings and Prince Edward Regiment)

The trouble with the 5th Div at that time, they had only one brigade of infantry, and once they had secured the Melfa River, they had no one else, so the 1st Brigade from the 1st Division was put in again and follow up Highway 6.

On May 26 the B.C. Dragoons and the Irish Regiment crossed the Melfa and began to advance on Ceprano. It was slow going, as the Germans continued to perfect their skills in conducting a fighting retreat. That afternoon the Cape Breton Highlanders and the Perth Regiment moved along the same route. Ceprano was on the other side of the Liri River, and that night members of the Irish Regiment swam across to do reconnaissance in the small town. The next day Royal Canadian Engineers built a bridge to get the tanks across the river while under fire. As it was being put into place, the bridge was damaged, forcing them to build another one. Meanwhile, the 5th Division waited anxiously to get across the Liri, while to the south the 1st Division was beginning to cross on their own bridge. By late afternoon the second bridge was built. Ceprano was secured by the Perth Regiment, and the advance towards Rome continued.

Telegrams brought bad news from the front, making their delivery in Canada an emotional event.

Fred Scott (Perth Regiment)
Going through we went up the Liri Valley and our first objective was a place called Ceprano. I lost four or five good friends in that battle too.

For a week the Canadians moved slowly towards the Italian capital, contending with German delaying tactics and struggling with the Italian terrain. The Germans were gradually moving back into their next defensive position, the Caesar Line, which was not fully prepared. The German 10th Army was moving relatively quickly so as not to be cut off by the Americans, who had broken out from Anzio to the west. The concentration of Allied forces in the area made communications difficult, as the airwaves were full of competing signals and frequencies from all of the different units in the area.

Jim Holman (48th Highlanders)
They had radios for inter-platoon communication, they were called 18 sets. They were just a little metal one, they would sit on your web, and it had a battery and a spare battery and set of old-type earphones. The throat pieces were about the size of your thumb that were on an elastic band that strapped to your throat. That was inter-platoon because I remember the company radios were big sets, and the one fellow carried them and the other operator walked behind him. I had to look for a fellow by the name of Carl one time, and he had a radio and we didn't know whether he got wounded or went bomb-wacky, but I was sent out to find him. He had it open, on "send," and he kept moaning, and it was blocking up the whole thing because we couldn't hear anything from the other ones. I was supposed to go and find him and shut it off, and I never did find him. I had to wear that thing and dive into trenches with this square thing stuck on your chest. It would break your ribs. The only thing was that was really good was we could listen to the BBC, and I would take the earphones apart and three guys would listen to one earphone, and three guys would listen to other earphone. We could hear the news of the BBC, and we could also hear Vera Lynn and Gracie Fields. A German lady would break in once in a while and tell us how stupid we were for fighting the Germans, and then she would tell us, "You guys out there got girlfriends at home and who are they sleeping with?" Heh heh heh — but I got rid of that thing, I hated that thing. It was terrible. You were attached to the officer. I was a runner, that's why I got it.

The advance continued, with the 1st Division and the 5th Division taking turns in leading the corps. The Canadians advanced along the Liri River, having to overcome obstacles and landmines left by the Germans. One town after

The arrival of the Canadians elicits a feeling of relief, not joy, in the locals. A week earlier the Germans had killed all of the males in this village.

another was taken … Pofi, Arnara, Frosinone, Ferentino, and Anagni. The advance had momentum, and Rome was tantalizingly close.

Albert Wade (Royal Canadian Dragoons)
It was late in the afternoon, word came to take my troop and we were going to escort the 48th Highlanders across the Ferentino airport to the Italian town that was sitting up on a slope at the northwestern tip of the

airport. It meant that we were going to be travelling on the airport property, and it was pretty wide open. The 5th Division had their tanks and they moved up, so it was pretty safe up to a point, but when we got a little over halfway we ran across two or three houses and there were Jerries. We had to get them out, so the infantry got in there and took care of that. Then we took them a little further up and we dropped them off just at the south entrance to the town. Apparently they were getting ready to attack.

Jim Holman (48th Highlanders)

We did a lot of walking. You come up against a rear guard of Germans, and they would stop you. They always had a good position, and of course they'd pin you right down where nobody could move. Then they had to call in some artillery support to get them out of there. And you'd think, "Well, here we go again," and all of a sudden there's another bunch you run into in another place. One day I ended up doing twelve slit trenches. Dig a slit trench and then just move a little ways, and they'd pin you down again, dig another slit trench. When they gave us our implements for digging slit trenches, they gave us a regular-size pick and shovel. Well, when you're pinned down by a machine gun, it was better just to lie there and take your bayonet and dig the hole and scoop it out with your hand or your helmet and get into the hole. You didn't stand up and dig a slit trench with a pick and shovel. The Americans had this little tiny shovel that folded up that they hung on their belt, and they could lie there on the ground and dig a slit trench. Why they didn't give us something like that, I'll never know. I dug more slit trenches with my bayonet. You had lots of time to study the ground when you're lying there with your face down in the mud, and you know, I never saw so many bugs in my life.

Albert Wade (Royal Canadian Dragoons)

The next day we advanced nearby the roadway leading north, called Route Via 6. It was a main highway from Naples up to Rome. The Canadian infantry had advanced up a little bit past the town, but there was a monastery on the right hand side of the road which hadn't been checked out, so we went in there. While we were in there we spotted this huge German Panther tank. Apparently it had either been abandoned or ran out of fuel — but the crew were lollygagging around. So we took them prisoner, we inspected the tank, and one of our drivers attempted to get into the tank to check the motor. He was immediately told to leave it alone, because it might have been booby-trapped. But it was a monster.

Harry Fox (Hastings and Prince Edward Regiment)

Well, the Jerry was retiring, so he'd leave machine gun posts to hold up to a certain time and they would scoot, and we were just pushing up against them. The idea being that the Americans were supposed to cut in from Anzio and cut that road, but they didn't do it, so Jerry escaped. So we just plugged up that road on foot. I think we were two days doing that because we went through Ceprano, Frosinone, a couple of the little towns, and we came to Anagni, and that's where we stopped.

On June 1 the Canadians were ordered to halt at Anagni. Politics came into play, and the Canadians were not to be the ones to liberate Rome. That glory would go to the Americans. After having broken through the Hitler Line and securing the bridgehead over the Melfa River, the Canadians now had to content themselves with being spectators, as they were put into reserve.

Herb Pike (48th Highlanders)

We weren't allowed to go any further to allow the 5th Army to take Rome. That didn't sit too well with the Canadian 1st and 5th Div at that time, we were a little upset over that Rome bit, we figured we should have had the pleasure of so-called taking Rome.

Al Sellers (Governor General's Horse Guards)

Rome fell without much fanfare and much incident. It was sort of political ... the Americans wanted to take Rome. It was in the 8th Army's path but they decided to let the Americans have it. They literally just rolled into Rome with no opposition. Nothing was damaged in it. The Germans just retired and let them have it. Normally when you go through any major place it was clobbered, buildings were shelled, mined — but in Rome I saw no damage at all.

The liberation of Rome met with little resistance but also little celebration. It was the first enemy-held capital to fall to the Allies.

The irony is that Canadians did lead the liberating forces into Rome. The First Special Service Force, the combined American-Canadian unit, led the way into the Italian capital. In the early hours of June 4 they seized the bridges over the Tiber River, and then entered Rome to secure it for the Allies. Several hundred Canadian members of the force played their part in this historic event. Soon after the liberation of Rome, the force was transferred to the south of France to fight there. While in Italy, Canadian members of the Devil's Brigade accounted for 185 of its casualties, with 62 of them buried in Anzio. Their story, while not a part of the Canadian Corps history, is an important chapter in Canada's role in the Second World War.

The Germans abandoned Rome to move north to their next major defensive position, and the Canadians were being moved to an area near Piedimonte d'Alife for reinforcement and rest. The past three weeks of combat had seriously weakened the strength of the corps, with almost 800 killed and 2,500 wounded.

Harry Fox (Hastings and Prince Edward Regiment)
We sat there I think for two days until they figured out what to do, and then the Canadians were withdrawn into reserve. They had to be built up to regular scale, which means hundreds upon hundreds of reinforcements — replacements actually. They had to be trained, so we were six weeks, maybe two months behind the lines doing that. At least we were getting a full night's sleep.

No matter where the Canadians were stationed in Italy, they constantly came face to face with the disaster that had befallen the Italian people when the war invaded their homeland. Poverty and starvation abounded, and the men did what they could to alleviate the pain.

The Canadians found a starving population as they advanced through Italy, and most shared their rations with the locals. Here Ralph Catherall of the Calgary Regiment feeds a young child.

Jim Holman (48th Highlanders)

There was always a lineup of kids, and the mothers would always try and dress the little girls up as pretty as they could in their rags, and scrub them until they just shone. They always had some kind of bucket or container so that when you were finished eating you'd dump your slops in. Of course the pretty little girls got most of the slops, and they must have been just starving too. They dumped the porridge and tea and everything right in the same bucket and took it home and ate it.

Harry Fox (Hastings and Prince Edward Regiment)

Well, naturally when we fed them, they appreciated it, but that didn't last long because we treated them almost like prisoners — send them back. We didn't want them in the way. They could get killed just the same as us, and all them that did get wounded passed through our Regimental Aid Post just like a wounded soldier. So they were something that you got rid of as quick as possible. So you passed them on back.

Jim Holman (48th Highlanders)

I often think about one little chap I saw. I was good friends with a stretcher-bearer, and his name was Jimmy Watt. We were dumping our food into these containers and this little guy was standing there and he would be about four or five years old, and he had his head down like this [on his chest]. Of course everybody is picking out the kid that you want to feed — if you were in a place any length of time you would pick one kid. So anyways this little guy had his head down and I stopped and I tapped him on the head. He lifted his head up to see and he had no jaw. It was blown right off. The lower jaw was completely gone and his tongue was hanging out, and it was full of scabs and was still pretty red, and he put his head back down again. I took him by the hair and lifted his head up and I said to Jimmy Watt, "Look at this," I

Chink Gades and Johnny Scott of the Royal Canadian Artillery's 11th Field Regiment share some bully beef with Italian children in Acireale.

166

said, "gee, this is awful." I still think about that. I wonder what ever happened to that kid? Like how did he ever survive? We were doing it and we got hurt — so what? But they weren't doing it.

The fall of Rome was the cause of great celebration for the Allies, especially on the home front. It represented the liberation of the first major European capital from Nazi tyranny, and more importantly it was tangible proof of success in the war effort. It drew the world's attention to the Italian Campaign. Then within forty-eight hours it was gone. The newspaper headlines and the radios crackled with stunning news: the Allies had invaded Normandy. Suddenly all of the attention turned to northwest Europe, and from that point on the Italian Campaign became an afterthought for the press. For the men in Italy, the dangers had not diminished, and the impetus of the campaign was as vital as ever: they had to continue to keep the Germans busy in Italy so that those troops couldn't be used against the Allies in France. The change in attitude towards the Italian Campaign was long lasting, as the men serving in that theatre no longer received the recognition they so richly deserved, both during the war and after it.

Fred Scott (Perth Regiment)

All of a sudden when D-Day went in — what shall we say? We got the feeling that we were second-class citizens. The Canadian Corps down in Italy seemed to be a forgotten bunch of fellas. But you carried on doing the same job all the time day after day.

Advance In Italy Continues

ROME, June 21.—(BUP)— British 8th Army troops have cleared the Germans from Perugia and advanced three to four miles beyond the town, a communique said today, while French and American units of the Allied 5th Army on the British left flank pushed slowly northward against bitter enemy opposition.

Driving rains slowed the Allied armies all along the central battle-front and desperate Nazi rear guards were putting up a fierce delaying fight everywhere, but there was no indication that the main German forces had been sent into action.

Eighth army veterans wiped out the last enemy resistance in Perugia yesterday morning after an all-night battle against snipers and machine-gunners entrenched in the streets and houses of the ancient cathedral city.

Latest reports said the British were fanning out swiftly beyond the town in full pursuit of the retreating Nazis.

Twenty-three miles to the west, other 8th army forces captured Chiusi and swept on northeast of Lake Chiusi to highway 73.

There was no major change in the 5th army front to the west, but headquarters spokesmen said the French and American troops were running into savage resistance in the Radicofani sector and north of Grosseto.

The Americans on the Tyrrhenian coastal flank captured Monte Pescali, a high feature 10 miles north of Grosseto dominating the intersection of highways one and 73, where stubborn enemy rear guards had been holding out for days.

On the American right, French colonial troops occupied a number of villages northwest of Radicofani yesterday, including Monticello, Seggiano, Vigo Corcia, Bagni San Filippo, Paucia, Palozzettta, Poggio, Majane, Pantano and Campo D'Orcia.

The French gains, averaging about four miles, were battered out after bitter street fighting in most of the captured villages.

On the Adriatic coastal front, the British 8th army forces continued their almost unopposed advance northward, driving four miles up the coastal road to the Menocchio river.

The British columns occupied San Benedetto Del Tronto, a big fishing port and pre-war resort town, Cossigiano, 10 miles inland, and Grottamare, three miles north of San Benedetto.

Advanced patrols moving through the hills inland also reached Ascoli Piceno, a provincial capital 17 miles southwest of Grottamare with acetime population of 42,000 \s.

Campaign in Italy Not Side-Show

WASHINGTON, June 22 (BUP). —Military observers today deplored the growing tendency to regard the Allied campaign in Italy as a side-show to the French invasion, pointing out that the fighting north of Rome is hastening victory no less than the battles on the Normandy peninsula.

While the cross-channel invasion has dominated the headlines during the past two weeks, observers here have not lost sight of the fact that its initial success was due in large part to the drain on German manpower and equipment presented by the Allied forces in Italy.

Prisoners taken by the 5th Army in its surge north of Rome testified to the effectiveness of the fighting there as a diversion. Some of the Nazi prisoners had been rushed to Italy from Belgian garrisons only four days before the Allies struck in Normandy. The outcome of the French beachhead battles could have been different if the Germans had not been forced to commit huge forces in Italy.

The campaign in Italy, it is felt here, has grown no less important since the cross-channel thrust.

Far left: *June 21, 1944, saw the Allied advance continue northward, clearing Perugia.*

Left: *As early as June 22, 1944, it became apparent that the Italian Campaign was no longer the focus of attention, despite the headline claiming otherwise.*

Harry Fox (Hastings and Prince Edward Regiment)
Well, you can't let yourself get worried about things like that. We did have newspaper people coming around and talking to us, and they would put little items in the papers saying so-and-so was just promoted, and so-and-so had been wounded and going home, and things like that. So we weren't exactly disregarded.

King George VI made numerous visits to Italy to bolster the spirits of the troops. Here he inspects a regiment of the Royal Canadian Artillery.

THE STAR WEEKLY

Page Eight

Toronto, July 8, 1944

Cutting an Army to Ribbons

By ARTHUR HELLIWELL

Allied soldiers slip into their dugout during a flurry of German shelling. This drawing was made on the Italian battlefront by English artist Edward Osmond.

Retreating Germans Turn on Allied Troops Along 25-Mile Front

ROME, June 23 (UP).—German shock troops have stalled the British 8th Army advance in central Italy with a series of savage counter-attacks on a 25-mile front north and west of Perugia, but other Allied forces are sweeping northward with increasing speed along both the Tyrrhenian and Adriatic coasts, a communique said today.

Allied headquarters revealed that crack German rear guards turned on their pursuers in the hill country surrounding Perugia for what appeared to be the first determined enemy stand since the flight from Rome began.

Exploiting to the full the time gained during the recent rains, the Nazis were disclosed to have sown the hills with mines and studded the highways with mortar and machine gun nests. Fierce fighting has been in progress for the past two days and nights on a battle line extending from a point just north of Perugia around the southern shore of Lake Trasimeno to the Chiusi sector, headquarters spokesmen said.

The main enemy counter-attacks centred on the Chiusi sector and Fontana, three miles above Perugia. All of the Nazi counter-blows have been repulsed, but it was indicated that the Germans were making their stand in considerable force and that a major effort would be required to clear the hills.

There was no let-up, however, in the swift thrust up the Adriatic coast by British 8th Army troops and supporting Italian units. Advancing more than 12 miles north of captured Termo, the Allied columns swept into Montecosaro and Morrowvale, only 20 miles from modern port of Ancona.

Other spearheads further inland were approaching the big highway junction town of Macerata.

On the Tyrrhenian coastal flank American tanks and infantry lunged ahead along highways 1 and 73 after overcoming fierce enemy resistance in the Monte Pescali sector at the junction of the two roads. One American unit thrust westward eight miles beyond the junction to Gavorrano, 15 miles northwest of Grosseto, while a second drove eight miles northwest of Paganico to Roccastrada, 17½ miles northeast of Grosseto.

The latter spearhead was only 52 miles below Florence, central pivot of the Rimini-Pisa line on which the German armies are expected to make their next real stand.

On the American right flank French colonial troops fought their way to within 35 miles southeast of Siena, capturing Castiglione d'Orcia, Cimgiano and Montenero.

As the ground fighting mounted in fury, the Allied air forces heavily attacked the enemy's battered lines of communication north of the battlefields.

While large forces of fighter-bombers and medium bombers smashed at Nazi gun emplacements, supply dumps and road lines in the battle area, a big force of possibly 750 American Flying Fortresses and Liberators blasted a dozen key railway and industrial targets in the north.

Two enemy aircraft were destroyed and 10 Allied planes were lost.

Thousands of Hun-Vehicles Captured

ROME, June 23 (BUP)—Allied 5th Army forces have captured or destroyed more than 2,100 German vehicles, half-tracks and self-propelled guns and 120 field artillery pieces, most of them north of Rome, and have smashed 129 enemy tanks, it was announced today. Headquarters spokesmen said the 5th Army booty included a complete ordnance shop captured intact on the march above Rome.

The majority of June and July were used for the Canadians to rebuild their units to fighting strength and to learn from their hard-taught lessons of the Liri Valley. One of these lessons was the need for a third infantry brigade in the 5th Division. It was a necessary addition in order to maintain momentum in battle. Two brigades would leapfrog each other in an advance, with the lead unit securing a position, then the next unit passing through to take the next position, and so on. A third brigade in reserve was absolutely necessary in order to respond to unforeseen shifts in the momentum of the battle. The 5th Division already had the Westminster Regiment and the Princess Louise Dragoon Guards. Several anti-aircraft units were transformed into the Lanark and Renfrew Scottish Regiment since the Allies controlled the skies and they no longer needed anti-aircraft support.

Above: *Feature newspaper article on the battle for the Liri Valley, published in July 1944.*

Right: *The Germans retreat, but are still dangerous, as reported on June 23, 1944.*

Allies Make
New Gains
In Italy

ROME, June 24 (UP).—
American armored forces
drove six miles through German mountain positions inland
from the Terrhenian Sea and
captured Roccastrada, threat-
ening the flank of Nazi forces
fighting a strong delaying
action around Lake Trasimeno
to the east it was announced
today.

The seizure of Roccastrada by the
American forces pushing up highway 73 opened the way to key road
junction of Siena, 23 miles to the
north and only 32 miles below Florence, the next major objective of
the Italian campaign.

Another column of the American
units on the left wing of the Allied
Fifth Army struck up the coastal
highway to the gates of Follonica,
12 miles west of Giuncarico and
55 miles below Pisa, anchor of the
next German defense line across
the peninsula.

"The enemy continues to offer
strong resistance on his present delaying position east and west of
Lake Trasimeno," the daily war
communique said in reporting little
change in the general situation on
the Italian front.

The Nazis were putting up stubborn resistance against the British
Eighth Army on either side of Lake
Trasimeno in the region of Chiusi,
which had changed hands a number of times, and above Perugia to
the east.

The official designation of the
opposition as a "delaying" action,
however, indicated that the Germans were bidding for time to dig
in along more defensible positions
farther north, probably along the
Rimini-Pisa line.

Front dispatches revealed that the
Germans had carried out extensive
demolitions at Roccastrada. Engineers described it as the most effective the Allies had encountered
north of Rome.

Three armored spearheads coll-
aborated in the reduction of German resistance in the Roccastrada
area. Two speared past the town
on either side but ran into stiff
resistance. The third crashed due
north, forcing the Germans to fall
back and surrender the town.

British United Press war correspondent James Roper reported
from Roccastrada that he found the
interior of many houses blackened
by flames, while undamaged homes
were nests of booby traps.

Herb Pike (48th Highlanders)

*We worked in threes, you had three sections to a platoon, and three platoons to a company —
infantry I'm referring to now — and you always had two up and one back. And the reason one
was back is you'd leapfrog, eh? We worked by infiltrating, by surrounding, by encompassing
different outfits. From regimental to company to platoon aspect — two up, one back. So you
were constantly mobile and when we were advised we were going into the line, you'd get on
trucks and they'd drive you up so far and let you off and you'd start to go in. You'd pass the big
guns, the five-fives. It seemed like you just got alongside the big guns and they knew you were
there and by this time you know your old heart is starting to pump a little bit and they'd let a
salvo go and the heart's in your throat. "You little sons of guns …," and you'd get up by the 25-
pounders and they'd pull the same thing. But once you got really involved, beyond the guns and
into where the patrols and fighting was, you settled down — at least I did, and the majority of*

Above: *While out of the line the Canadian troops kept busy, including holding a track and field
championship on June 24, 1944. Here the West Novas' tug-of-war team battles the Saskatoon Light
Infantry in the finals.*

Left: *Success still gained headlines, albeit smaller ones located further back in the newspapers.*

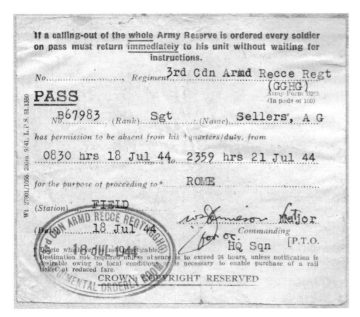

Above: *Treasured possession: a four-day pass to Rome.*

Top right: *While on leave in Rome, the men visited historical sites such as this ancient monastery.*

Centre right: *St. John's Basilica in Rome.*

Bottom right: *While on leave in Rome, the soldiers would visit the famous historical sites such as the S. Maria Maggiores Basilica.*

The Forum in Rome as seen during the Second World War. *Via Appia in Rome.*

the guys did too. We'd have a designation of what we'd have to take over. Jerry was set up with the defence positions there, and he had lines of fire, and we would have to try to infiltrate to take this group of homes and get them out of there. That's the way the action was in most cases.

Peter Routcliffe (Governor General's Horse Guards)
They did a lot of sports activities and stuff like that. Had a rest, clean and polish your uniform, got everything dressed, and they were able to go off to town once in a while.

Al Sellers (Governor General's Horse Guards)
When we got a leave in Rome, that was the greatest experience in my life. That was the one plus of the Italian Campaign to me. I had the opportunity to see Pompeii, and when we were there, Mount Vesuvius had a mild eruption. I had the opportunity to go to Vatican City, St. Peter's Square — I got splashed with some water by the Pope, and I'm not RC! To see all these guys hawking goods like that little statuary of the Pope and that wolf that suckled the two orphaned kids. They're selling those, and the prostitutes were there. Really to go to St. Peter's Square is quite the experience, and to see Tivoli — that beautiful fountain, it's something. Rome was a beautiful city. To see the Coliseum in Rome, to see the aqueduct — it had its pluses.

During this period of recuperation, the 1st Canadian Tank Brigade was still in action, supporting the British advance north to Florence.

John Richardson (Ontario Regiment)

We went through Rome at three o'clock in the morning and hightailed it north from there. I guess one of our main battles from then on was in the Lake Trasimeno area, and again we ran into our old friends the 1st Para Division. They had a couple of divisions up there and we were trying to force the main road up to Arezzo. So for quite a number of days we were having some real fun with that gang. That's where I first ran across the Germans with bazookas. We were in kind of a flat area but there was a drainage ditch around there, they were quite deep, I'd say about ten feet across and maybe four feet deep. I got out and had a look and there was a bazooka facing right at me. I guess he was just as afraid to lift up and shoot at me — because he knew damn well that I probably had the gun ready facing him too, so I guess discretion was the greater part of valour! That was the first time I saw one of them. Thank goodness he didn't have enough guts because he would have got me easily there. I couldn't have been any more than fifty feet away from him. Anyway, those are the things that go on in wars.

The Three Rivers Regiment suffered heavy losses in a battle around Lake Trasimeno. The 1st Division re-entered the line briefly at Ponte Vecchio. Early in August, the tanks of the Ontario Regiment supported the 8th Indian Division during several days of fighting, and on August 17 they crossed the Arno River. In the meantime, the Americans were moving up the west coast of Italy towards Pisa. In August the Canadian infantry went back into action, well rested and ready for action.

Sherman tanks of the Three Rivers Regiment accompany the 21st Indian Infantry Brigade to Montespertoli.

Above: *Trio of Governor General's Horse Guards pose by a river in Italy. Al Sellers is on the left.*

Left: *Al Sellers by a river in Italy.*

Al Sellers (Governor General's Horse Guards)

Summer in Italy was terrible. It was hot. It was dirty. We all watched on the advance that if you have an opportunity to get shelter — it was always nice to get under some shelter. I'd never go into some of these houses because they could be lice-infected. If you were at the front and the attack had just finished, it could have been booby-trapped. The dysentery was the worst thing because they had all these grapes there and it was kind of enticing if you were going through some guy's vineyard to pull off a bunch of grapes and chew them. Flies — I never saw so many flies, and we had our share of dysentery.

Jim Holman (48th Highlanders)

Of course we were told not to eat any — in some of the towns that had been liberated, you'd go on leave they were told not to eat ice cream because it wasn't pasteurized. It would give you the trots too.

Al Sellers (Governor General's Horse Guards)

That's pretty uncomfortable in a tank when your crew member has to go and you're stuck in the tank and the tank's moving somewhere. The tank doesn't have a restroom, so it was not all peaches and cream in the tank.

Jim Holman (48th Highlanders)

The dysentery was just terrible. Especially when you're up where the action was and you had to go, and you couldn't get up and go. A lot of guys just did it in their pants, you couldn't hold it because the pressure was so great.

Al Sellers (Governor General's Horse Guards)

The tanks — the turrets rattled, and the wheels rattled, and the springs squeaked, and then that lousy engine was roaring. Then again you didn't have a restroom in them, you were a captive audience in a tank, and when the convoy stopped — that was an opportunity to get out and do something.

Peter Routcliffe (Governor General's Horse Guards)

Yes, there was quite a bit of dysentery. There was some cases they'd have desert sores, sores on their legs, and one day the medical officer had seventy-two men with it. So he said, "Take them down, march them into the ocean," and within two days they were all gone because the salt in the saltwater and the iodine and the phosphorus in the water just cures it.

Jim Holman (48th Highlanders)

Water was another thing, trying to find water. We had little containers of pills they gave us to purify the water — you could get water out of the puddle and drop a pill in it. I guess it was chlorine or something, and you'd check and some were pretty murky looking. The Germans would either salt the wells or they would poison them. We weren't allowed to drink any water out of the wells until it was tested.

Al Sellers (Governor General's Horse Guards)

When I think of the pills that we had: quinine for malaria, and then we had the water purifying pills — God knows what it was — and then that famous number nine pill, which most of the fellows said could cure gunshot wounds — anything! You had to pretty well use your own judgment.

Herb Pike (48th Highlanders)

There was another thing: the hygiene. You'd go in the line and you'd wear the same thing for a week. They'd bring up the mobile showers, when you come out of the line and you get into those and try to get a change of underwear. You get all your dirty stuff together and you'd get some Italian woman and give her a couple of lire and she'd beat it on a rock.

Gord Outhwaite (48th Highlanders)

… and the soap, I don't know what kind of soap they used but …

Herb Pike (48th Highlanders)

You had to fend for yourself pretty well. There weren't too many aids for infantry — you couldn't send it to a laundromat. You fended for yourself as much as possible.

John Richardson (Ontario Regiment)

The countryside was hilly and kind of pleasant — a lot of fields and a lot of grapevines and farming. So we had little battles here and there, but nothing major. One time I went to take a shortcut in this Trasimeno area with the British. We were taking a side road and unfortunately I had two tanks blow up on mines so I wasn't much help to anybody then. We stayed there a couple of days. Had I gone on I was heading right into a whole damn German division who were lined along the main highway into Trasimeno del Lago, and it would have been nasty, so they did me a favour by stopping me.

Herb Pike (48th Highlanders)

Another problem with fighting in Italy were these damn vineyards. Jerry had a habit of mining these places. You had to be very careful. They had a shoe mine, it was a little box, probably eight inches by eight inches, and there was a quarter stick of dynamite in it. You step on that thing and it would blow your foot off. We wore putties and they were wound around your leg. Luckily the binding of the putty would stop your leg from basically shattering, so you'd only lose a foot instead of a whole leg because of that. Then there was another mine Jerry had that was called a ratchet mine. A tank would roll over it and it wouldn't go off right then. But as a multitude of things would happen on top of this, it was like a ratchet — it would keep winding up, winding up, and all of a sudden it reached a point and the next guy who would step on it, or the next truck or whatever, and off she'd go.

John Richardson (Ontario Regiment)

The Engineers came up to take a look at all the mines and to dig them up. They pulled one out right from under my back track — I missed it by about three inches. Motorcycles are running right over cross the top of it, people are walking over it, but those Teller mines are aimed at doing tanks not infantry. Some of them put two of those Teller mines together and boy they sure make a hole. They blow a hole about four deep and they really smash a tank and the track up, flatten the undercarriage and everything else. Sometimes crack the engine block too.

Jim Holman (48th Highlanders)

I had been on quite a few patrols, day patrols and night patrols. Day patrols were fine, like you just had to go reconnoiter and see if you could raise some fire. Some of them call them a contact patrol, and you had to try and find out the strength of the place by making them shoot at you, like you're drawing fire. That I didn't like that at all. I remember because there were incidents where we were going across the field and guys on either side falling down and dying beside me. I hated night patrol, I hated it with a passion. Sometimes you never wear a helmet, your face had to be blackened, and the backs of your hands. One guy trips and falls and the next guy trips and falls and making a racket, and then all of a sudden you're all trying to get away from each other and you're lost, it's night, and you can't find out where you are. I spent two days getting back to my outfit one time because I got lost. Instead of walking towards the Germans or walking towards our line — I was walking between them. I ended up in some American outfit, and they took me back. It's weird, like you're listening for shellfire — which way is it coming from, now which one is it shooting? I was almost sick that time, I was so shook up. But luckily I got in the right direction in the end. And this big black fellow in the night says, "Hey man! Where are you going?" Scared the daylights out of me!

Harry Fox (Hastings and Prince Edward Regiment)

It was lousy. You went out on these long sojourns. You didn't know what was going to happen. You never got to where you were supposed to get because the Jerries didn't let you. Jerries didn't patrol too much, they were in defensive positions with their machine guns. You blunder around in the night, you're scared stiff, you're not happy, so you don't push it to a conclusion. You're moving along and you get close to your objective, the Jerry lines, and he opens up the machine guns and that's it, you know where he is, and you bugger off. It was a waste of time and men really from my point of view. You do that one night, why do you have to go out the second night and do the same thing? And yet we did it for months. When they're in a defensive position, that doesn't mean much. They're just going to hold and that's all there is to it. So why go there and stick your neck out?

I remember one recce patrol where a young officer turned around and came back. They asked him "Why?" "Well," he says, "I don't know why, I just didn't feel right." So they practically called him a coward and sent him out the next night. So he gets about fifty yards from where he was the previous night and rat-a-tat-tat, gets killed. So a good officer wasted. He didn't know why he turned back the first night, but he was right, there was something there and he knew it. So he got killed, and there's no reason for a thing like that.

John Richardson (Ontario Regiment)

At Lake Trasimeno there was an 88 right in the village square, overlooking this area where we were approaching. The Italians advised us of this gun and showed us where it was, and then we had the artillery knock it out. Thank God because it would have picked me off so fast it wouldn't even be funny. I stayed in the line one night. I said, "You fellas, I want you to guard my tanks and keep a patrol around there. I'll stay with you and I'll have the guns facing this way so that you'll have an all-around defence." Nothing happened during the night, everything was fine. As soon as it got nice and bright we saw that the Germans were only a hundred yards away. You just wouldn't believe it — nobody bothered us, they could have potted us off at first light. But nothing.

We eventually got into Arezzo then we headed for Florence. We didn't have too many scraps at that time, just a lot of hit-and-miss — the Germans were obviously phasing back to the mountains north of Florence where they prepared their next big line to stop us. We eased the Germans out of Florence — it was an open city, the only thing we did there was the air force bombed the railway tracks and the station, outside of that the city was not touched at all. We didn't want to smash that city because it's a beautiful city.

Jim Holman (48th Highlanders)

There was a river running through the middle of Florence and it was an open city. They didn't want any destruction. We were dug in on a rise to the south where we could almost look down in the city and see the lights on. The Allies were on the south side of the river, and the German front was still in the city on the north side of the river. But there was nothing going on. I imagine they did some obscene motions to the guys on each side when they saw them over there.

Herb Pike (48th Highlanders)

We were shipped back to the Adriatic again. The next thing we know we're going into the Gothic Line …

THE GOTHIC LINE

THE GOTHIC LINE CUT ACROSS THE entire width of Italy, from Pisa through the northern tip of the Apennines to Rimini. It was in place to stop the Allies from advancing into northern Italy and its vital industrial and agricultural region. Beyond it the next major defensive line for the Germans was the Alps, and in between was the Po Valley and the vast Lombardy Plain — a flat stretch of land that would make it easy for the Allied tanks to roll unimpeded to the mountainous frontier. The security of this zone was vital to the Germans to maintain their conduit to the Balkans and Greece, but most importantly it protected Austria and the southern border of Germany. It was vital for the Germans to halt the Allies at the Gothic Line, because if it were breached, the results would be disastrous for the Reich. Undoubtedly the Germans would put up a desperate and hellish fight.

Albert Wade (Royal Canadian Dragoons)
The Gothic Line went through a series of high-rise areas, mountainous country — hilly anyway. The 1st Division had deployed several regiments along the ridges of that particular area, it ran from the sea back inland, almost to the centre of Italy. The British had one end of it. We had various duties there to patrol,

Gothic Line & Beyond

and then we prepared for the main battle, which was to attack the towns on the Adriatic, to clear them of Germans.

The Gothic Line was the most fortified line that the Allies had faced in the Italian Campaign. Like the Hitler Line, it was a series of mutually supporting gun positions, located for strategic advantage and organized for maximum efficiency. A year in the making, the line was well designed and ready for battle. To assault the Gothic Line, the Allies would have to first contend with a fifteen-kilometre battle from the Metauro River to the Foglia River, where the

Canadians head for the Gothic Line through the dust and heat.

Germans would slow them down and inflict as much damage as possible. Then they would have to fight their way through the emplacements and gun positions — a five-kilometre gauntlet of firepower and death that far exceeded what they had experienced at the dreaded Hitler Line. Kesselring put his infantry units along the line, with the 14th Army in the west facing the Americans, and the 10th Army in the east to face the British and Canadians. Behind them he positioned his mobile units, poised to respond to attacks anywhere along the front. This group included his panzer and panzer grenadier divisions. He knew that the attack was coming, he just didn't know where.

This uncertainty weighed heavily on Kesselring, and he was determined to find out where the Canadian troops were positioned. The Allied modus operandi was to spearhead their attacks with the I Canadian Corps, so for Kesselring, to know the location of the Canadians was to know where the attack was about to take place. Knowing this, the Allies planned on a surprise attack in the east, yet positioned the Canadians in the west near Florence to throw the Germans off. Orders then went out, and the Canadians removed all of their shoulder patches and any form of identification. They loaded up on the transportation vehicles and secretly moved across Italy to the Adriatic coast to join the British for the impending attack.

Jim Holman (48th Highlanders)

I think the whole 1st Div must have been there, dug in all over these fields, a lot of soldiers and equipment. One night you could hear the throttle of these big engines, aircraft, and you could hear them coming. We couldn't see them, but you could almost feel the vibration of the engines. As they flew over, they dropped what they called candle flares, or parachute flares, where the flare itself keeps the parachute afloat. They're just hanging in the air, lighting the ground up because the parachute acts like a reflector. Then the second one came over and dropped canister bombs. The canister bomb is like a forty-five-gallon drum just full of tiny anti-personnel bombs. It breaks open so far off the ground, and all these little things rain out and drop straight down into slit trenches, and it was just awful. The screaming and the hollering on these things as they pass by. They just made the one pass and then they were gone. There were a lot of casualties that night, they spent the rest of the night sorting the ones killed out. These little bombs would blow your legs off, that's how powerful they were. That was a terrible night. We were very lucky that night when the bombers went along the perimeter of the group and didn't get into the main body of where the guys were dug in.

The orders came to "Take all your patches off! Take the trucks out!" We went from Florence all the way across to the other side of Italy in secret because they didn't want the paratroopers to know where we were. We got over there and the paratroopers were there.

The Allies' battle plan was severely hampered by a recent transfer of seven divisions to the south of France for the fighting there. The plans had to be made taking this disadvantage into consideration, so it was decided to have the British and Canadians attack on the eastern sector of the Gothic Line, crossing the Foglia River where the Germans were in strength. This would force Kesselring to commit his reserves there, leaving the western segment of the line vulnerable,

and that would be where the Americans would then launch their attack. The goal was to envelope Bologna and move into the Po Valley. Speed was of the essence, though: they needed to break through the Gothic Line quickly in order to advance across the plain prior to the September rains, otherwise the Allies would get bogged down by mud. The plan would exploit the Allies' advantage in artillery, armour, and air power, but they faced numerous rivers to cross along the Adriatic coast, which would slow the advance. The Germans were adept at stalling tactics, and their defensive positions, built around the neutral principality of San Marino, were perfectly situated to bring the Allies to a standstill.

The Canadians moved into position south of the Metauro River during the last week of August. There were three corps along the narrow thirty-five-kilometre front, combining the forces of the British, the Canadians, and the Poles to face the Gothic Line. The objective for the Canadians was to cross the Metauro, secure the territory beyond it to the Foglia River, break through the Gothic Line, and then push on to Rimini. The route would force the Canadians to fight through some of the most strongly held German positions, over six rivers, all without adequate manpower. The men of I Canadian Corps were about to descend into hell.

Snipers made every step hazardous near the front. Here L.V. Hughes of the 48th Highlanders takes aim on a German near the Foglia River.

At 2300 on the night of August 24, 1944, the Canadians silently launched their assault across the Metauro River. Under the cover of night they advanced in the direction of the Foglia River, with the intent of capturing the ridges ahead. Foothills rippled across the front on the approach to the Foglia, and the Germans were well entrenched there. As the men moved across the lowlands, the Allied artillery began to mercilessly pound the German positions along the ridges. As the sun rose on May 25, the Canadians marched through the foothills, enduring sweltering heat and German delaying tactics. They cleared the ridges, and finally they approached the Foglia River, with the Gothic Line in sight on August 29. On either side of the river were flat meadows that had been cleared of every tree, building, or any form of cover by the Germans. Along the river were minefields, followed by wide tank ditches and backed by concrete gun emplacements. Flamethrowers, anti-tank guns, and permanently installed tank turrets controlled the field, making it a veritable death zone for anyone who dared to cross it. Exploiting one of their advantages, the Allies had the air force bomb the Gothic Line to soften it for the impending assault.

Above: *The 48th Highlanders head for Point 146 near the Foglia River during the battle to break through the Gothic Line.*

Right: *A Canadian takes cover in a slit trench near the Gothic Line.*

Kesselring wanted to know who was on the ridge facing the Gothic Line and ordered that a patrol go out and pick up a prisoner. Instead they came into possession of a letter to the troops by General Leese, complete with the order of battle. Kesselring had all of the intelligence that he needed, and he promptly ordered the 26th Panzer Division to the front to repel the attack. Meanwhile, Allied intelligence for the area in front of the Canadians was inconclusive, so patrols were sent out. When word got back that the area appeared to be lightly defended, the Canadians launched an immediate attack to take advantage of the situation. General Leese's original plan called for the attack to be launched on the night of September 1–2, but the Canadians moved out on the afternoon of August 30, much to the surprise of the Germans — and their own Allies. This audacious move was the work of the newly promoted General Burns, and it proved successful. The German reinforcement troops were not yet in position, and the attack was not expected by the troops who were there.

The West Novas crossed the Foglia River to be the first to test the defences of the Gothic Line. They advanced right through a minefield and faced the onslaught of the German guns. At the other end of the Canadian line the Cape Breton Highlanders launched an attack on the ridge behind Montecchio known as Point 120. The Perth Regiment attacked up the centre, assaulting Point 111. Tanks roared in with the infantry, supporting the attacks. One company of the Perths were turned back by the Germans defending Point 111, but the follow-up company would not be denied. As tanks pounded the German defences at the summit, the Perths crept up the hill and made a terrifying bayonet charge to seize the strategic position. The valiant action by the Perths had outflanked Montecchio. Another Perth company moved in behind Point 147 and surprised the defenders there, taking the highest vantage point in the region. From the two key high points, the Perths were able to shell the Germans and eliminate their attacks on the advancing Canadian units.

While the Perths were capturing their objectives, the West Novas were pinned down on their front, and the Cape Breton Highlanders were in trouble as well. The 5th Division then quickly moved in to support the gains that had already been made. The Irish Regiment and the 8th Hussars attacked Montecchio and took the town before the Germans could respond. The B.C. Dragoons were sent to link up with the Perths and to push forward to Point 204, which was two kilometres into the Gothic Line defences. After having problems crossing the Foglia, the B.C. Dragoons were engaged by a German company, which they destroyed, but lost several tanks in the process. Unable to find the Perths, the B.C. Dragoons advanced to Point 204 on their own across the valley. Fifty Sherman tanks headed out, and were quickly targeted by the Germans. Only eighteen reached Point 204, and they began using the high ground to their advantage as they fired down onto the Germans. Among their casualties was their CO, Colonel Fred Vokes, who was killed by a mortar blast. The surviving members of the B.C. Dragoons were soon joined by members of the Perths and Strathconas. Unbeknownst to them, they were surrounded on three sides by the Germans, who subsequently launched a counterattack at midnight in an attempt to dislodge the Canadians from the key stronghold. As the Germans shelled them and put in an attack, the Canadian tanks and infantry worked together to push the enemy back. The 17th Field Regiment unleashed the fury of their guns on the Germans from close range, annihilating them on the hillside, and destroying any future attempts to retake Point 204. It was the key battle of the Gothic Line, and the taking of that hill signalled the beginning of the end of the Germans' grand defensive position.

As the 5th Division made great gains, the 1st Division moved into the area between the 5th Division and the Poles who were fighting near Pesaro. The PPCLI and a squadron of British tanks fought through the Gothic Line; then it was the turn of the Seaforths along with another squadron of British tanks to take the lead. As darkness fell on August 31, the 1st Division had breached the Gothic Line. The next day the Canadians faced the task of clearing Monte Peloso and Monte Luro, two peaks that towered over the area, controlling the defences in all directions. At 1000 the Princess Louise Dragoon Guards put in the assault on Peloso, and immediately faced a hail of bullets and shells. The losses were staggering: 130 casualties in one morning, with only 40 men reaching the base of Peloso. The pressure on the strongholds continued as the Strathconas lent support to the beleaguered unit, and in the end the Germans began a withdrawal from Monte Peloso and Monte Luro. In the meantime the Irish Regiment, the Westminsters, and the 8th Hussars cleared Monte Marone and Tomba di Pesaro, while the Vandoos faced a tough fight. After several attempts to assault the high ground near Borgia San Maria, the Vandoos overcame the intense fire from the Germans, who were protected by concrete bunkers connected by a network of tunnels. The intrepid Canadians engaged the Germans with machine guns while other members of the unit snuck up on the bunkers and threw in grenades to clear them. Simultaneously the Seaforths were fighting at Pozzo Alto, and by securing that position, they strengthened the hold that the Canadians had taken in the Gothic Line. That night the Loyal Eddies made the ascent of Monte Luro to clear it of the enemy, only to find that the Germans had deserted the site.

The advance did not stop that night. The Canadians had the momentum and they wanted to exploit it as thoroughly as possible. The Germans were reeling from the speed of the Canadian assault and were unable to prepare a proper defence of their positions. Ironically, the Germans were falling victim to their own concept of blitzkrieg. Their retreat was not as orderly as in the past, and erratic encounters occurred. The Governor General's Horse Guards moved north, as well as the Westminsters and the Lanark and Renfrews — sweeping the area up to the Conca River. That night had an unearthly feel to it, with the landscape being lit by fires all across the front. Moving in the direction of Cattolica and Riccione was the Royal Canadian Dragoons along with the 21st Armoured Brigade. The RCRs took the Via Adriatica north and came across the 1st German Parachute Division that seemed to always meet up with the Canadians in battle. It was a bitter clash.

Jim Holman (48th Highlanders)
Tanks were burning into the night. You could see them lighting up all over the place. I remember the first time I saw a German Tiger tank, it had six inches of concrete poured on the front of it. I couldn't believe this, it was huge, it was so much bigger than our tanks. Holy Moses, they were big!

Albert Wade (Royal Canadian Dragoons)

Orders came through that we were to do reconnaissance in around a town called Riccione. We were to do a reconnaissance down in this one roadway leading towards the seashore. We advanced and something went wrong with my radio system in my car and I was out of communication. By this time we received a new troop officer who took charge of the troop, a fellow called Sammy Stokes. He was an awful nice chap. He was from the St. Catharines area, of the Stokes Seed and Feed people. He was the son of the owner. Anyways, he said, "Lookit, Al, you better stay there and I'll get somebody down back in here to look it over for you." So I did, and that was where he had turned to go down this side road. So he proceeded along with the two armoured cars. He got about halfway to the seashore and they encountered German marines. They were dug in. So he's in this scout car and he didn't have too much experience in battle. He made the mistake of stopping, and they stepped out and they killed him and his driver. His driver was a very, very good friend of mine — Danny Dailey, he was from the Boston area. He'd come up to Canada and volunteered because he had had a little tough luck in life and he was looking for a different place to settle, but instead of that he ended up in Italy. So we lost two of our men there, two very good fellows, and the car was a mess. Soon after that, these German marines had vacated the area. Apparently in the darkness that same night some boats were seen coming in, and they picked them all up and took them away. We never even got a crack at them, that's how fast it happened.

By the following morning it was clear that the Germans had been defeated in the forward positions of the Gothic Line and the area was secure. The seemingly impregnable defensive line had been cracked wide open by the Canadians in a matter of days, and it would stand as one of Canada's proudest military achievements. The Germans were quick to respond and shifted troops into place to slow the progress to Rimini.

On September 3 the Westminsters and the Strathconas crossed the Conca River and drove towards the Marano River. The region was a series of rivers and ridges, and they progressed cautiously, not knowing which ones would be defended by the Germans and which ones would be conceded without a fight. These ridges gradually rose higher as they stretched inland, joining the mountain range, which ran parallel to the coast. The Germans could slow down the Canadians from the ridges, while large guns in the mountains could hit them with deadly enfilade fire. Near the coast the RCRs put in an attack on Riccione to drive the Germans out of the resort town. Facing the Canadians off in the distance on the left was the San Fortunato ridge, which stretched across the horizon and ended at San Marino. The small principality was on a mountain peak on the northeastern part of the Apennine range, which made it the dominant feature in the area. While San Marino was neutral in the war, that didn't stop German "visitors" from observing the artillery fire and communicating back to their gunners to make adjustments.

Herb Pike (48th Highlanders)

I recall we were in a column, we come over this hill and there's a town down in the valley. We come down into the town and started to go up again, and all hell breaks loose. Jerry let us walk through and they had us surrounded. The whole regiment is in this valley and as the guys were filtering down the road they split into a "V" and right in the top of the "V" there was a mortuary and there were a couple of stiffs in there. The guys were coming in and it's dusk now and the password at that time was "Russian Bear." You had to say "Russian" or you got to answer "Bear" — "Okay, come through" — and as the guys are coming through we were challenging them. All of a sudden there's one … I give the password and there's no word. I said, "I'll give it to you one more time." He says, "It's Colonel MacKenzie" — he had forgotten the password! But I recognized his voice, so anyway he comes through. Unbeknownst to us, the Hastings and Prince Edward Regiment had been through there about three or four days earlier, and communications didn't get back to us to beware of the possibility of entrapment. So when all hell started breaking loose, I dove into a slit that had already been dug by one of the Hasty Ps and unfortunately when I dove into the trench I landed right on top of a poor Hasty P that had got a machine gun burst. They had pulled his tunic off him and his back was just riddled — he was dead, of course, and I had to stay in that slit with him. A slit is, what? Five feet long, and if you got down four feet you were lucky. He had dug it evidently but he tried to get out and was hit by a burst of machine gun fire. I'm on top of him, and I had to stay in there — I must have been in there four or five hours. Now he had been out in the hot Italian sun for probably three days since he had been shot, he wasn't too healthy…

Gord Outhwaite (48th Highlanders)

Yeah, there was a slight odour …

Herb Pike (48th Highlanders)

But things like this would happen. Anyway, lucky enough our company commander had got back and he had got a group of tanks. They came in and we fought our way out of that situation.

The Canadians were attempting to maintain the momentum they had gained when they broke through the Gothic Line, but it was dangerous as both divisions were under strength. They were attempting to do the job of a much larger force, and by being spread so thin, the Canadians faced potential disaster if they engaged a large German force. They were operating without a reserve, so any weakness along the front could not be reinforced when exposed. This problem stemmed from a last-minute decision by General Leese just prior to the assault on the Gothic Line. He had switched the 1st Canadian Corps and the much larger V British Corps, having the Canadians spearhead the attack. Forced to fulfill the task of a larger corps and then to follow it up with a rapid advance with depleted regiments left the Canadians in a precarious position.

Jim Holman (48th Highlanders)

We went up this roadway, and this was quite hilly country. The sergeant says to us, "Come down, we're going to make a bayonet attack." Have you seen the bayonets we used in the Second World War? They look like a big nail. On our left was this big field and way out in the field was rubble and growth on it. There were a lot of guys there. They were stretched from where I was maybe more than a quarter of a mile. Word came, and we were to charge into this field and then turn and go up towards three houses. There were Germans in there. They hollered charge, we ran out into this field towards this here rubble pile, and it was a long ways away. A machine gun was in there, and we didn't know it. It was one of those MG42s, and they just started grrrrrrrrr, they just growl, and the whole bunch of us just went down, and it just kept it up. Every once in a while it would stop, then it would fire again. The guys would get up and try to run and it would fire. So it finally got to the point where you couldn't move at all. I stuck my head up in the grass, and I saw the fire coming out of this brush. Well, I got up on my elbows, took my helmet off, and I got up so that I could just see above the grass. I put my rifle on my elbows and I waited until they fired and I saw the flash, and I moved it into the flash. The next time he fired, I fired and it stopped, and it never fired again. So everybody starts to get up and we continue up to these houses. When I got up, this fellow beside me never got up. I hollered at him, and he didn't get up. I had to just keep running, so he must have got hurt bad, I don't know what happened to him. The houses were on the other side of the railroad. There was a German tank up there and you could hear it roaring back and forth, and about halfway down the field — our two-inch mortar man was firing at these houses. Everything was so exciting, everybody was pumped up, and the screaming and the hollering it was just, ohhh. As I was getting close to the road, maybe a couple of hundred yards away, I heard this scream like I never heard before in my life. The scream — I can still hear it — it was something, oh, just unbelievable. By the time we got up there, this tank had moved off behind the houses and the Germans were moving out. I looked in the ditch and there were one of our guys lying there and this tank had run right over him. I imagine that was the scream that I heard when this tank went over this guy — I still hear it. It was just awful.

Having driven the Germans back over the Conca, the Westminsters and Strathconas gave the lead position to the Irish Regiment, the Cape Breton Highlanders, and the 8th New Brunswick Hussars. They were to put in an attack on Besanigo as a part of the drive up the Adriatic coast.

Harry Fox (Hastings and Prince Edward Regiment)

Ninety percent of the cases of extreme bravery were never noticed, or at least never passed on because you don't get a medal unless an officer writes out a citation. Quite a lot of things happened when there was no officer around. So there was one guy, for instance, he was leading his men through a big building, searching room by room, and when he came to the very end there was a bit of a veranda, and below the veranda was a courtyard. There was three Jerries running across this courtyard, so he shot two of them and the third man went down the well. So this lance-sergeant jumped over the balustrade down onto this courtyard, over to the well, dropped a 36 grenade down, and went down the well himself. He didn't know how deep, if there was water in it, how many Jerries, or anything — he went down that bloody well. Now that's something I don't think I could have done. There were Jerries down the well, and, well, there was a bit of a skirmish down there, and they were stunned by the explosion of the grenade, so they weren't a hundred percent, but he was out to kill, and he did that. The lance-sergeant got recognized, he got the distinguished conduct medal. Yeah, that was guts.

Jim Holman (48th Highlanders)

The Germans were coming and we had to get out of this one place — so we're running down this road, and as we were going by this bank, it was high, one of our guys was standing up there hollering like hell, "Wait for me! Wait for me!" So when I looked at him, his heel had all been blown off. He slid down the bank right where I was so I said, "Okay, jump on" and he jumped on my back and sat on my gas cape rolled up at the back, like a saddle. "Hang onto my rifle," and I took off down the road. I went up over into the vineyard, I just kept going until I collapsed, I couldn't run anymore. I was just trying to get my breath, I thought my lungs were going to burst. It ended up he stayed there, I went down and I could see a house and some of our vehicles there. So I went and told them about this guy and they went back to get him.

About a kilometre away a ridge ran parallel to their route, and suddenly they found themselves under heavy fire from that position. The 1st German Parachute Division was dug in all along the ridge, halting the advance with deadly fire. It quickly became apparent that the Germans had an incredible defensive position in place, and it would have to be dealt with before the advance could continue. The British 1st Armoured Division put in an attack, only to get hit mercilessly, losing 79 of their 156 tanks in that one day. All along the ridge the battle raged, with both sides suffering grim casualties. The assault on the ridge continued through to the evening of September 5th, when the two sides began to reinforce and prepare for a major engagement. The battle for the Coriano Ridge would be a nasty affair.

The buildup to the second phase of the battle for Coriano Ridge varied between the two sides. Kesselring could see the problem facing the Germans if the Allies broke through, so he decided to heavily reinforce his units along the ridge to stall the advance. He moved in the 98th and 162nd Infantry, 26th Panzer, and 29th Panzer Grenadiers along the Coriano Ridge. Eighty artillery batteries provided support from the highlands. In the short term he wanted to stall the Allies until the fall rains arrived — then the mud would do more to stop them than his army could. With the advantage of the high ground the Germans could control the entire area all the way up to Rimini. For the Canadians, they wanted to strike at the strength of the German defensive line, but that was in a position that was on boundary between the Canadian and British corps, so some jurisdictional wrangling had to occur before an attack could be launched. The British delayed a Canadian assault so that they could secure the inland flank, but this action dragged on for eight days, allowing the Germans to strengthen their position in the meantime. Meanwhile the Canadians held the line facing the Coriano Ridge, with the Cape Breton Highlanders and the Irish Regiment enduring constant barrages along the front. The tanks of the B.C. Dragoons and the 8th Hussars would remain out of sight behind another ridge, pull forward enough to fire from the top of the ridge, and then quickly back up to avoid the inevitable return fire. The position for the Canadians was so deadly that it was nicknamed Graveyard Hill.

Herb Pike (48th Highlanders)

There was a time at the Coriano Ridge, the area in Italy just off from San Marino. We fought around that state, I can remember very vividly looking up and seeing the mount with this tower that was right on the top of this place. It got so hot and heavy with wounded right there that the powers that be decided we'd call a ceasefire for an hour to allow both sides to send their stretcher-bearers out to pick up wounded and bring them in. I've often thought of that, and when you stop to think of it, it's really silly, isn't it? Two intelligent races get together and they're fighting and killing one another, and then all of a sudden they say okay fellas, let's play fair. We won't shoot each other and go out and bring each in and at the prescribed time go back at it again. Ridiculous when you think of it.

Harry Fox (Hastings and Prince Edward Regiment)

I can tell you that the bulk of our wounded, if they weren't too bad, they were always worried "Oh geez, Sergeant-Major — did I do a good job?" They were worried that they hadn't been good enough, and now that they're wounded, they couldn't do anymore. That sort of upsets me in a way, but I would say, "Oh yes, you did all right. If I had a thousand guys like you, we'd be in Berlin next week." Send them away happy. But most of them were worried that they hadn't done a good job. It is tough. You can get quite angry when you know that some of your friends have been hit. Some men you had to almost restrain them, they were just going to revenge them, which would mean of course that they'd only get themselves killed.

The British made an attempt to clear their inland position, but were unable to dislodge the Germans. In the end, General Leese decided to move the boundary between the Canadians and the British so that the Canadians could put in the attack on the Coriano Ridge. Elsewhere the Canadians had secured a bridgehead at Riccione, with the RCRs and the Hasty Ps holding the position. They were unable to advance since their flank would be exposed, so the attention of everyone along the Adriatic coast was focused on the Coriano Ridge. On September 12, 1944, British and Canadian units moved into position. That night the attack went in.

The Allied artillery initiated the action with an overwhelming barrage while bombers flew sorties over the ridge and brutalized the German positions. Flares dropped from the aircraft enveloped the battleground in an eerie light. The British put in their attack around San Clemente in the south while the Canadians made their attack around the town of Coriano in the east. A creeping barrage of nine hundred guns led the Cape Breton Highlanders and the Perth Regiment across the Besanigo River and up to the Coriano Ridge. The Germans were forced to hide from the artillery until it had passed them by, then they re-manned their positions and began to fight back. By dawn the Canadians had reached Coriano, but it was heavily defended. They fought off German tanks as they counterattacked, and as the morning wore on, the Westminsters and the Irish Regiment joined them to attack the town. Fighting along the ridge continued, with the New Brunswick Hussars and the Strathconas playing a pivotal role in the battle. The Allies continued to pound the Germans with their air force and artillery, dropping more than five hundred tons of explosives on them in a period of twenty-four hours.

Al Sellers (Governor General's Horse Guards)
We did have a change in personnel at the Coriano Ridge, our C Squadron attacked an area there and they brought back about fifty or sixty prisoners — old guys, not very young fellows, not in the best of shape. They had just been conscripted, and they were just happy that the war was over. The infantry would see more of the crack German troops. The front got narrower as we progressed north.

Jim Holman (48th Highlanders)

This is where there was one hell of a big charge, all of us going down into this lowland and up the other side, and it was almost a massacre. The Germans had that whole field of view, they had it covered. But we took it, we done it, went up and chased the Germans off the top. There were a lot of casualties. There wasn't even hedgerows or someplace to hide. A lot of it was just the weeds in the field, and when these Germans were up higher than you and they can look down, they can see in the weeds.

Albert Wade (Royal Canadian Dragoons)

We were encamped along this main road, just south of what we would call a lighthouse, only it was a very poorly erected looking thing. It was sitting on the side of a hill and the Carleton and Yorks the night before had taken a hell of a shellacking, and the RCR had been in a battle along this ridge and they had taken a lot of casualties. It was in this yard where they had made a makeshift hospital out of a barn. They were bringing the casualties down. I experienced a major that was absolutely completely mutilated, blown almost in half on a stretcher, and they were carrying him in. He died when they were trying to sew him up. So we knew that there was something pretty heavy going on along up this ridge. I was sent forth again, as I went

up the ridge up along this roadway. The troops that I met up with, our own men, they were reporting about this strange-looking building, and gee whiz it no sooner happened than the Germans had anti-tank guns up there and they were pelting us. They got two more of our officers and two or three of the crewmen from two of the armoured cars. We either lost two or three right there and then. They bounced a couple off the back of my car, but I guess I was too small a target.

A pair of Canadian soldiers check out a German MG 34. The formidable weapon was capable of firing nine hundred rounds per minute.

The Irish Regiment led the way through the town of Coriano, having to clear the position street by street, building by building, in close quarters, in a manner that was reminiscent of Ortona. Painstakingly the Canadians cleared the town, securing it ever so slowly. By September 14 the Coriano Ridge was taken and the town was secured. The men of the 5th Division were put into reserve for the next three weeks. The units had been ravaged by the previous three weeks of fighting, and they were in dire need of replacements and more equipment. In the meantime, additional units were put under Canadian command for the continuation of the battle to destroy the Gothic Line. The British 4th Division, the New Zealand 2nd Division, and the Greek 3rd Mountain Brigade all joined the Canadians for their next task: Rimini and the clearing of the San Fortunato Ridge.

Herb Pike (48th Highlanders)

Jerry didn't have any air force left down there, but there was an old Junkers. He'd come over and dropped an anti-personnel bomb — this is a bomb probably six feet long, but halfway down it split open and little tiny things about the size of a two-inch mortar bomb would come out and they'd spread all over the place. We'd been under fire and we were in a dried-up riverbed. Now the bed came down and then it swung off at right angles and I was in the cut-off and right behind me was the sergeant-major of the company, Gordie Keeler, and his head was actually touching my feet. Behind him was another sergeant called Jimmy Harker. This plane come over and dropped these anti-personnel bombs and one of these things hit Harker right in the back and actually cut him in half. The other hit Gordie Keeler right behind the knees and it took both his legs off and went right on by me. Well, we got Gordie out to casualty clearing, and when we came out of the line and went back to see him, the nurse said, "Gee, I'm glad to see some of his friends back here, this guy's unbelievable — he's trying to chase the nurses." Chase — with both legs off!

With the new additions to the Canadian Corps, General Burns arranged his forces with the Canadian 1st Division in the middle, the British covering the inland flank, and the Greeks on the coast. The New Zealanders were put in reserve. The next objective for the Canadians was to deliver a final death blow to the Gothic Line by capturing Rimini on the coast and taking San Fortunato

A Perth anti-tank gun mired in the mud being extricated by a tank of the Sherbrooke Fusiliers.

Ridge. The approach to the Rimini Line was across a coastal plain that gradually turned into hills that were progressively higher until reaching the height of the San Fortunato Ridge. From this high ground the Germans used their familiar tactics of shelling the advancing Allied troops in the low-lying areas. The plains were broken up by several streams, and with the autumn rainy season in progress the entire area was quickly becoming a quagmire of mud. The Rimini Line spanned from Rimini on the coast to San Marino on the inland, with the San Fortunato Ridge stretching between the two. Slowed by the mud and harassed by the shelling, it was a difficult advance. Great feats were accomplished just to keep the roads clear and bridges intact. The men suffered through miserable conditions with the constant wetness, with some even developing trench foot.

Jim Holman (48th Highlanders)
We had mud. It's all rain, and I remember when I took my shoes off one day my feet were like prunes.

The plan for the attack on the Rimini Line put the Canadian 1st Division at the forefront of the battle once again. Facing them would be their old familiar foes, the 1st German Parachute Division. For the 1st Division the assignment was split between two brigades. The 1st Brigade was given the task of taking Rimini's airfield, the 3rd Brigade was to take San Fortunato, and the 2nd Brigade was kept in reserve.

In the early hours of September 14 the attack was launched. All along the Marano River the Canadians fought to cross the swollen waters and to overcome the German defences along the riverbank on the far side. The 1st Brigade successfully made the crossing and battled to their first objective: the Rimini airfield. They met with tough resistance there, and as the shelling intensified, they dug in for protection. To their left the 3rd Brigade advanced on the Marano River, and the West Novas were stopped from crossing by tough German resistance. The Vandoos were able to fight their way across the Marano but were driven back by a determined German counterattack. The next day both the West Novas and the Vandoos successfully made the crossing and pushed forward to the ridge just beyond the river. Two towns dominated the ridge, with San Martino to the north and San Lorenzo to the south. It was incumbent on the 3rd Brigade to clear the two towns, so the Vandoos focused their efforts on San Martino and the West Novas headed for San Lorenzo. After a tremendous battle, both towns were taken, and the ridge was secured for the Canadians on September 15, putting them in position to make an attack on the San Fortunato Ridge.

The next day events unfolded that left the Canadians in a perilous position. The Seaforth Highlanders were sent forward to relieve the beleaguered Vandoos at San Martino, and during the transition the town was left unoccupied for a short period of time. The Germans quickly re-occupied the pivotal town and defended it fiercely. Three times the Seaforths made a brave charge up the hillside in an attempt to dislodge the paratroopers, and each time they were driven back. As their numbers were depleted by these attempts, the Seaforths were relieved by the Loyal Eddies, who immediately came under fire from the town that towered above them. To the west the PPCLI and the Hasty Ps were suffering the same fate as they attempted to advance past the ridge. At the airfield the RCRs and the 48th Highlanders were barely hanging on. The success of the operation was in jeopardy, and the Canadians were pinned down all across the front.

In a bold move, elements of the Canadian units moved west and across the open ground to outflank the Germans at San Martino. Realizing that they were on the verge of being surrounded, the Germans quickly withdrew and the hilltop town was once again in Canadian hands. With the elimination of fire from this stronghold, several Canadian units were no longer pinned down and were able to join in the advance.

The battle moved forward to the Ausa River, and after some resistance the Carleton and York Regiment made the crossing and secured a bridgehead. Quickly the West Novas and the Hasty Ps moved through this secured area and advanced up to the foot of the San Fortunato ridge. The air force began a terrific bombardment of the German positions along the crest of the ridge.

Sydney Frost (Princess Patricia's Canadian Light Infantry)

Well, it was wonderful to get back to see my friends that were left. Of course, everybody had been promoted in the meantime and I'm still a lowly lieutenant, and all my pals are captains and majors. At least I was back among friends. I couldn't stand the holding units in England. They were full of what we called zombies who didn't want to fight, they wanted to stay there and have a good time with the pubs and the girls. So it was a relief to get back. I wasn't in very good shape. I had malaria again in England and I almost missed my boat. The thing about malaria is it strikes you in the initial stages every second day. So on the days off I would try and pack my kit and get ready to be shipped back again. So on the final day when my ship left I was in terrible shape, I didn't know how I'd make it, but my friends helped me out and carried my kit. I got aboard and then collapsed and confessed that I had malaria. Well, the ship's captain was as mad as hell that I had been allowed to come on the ship in this condition and he was about to have me taken off. Luckily on the ship was another PPCLI officer, by the name of Captain George Corkett, a great friend of mine and RMC graduate. He happened to know the medical officer on the ship. He said, "Don't worry about young Frost, he just has a little constipation, that's all — give him a 222 and he'll be fine!" So they kept me on the ship, thank goodness, and I finally got back to my home — the regiment. It was a different war when I got back. Because all the originals are gone pretty well, not all killed — casualties, malaria, jaundice — you name it, we had it. But instead of the devil-may-care happy attitude that we had in Sicily and southern Italy, it was one of cold resolve. We're going to kill those SOBs and we're going to win this war and we're going to do it quickly. They were professional soldiers. After I came back, I was put in charge of the machine gun platoon — that was kind of a specialist job, but it was a great job because we're all mounted on carriers, so we didn't have to walk anymore. We could give support to the poor guys who were doing the fighting.

The San Fortunato Ridge towered above the Canadians, rising fifteen hundred metres on a slope that was possible to run up, but too steep to include the tanks in the assault. They would fire from the ridge facing San Fortunato in support. The Canadians decided that their best shot at taking the ridge was through audacity: they would simply run straight up the slope as fast as they could and try to overwhelm the Germans. It would be a long run through purgatory. The plan called for the men of the 3rd Brigade to make that mad dash, while the 2nd Brigade would simultaneously outflank the position by moving beyond the ridge and crossing the Marecchia River to the north of it. On the night of September 19, the units moved into their positions at the base of the ridge. The signal was given and they raced up the hill. As they reached the crest, the Canadians attacked an astonished enemy. The Vandoos poured over the top of the ridge and quickly neutralized the sentries. In many cases they captured prisoners before the Germans knew what happened, but soon there were firefights, and the skirmishes were fought in close quarters, with rapid and deadly results. The Vandoos quickly seized Villa Belvedere and began to clear the area.

Sydney Frost (Princess Patricia's Canadian Light Infantry)

San Fortunato was sticky in that the shelling was so terrible. The Germans had this habit of shooting airbursts, this is something from the first war, where the shot goes over and explodes in the air and comes right down on top of you. And that's what they used at San Fortunato because it was a high peak and they couldn't fire direct, so they shot up in the air, and a lot of my men got cut from shell parts.

Harry Fox (Hastings and Prince Edward Regiment)

At that particular time the Hasty Ps were on Fortunato Ridge, which observed all the Rimini plain. It had to be taken before Rimini could be captured. I think there must have been five or six battalions at least, fighting on Fortunato before it was captured. The ridge was very steep and it was sandstone. So it was fairly easy for the Jerries to dig positions into it, and being steep, it was hard to get up. Of course, once again they had the observation, and these mortars on the back of the ridge could reach every part of the area. Well, we were just taking casualties and not getting too far, so the battalion commanders began to complain. So a plan was figured out — all Canadian troops were called off the ridge, and the ridge would be hammered all night by artillery. In places you went up on your hands and knees, and in other places there was a road going up, but Jerry knows where they are, and he hammers them, so it's a bad place. So it was just a matter of grit your bloody teeth and keep on going. The attack succeeded. It took a day to do it, just the same.

Following close behind the Vandoos were the Loyal Eddies, who passed through looking to move in behind the ridge. At that time the Germans were sending troops to San Lorenzo on the far ridge to battle for the town that the Canadians had already taken. As they passed through San Fortunato Ridge, which they thought was securely in German hands — at least it was when they set out. They quickly found themselves in an ambush and they didn't have a chance. Over the next few hours the same action repeated itself as the Germans continued to send more troops forward. The Canadians had seized a portion of the ridge and were expanding on that position. By the afternoon of September 20, Kesselring realized the futility of his men's position at San Fortunato and gave the orders to withdraw. The Germans moved back to the next natural obstacle to set up their defences: the Marecchia River. As the rain poured down on September 21, the soaked men of the PPCLI battled with the Germans at the Marecchia River, crossing it and securing a bridgehead on the far side.

Sydney Frost (Princess Patricia's Canadian Light Infantry)

From then on it was the Po Valley, and the generals had told us, "We're going to go through the Po Valley and finish the war up in the Alps." Well, that was great. So after a lot of hard fighting we dislodged the Germans from San Fortunato, and then we went down into this wonderful plain. And I thought, "Isn't this great, well, the war is just about over." But there was still one more river to cross, the Marecchia River, and there was this little village on the south side of the river. I thought, "Well, we'll halt here for a moment or two and get our breath," and I saw a nice strong Itie house. One thing about Italian houses, they were built generations ago and they are solid — four feet thick, and you were usually pretty safe in them. So I got my platoon together and I said, "We'll rest here for a half an hour or so, and then we'll carry on across that river." As soon as we got into the house the first shell struck and it was a big one and blew away one of the rooms upstairs. I have about twenty-five men or so, and I'm trying to decide whether we should occupy every room or put everybody in one room. Well, I thought for the moment I'll spread them around. The next shot — a shot comes in, a big heavy one again, destroys another room. Well, now I'm down to about three rooms — what do I do with my men? I still distribute them around a little bit. Before the hour is out, another room goes. So finally I said, "Enough of this" — it's like playing a hand of poker, what do you do? What do you throw away? I threw away three rooms, let's all concentrate in this one big room. Well, it was a lucky one because the rest of the rooms were soon blown away and there was only one big room left. I was down to about fifteen men and we're all lying flat on the floor like sardines. One man, it was too much for him — a religious type, a new recruit — he started to cry and pulled a Bible out of his pocket and said, "We're all doomed, we're all going to hell, and let's pray." Well, I was having none of that. I said, "No one is going to hell, we don't need to pray at this point, give me that Bible." He wouldn't give it to me, I took it from him and I hit him with the back of my hand slightly, and that seemed to knock some sense into him and he quieted down. Well, then we hear tanks coming, German tanks. I was looking out a window, I could see this tank, and he could see me too. Whoosh! It went right through the window but above my head. I ducked down and the next shot went right through the window, and one thing about the armour-piercing shells, they don't explode, they go right through, and that's what happened with the second one, and the third one. By this time it was pretty desperate, we didn't know what was going to happen until finally the Canadian tanks arrived and saved the day.

For the Germans the situation was deteriorating badly. Without the advantage of the San Fortunato Ridge, they knew that Rimini could not be held, and any losses that they would sustain there would be pointless, so they withdrew without a fight. The Germans moved back to a defensive position to the north, and they didn't leave much of a town behind. The constant Allied bombings over the previous few weeks had reduced the once beautiful resort to rubble. On September 21 the empty town was taken by the Greek troops that were advancing along the coast as a part of the Canadian Corps.

Canadians, Greeks Unhinge Gothic Line

Rome, Sept. 22 (AP).—German hopes of holding Northern Italy through the coming winter were blasted today as battered remnants of 12 Nazi divisions fell back into the Po Valley before the victorious onslaught of Canadian and Greek troops as the British 8th Army forced a crossing of the Marecchia River west of the captured Adriatic stronghold of Rimini.

Rupture of the enemy's Gothic Line defenses at Rimini and to the west of the shattered resort city gave Gen. Alexander, Allied commander-in-chief in Italy, the opportunity he had long sought to throw his great armored superiority against the Germans where there was room for manoeuvre.

"The Battle of Italy is not yet over," wrote Associated Press War Correspondent Lynn Heinzerling from Rimini, "but it appeared to be entering its final phase today."

British 8th Army tanks from their foothold across the Marecchia were ready for quick smashes in two directions—northwest along the ancient Via Emilia toward the big industrial city of Bologne, and northnorthwest toward Ravenna, Ferrara and the Po Estuary. The Nazis, with much of their transport lying in rusting heaps beside Italian roads, appeared literally to face a fight for their lives.

The Canadian and Greek crossings of the Marecchia River beyond Rimini were accompanied by fierce British attacks further inland on and near Ceriano Ridge, six miles southwest of Rimini. The Nazis threw in several savage counterattacks, and the Town of Ceriano changed hands several times before British troops won possession both of the town and the ridge.

Greek troops smashed into Rimini Wednesday night, and by yesterday morning had cleared the greater part of the town. Canadian armor and infantry, in the meantime, had surged on to the Marecchia River west of the city, forcing the German garrison to retire hastily to avoid entrapment.

Rimini, once one of Italy's most fashionable resort cities, was found heavily damaged by Allied air and artillery bombardment. Its railway station was a heap of wreckage. The Church of San Nicolo al Porto was badly wrecked.

Beyond Rimini stretch some of

GOTHIC LINE—Page 2

Above: Canadian and Greek troops get recognition for their success at the Gothic Line.

Right: Canadian and Greek troops enter Rimini across the only bridge that was not destroyed by the Germans.

Jim Holman (48th Highlanders)

I remember going into Rimini. In the outskirts there was a lot of mortaring, a lot of Moaning Minnies and stuff like that coming down. They shoot you from a mortar from a long ways away, you don't see them, unless they're up on a ridge and you see the smoke. The Germans had pulled back from this river so we didn't come up against any resistance at all, only a machine gun down the street. If we had ventured down the street a little bit farther we probably would have. We came to this bridge and it was the only bridge the Germans didn't blow. So our section had to go across the bridge, on the German side, and put a guard on. We had to make sure that the Germans didn't come back to blow the bridge. I have two pictures in the archives, I'm third on the right in the one from Rimini. I remember the day the photographer took it, it was kind of a phony picture. We had no web equipment on, just our rifles, and he said, "Now sneak along those buildings and make like you're clearing houses." So we did it and he said to us, "Just like you're disappearing around the curve." Well, around the curve there was some German machine guns, just roaring and screaming, and the first guy turned around and you should have heard what he said to that photographer! Heh heh heh. Anyways the building that we're up against, you can see where a shell had hit one of those steel doors and blown it in. It happened to be a barbershop, so we went in and we had this guy cut our hair.

A group of Canadians man their gun in the ruins of Rimini. At one point in the battle they withstood a German attempt to break through the Canadian line.

The ruins of the railway station at Rimini.

RIFUGIO

Above left: *A patrol of 48th Highlanders move carefully through Rimini. Jim Holman is third from the left.*

Above right: *Feature newspaper article on the Irish Regiment from September 23, 1944.*

The Gothic Line had been shattered, thanks to Canadian troops who bravely battled through the worst that the Germans could throw at them. In the month of fighting, the Canadians suffered nearly four thousand casualties. One in four were fatal. For the severely depleted Canadian 1st Division, a break was in order. They were relieved by the New Zealand Division and the 5th Armoured Division, and they moved to the rear to rebuild and to refit after a month of hell.

Clearing the rubble in Rimini after the city was liberated.

GOTHIC LINE IS UNHINGED

(Continued From Page 1, Column 3.)

Italy's finest roads, ideal for Allied armor. The Po Valley, however, is laced by a good many rivers, which will give the Germans opportunities to make delaying stands, and the Allied Command cautiously avoided making optimistic statements.

Nevertheless, the enemy's plight appeared fully as bad—perhaps even worse—than when the Allied offensive from the Garigliano River in May and June almost destroyed the Nazi 14th Army and severely crippled the 10th Army.

What few German units still have motor transport will become highly vulnerable to Allied air attacks once they get on the roads northwest of Rimini, and their escape routes through Northern Italy already have been virtually closed by the destruction of bridges over the Po.

An official Allied report said that two German infantry divisions had lost the greater part of their effective fighting strength in a vain effort to hold the Rimini area, and that "losses heavier than Cassino" were inflicted by the Canadians on the 1st Parachute Division and by the 8th Army as a whole on four other divisions.

As the four-week assault on the Gothic Line thundered toward a climax, American troops of the 5th Army stormed into Firenzuola, an important road junction 26 miles south of Bologna, and seized the southern slopes of Monte Coloreta, a mile and a half northeast of Firenzuola.

As they moved up, the Americans found large numbers of enemy dead littering the slopes on which withering artillery and machine-gun fire had been laid preceding the advance.

An American column pushing along strategic Highway 65 toward Bologna was within a mile of Futa Pass, where the Nazis were believed to have installed some of their most formidable defenses. Rain and low visibility precluded air support for the attacking troops.

Near the Italian west coast Brazilian troops beat steadily northward and captured the important town of Pietrasanta, 19 miles northwest of Pisa.

BRIDGE TAKEN

R. THIBERT   **H. E. DETLOR**   **G. F. STUART**

L.-Cpl. Roland Thibert, 22, of Niagara Falls, was severely wounded in France, his wife, Mrs. Pearl Thibert, has been informed. Pte. Hugh Edgerton Detlor, wounded in Italy, observed his 20th birthday in hospital, according to information received by his father, A. B. Detlor, Niagara Falls. Cpl. George F. Stuart, 28, has been killed in France. His wife resides in Fort Erie.

Slept Through Battle

By DOUG HOW
(CP War Correspondent)

WITH THE CANADIANS ON THE ADRIATIC FRONT, Sept. 23.—For six hours the German paratroopers counter-attacked the Perth Regiment and the western tanks dug in on Point 204. Tankmen shot them off their Shermans. Infantrymen fought with rifles, grenades and machine-guns.

The Perths were ordered to make a slight withdrawal to allow an artillery concentration to be brought down on the enemy beating at this force which had broken through his Gothic line and now was mounting the slope behind it.

After dawn they retook the positions and found Pte. H. E. Detler of Niagara Falls, Ont., Cpl. Roy Martin of Kitchener, Ont., had to shake him to get him awake. A mortar bomb had caved in part of his slit trench. Paratroopers had dug within a few feet of him. The fight raged with intensity for hours. And Detler slept through it all . . .

L. Cpl. Abraham Rochlin, Montreal, guided a company under Capt. W. J. (Sammy) Ridge Millbrook

While the battle against the Germans at the Gothic Line had been a success for the Canadians, the Germans had been successful in one thing: they had slowed down the Allied advance until the rainy season. As the Allies looked to enter the Romagna, the rain poured down, transforming the land into a sea of mud. The once shallow streams had morphed into swift moving rivers with dangerous torrents. It was clear that they were not going to get far through the coming winter. As beaten as they were, the Germans continued to put up a fight, tenaciously hindering every attempt to advance. While the Germans knew that the fight for Italy was a lost cause, Kesselring still requested additional troops to continue the war, and Berlin obliged him. The Nazis were going to fight until the bitter end in Italy.

Far left: *Newspapers herald the success of the Canadians at the Gothic Line.*

Left: *Local casualties reported in the Niagara region on September 23, 1944.*

A destroyed tank left in the wake of the battle to crack the Gothic Line.

Sydney Frost (Princess Patricia's Canadian Light Infantry)
Well, it got fiercer all the time. I don't know how they did it, but they fought like demons. I don't know where they got the equipment from or the men from, because by that time the second front was in big swing, and yet they seemed to find the men. Paratroopers. I think they perhaps sent their best men down to Italy, because they didn't have too many and they thought with the nature of the terrain and they had a good solid professional corps down there, who knew how to defend — that that would be enough and they wouldn't have to put a big army or two down there.

Herb Pike (48th Highlanders)
I recall a time north of Rimini around what we called the Jam Factory. Jerry had six self-propelled guns and mortars and they were shelling us pretty good. We heard tanks coming down the road, and we called for our 17-pounder platoon to come up. The sergeant of the platoon was Porky Adams, and the other fella —

Gord Outhwaite (48th Highlanders)
Bobby Shaw?

Herb Pike (48th Highlanders)

Bobby Shaw! I was the last guy talking to him when they left to go back to get the guns to bring them up. I said, "Stay in the verge, don't go down the road, it's mined." This was one of the ratchet mines. I don't know why they did it because they were well-trained soldiers, they walked out of that farmhouse and down that road and stepped on one of these ratchet mines and off it went. We went out and brought them in. Bobby Shaw was cut right in half, and Porky Adams — he was just hamburger meat. It was just damn ridiculous that they would do this, but again they're probably thinking about what they are going to do with the guns when they brought them up and where they were going to set them up. They just walked down the side of the road and that was it. Things like that can happen.

CONSCRIPTION CRISIS

WHILE THE GERMANS CONTINUED TO RECEIVE reinforcements and equipment, the same could not be said for the Allies. With all of the attention on the fighting in northwest Europe, the campaign in Italy was all but forgotten. All of the resources of the Allies went to the fighting in France, Belgium, and, as of September 1944, the Netherlands. The capture of Antwerp and the Battle of the Scheldt was getting all of the press and all of the supplies. The result was a dangerous situation in Italy, where all units were severely understaffed and the substantial loss of officers was taking a huge toll, as they were not being replaced. The problem affected the divisions in northwest Europe as well, but none suffered as greatly as the Canadians in Italy. Where there should have been 150,000 men, only 85,000 were on duty. With smaller units being sent out to do the job of full-strength units, they faced more dangerous situations, and often suffered greater losses because of it. Then the unit would have to fight again, with even fewer men. Those who were wounded would be nursed back to health only to be sent to the front again. Many were fighting after being casualties three or four times. Some who sustained major wounds that would have normally sent them home found themselves back in action after a lengthy convalescence. The result was devastating on the morale of the men. Many felt that they were going to have to fight until they died, and that getting wounded was only putting off the inevitable. This situation led to the Conscription Crisis of 1944.

Harry Fox (Hastings and Prince Edward Regiment)

We were basically shorthanded. We were only built up to full strength after the Hitler Line, and then of course we gradually went down, and down, and down — and we were never at full strength again until we got into Holland. The troops weren't happy, and they figured, "Here we are, slugging our ass off in Italy, and there's thousands of zombies back in Canada. We're here, there's a job to do, well, let's do it." That was their way of looking at it. Let's get the job done and go home.

Herb Pike (48th Highlanders)

It affected some, but remember these guys were veterans. You know the pity was a guy would get hit, and he'd get hit in such a way where normally he would have been sent home, but because of the reinforcement situation down there they would patch these guys up and send them back. I had one man, he was hit three times in Italy, should have gone home on the first time he was wounded. We crossed the Ijssel River [in the Netherlands, April 1945] and he got killed the next day. Now, there's no way that man should have been there, but because of no reinforcements that's what happened to many a guy. He should have been home.

The rate of casualties was higher than anticipated in Italy, primarily due to the nature of the campaign. It was expected to be a war more dependant on tanks and aircraft, but Italy's terrain made it primarily an infantry war, so the casualties were much higher. Then the environment took its toll — thousands of men were incapacitated by illnesses such as malaria and jaundice, another aspect of the campaign that had not been anticipated. As the campaign progressed, the losses increased so that by the spring of 1944 the Canadian Army was forced to re-muster (replacing troops by drawing on the support staff, such as drivers and cooks, and the wounded). Other units were transferred, such as the anti-aircraft gunners, since the Luftwaffe had become non-existent by that point in the war. The problem was that these men were not trained as infantrymen, and they became casualties quicker because of their inexperience; they were also a liability to the experienced men that they were serving with.

Fred Scott (Perth Regiment)

Lack of material, lack of reinforcements, and yet we carried on and did our job as best as we could. You never hear any of them complain too much about it, they just done what they were told, and we done it.

Herb Pike (48th Highlanders)

We were fighting with equipment that was nothing like the boys had in the invasion on D-Day had. Sure, I carried a Thompson sub. A Bren gun and a Lee Enfield rifle. Our tanks, the old Shermans and the Churchills and whatnot, this was the first generation of Sherman. All the good stuff was being held for Normandy — and we had to do the same job with lesser equipment. The job was done, there's no two ways about it.

Al Sellers (Governor General's Horse Guards)

Our equipment was pretty well worn out and so was our rations, so was our clothing — I think I wore the same uniform all the way through Italy. We were shortchanged in so many ways, they had all sorts of stuff available to them. We had nothing. In our outfit we had the Sally Ann captain, Captain Mercer, and he was a great guy. From time to time he'd get a supply of chocolate bars and whatnot, and he'd dole them out to the guys. But we didn't get canteens, we didn't get theatres, we had no entertainment. We were undermanned, and the reinforcements were not trained well. One tank I had, my loader was eighteen years old, and that was in 1944, five years after the war started. So this little guy comes up and he had virtually no training at all. The gunner was another one. You could tell by the regimental number when they must have joined up — most of our numbers were five digits, but then we had the reinforcements with their six-digit numbers, we knew "Oh-oh, we got to train this guy." We didn't have conscription in Canada; it was a volunteer army, a volunteer air force, a volunteer navy.

Herb Pike (48th Highlanders)

When you talk about casualties, the biggest problem is that the reinforcements we got were restructured guys who were probably in an anti-aircraft outfit and they sent him to a couple of weeks of infantry training, and then sent him up. Now you don't train an infantryman in two weeks, and a lot of guys come up today and they're gone tomorrow. Training was so vital.

The issue stemmed from the fact that the Canadian Army was an all-volunteer army. While over a million Canadians answered the call, it put a huge strain on the country's infrastructure as 10 percent of the nation went into the service. As the need for more soldiers increased, the idea of conscription was a touchy one in Canada, and was not universally supported. As such, the politicians of the day tried to walk the tightrope of public opinion by deciding to implement conscription but keep anyone drafted to serve only in Canada. This did not do the fighting soldiers any good as they were fighting with units that were only at half strength or less. To go on the offensive, an army needs an advantage of triple the amount of troops that the defender has. The Canadians were attacking with equal numbers to the Germans, and were suffering catastrophic losses as a result. Even by cannibalizing their own support system, the Canadian Army in Italy was heading for disaster. It was estimated that they would run out of troops by the fall of 1944.

Herb Pike (48th Highlanders)

Our reinforcements were nil. We were operating with a platoon with fifteen or sixteen guys — it should have been thirty-three men in it! We just weren't getting the reinforcements. I was a sergeant of a platoon at the time and I went six months without an officer. We just didn't have them. You're operating with …

Gord Outhwaite (48th Highlanders)

… partial strength.

Herb Pike (48th Highlanders)

Yeah. It's amazing quite frankly, that we were able to do anything — and it wasn't just our regiment, but everybody was the same.

Gord Outhwaite (48th Highlanders)

Well, they took most of our support over for D-Day, and that's why we were left high and dry. Fortunately we made it, but still we were in a very precarious position.

While the debate dragged on in Ottawa, nothing was being done for the fighting men — particularly those in Italy facing the most dire of circumstances. The situation came to a head in late September when the Minister of Defense, Colonel J.L. Ralston, visited the troops in Italy. The reception he received was less than warm, and he was brought face to face with the crisis, and its impact on the men and their morale.

Joseph Reid (Calgary Regiment)
One time the Minister for National Defense came to see us through the campaign and we said, "Send us more troops, more reinforcements."

Upon his return to Canada, Ralston pushed to send the conscripts overseas and into action. Prime Minister Mackenzie King feared that such a move would be political suicide, and so he fired Ralston. General MacNaughton was named as the Minister of Defense, and he promptly promised more volunteers. Precious few ever made it to Italy.

Harry Fox (Hastings and Prince Edward Regiment)
They were completely teed off by it. We were short of men, junior officers right down to the last rear rank soldier, and yet we knew there were thousands of trained men in Canada just sitting on their backsides. We could have used them, and had they been there, possibly we wouldn't have had so many casualties.

For the men in Italy, they were resigned to their situation and tried to make the best of it. Even if Ralston had been able to send the conscripts into action, the experienced men feared the dangers of putting "zombies" into combat units. They would be risking the lives of the men who were willing to be there. Sadly the leadership in Ottawa did the fighting men of Canada little good in the war, supplying them with cheap or outdated equipment and refusing to maintain an adequate fighting strength throughout the entire campaign. Such political machinations cost lives, adding outrage to the despair of war.

As the Conscription Crisis played out, the Canadians in Italy stoically fought the war, shrugging off the frustration of the debate and single-mindedly focusing on the problem at hand: to defeat the Germans and bring the war to an end.

Harry Fox (Hastings and Prince Edward Regiment)
Oh, we knew all the way along it was going to come to an end, but we didn't know when. It was going to just drag on, but every time we went into a big attack, we won. It happened every time so that basically we knew in the back of our heads that we were winning, but it would just take time.

Gord Outhwaite (48th Highlanders)

They took away our automatic weapons — well, we had the Thompson and they took it away from us and give us a Sten gun, which is a plumber's dream — it was useless.

Herb Pike (48th Highlanders)

I wouldn't carry one.

Gord Outhwaite (48th Highlanders)

A useless damn weapon. They were actually made for the airborne for close fighting. They would fire out the breach, you could drop them and they would fire a half a dozen rounds. They were a lousy gun.

Herb Pike (48th Highlanders)

I wouldn't take one, I carried a rifle.

Gord Outhwaite (48th Highlanders)

Well, actually I did a little better, I carried a Schmeisser. It's a better weapon. Unfortunately the Germans had it, but this one I sort of liberated from a German. I thought, "Well this one works better than mine, so I'll use that."

THE PO VALLEY

THE PO VALLEY SPREAD OUT BEFORE the Allies with its flat plains. Initially the hope was to send the tanks across this low-lying area, to rapidly advance against a devastated enemy. But there were many obstacles: the Germans had been reinforced, the weather had turned bad, and the Allies were facing a series of river crossings again. Ahead lay the Fiumicino, Savio, Ronco, Montone, Lamone, Senio, and Santerno Rivers. The difference in the Po Valley was the addition of innumerable canals that crisscrossed the terrain as a part of the agricultural infrastructure. Both the rivers and the canals were controlled with ten-metre-high banks, diverting the water into farm fields, vineyards, and orchards. These fields in turn were surrounded by stone walls or hedgerows. Each of these elements presented an obstacle that the Germans could exploit in slowing down the Allies, and the sum of all of them presented a major challenge. Every field, every river, every road, and every dyke would be hotly contested.

Due to the mud created by the rain, the advance would have to be confined to the roads, where it would be less of an issue. Advancing along these open thoroughfares was particularly dangerous for tanks since they were exposed, so the infantry would have to scout ahead and ferret out the hidden German positions. The routes were mined by the Germans as they retreated, and the advance was slow and dangerous.

Rivers Along The Adriatic

Canadians Over River Pouring Into Po Valley Yanks Continue Advance

Canucks Hold Beachheads From Marecchia — Foe Disorganized to Limited Extent

Rome, Sept. 23—Canadians with the British 8th Army drove beyond captured Rimini into the Po valley today and established beachheads three miles wide and two miles deep across the Marecchia River.

Rimini fell Thursday to Greek forces under Canadian command.

American infantry of the Allied 5th Army widened their breach in the centre of the Gothic Line with the seizure of Monte Citerna and Monte Tronale, both west of captured Firenzuola. High ground north of Firenzuola was occupied.

These advances placed the 5th Army on the threshold of the strategic Futa Pass.

Columns spearing northward along the mountain roads were meeting an enemy which Allied headquarters declared was becoming disorganized "to a limited extent."

IS VITAL PASS

Futa Pass is approximately 29 airline miles south of Bologna.

British and Brazilian forces with the 5th Army continued to make gains "against varied resistance," said an Allied Headquarters report.

The Brazilians, operating on the left flank of the 5th Army near the Ligurian coast, were last reported smashing forward from Pietrasanta in the direction of La Spezia, 23 airline miles distant.

Today's communiqué said the 8th Army had mopped up all resistance south of the Marecchia River which empties into the Adriatic at Rimini, and that the bridgehead across the river, over which the thrusts toward Ravenna and Bologna have been launched, was "considerably enlarged."

The bridgehead was reported three miles wide and two miles deep. Advancing 8th Army troops were taking an increasing toll of prisoners.

ROAD TO MILAN

Advance elements were astride highway 9—the ancient Via Aemilia—which extends northwest on the southern edge of the Po Valley through Forli, Bologna and Modena toward Milan. They were also astride parallel rail lines and began pounding northward up highway 16 toward Ravenna and the Po estuary.

Clearing skies enabled the Allied air forces to begin a new offensive against enemy communications behind the battle lines. From the Piave River northeast of Venice to the Milan and Alessandria areas far to the west, Marauders and Mitchells attacked dozens of highways and rail bridges in a renewed campaign to maroon the Nazi armies.

The Allied Command paid special tribute to the 1st Canadian Infantry Division for its leading role in the offensive which carried it from the Metauro River through the Gothic Line to the new bridgehead over the Marecchia and the gateway to the Lombard plain.

Herb Pike (48th Highlanders)

Not only the terrain was a problem, but also the rivers. We would just get over one river and you've got another one to cross — or a canal.

Al Sellers (Governor General's Horse Guards)

I forget all of the names of the crossings. These things may have been anywhere from thirty to fifty feet wide, but in the dry season they would be just bone dry. If there was a storm somewhere farther away from where you were, a couple of hours later those things were just a raging torrent. We had tanks get caught and we had to tow them out, or else we'd lose them. The Engineers couldn't always be up there with us because the people with us, they were the infantry. They had to come up later on, and sometimes they did put in those Bailey bridges — constructed them under fire. The farther north we got, we got into the canals, and the enemy was very adept at using them to stop our advance simply by flooding an area.

Left: *Canadians advance into the Po Valley, as reported on September 23, 1944.*

Above: *Bailey bridge over the Marecchia River becoming engulfed by the swollen river. Shortly after this photo was taken the bridge was swept away by the current.*

Harry Fox (Hastings and Prince Edward Regiment)

All bridges were smashed, so we couldn't use them. The areas around the bridges were mined, so the mines had to be cleared away before anything was done. The next point would be: they were on high ground on one side and we were coming along and had to go down the river slope, and they could see. They had that all previously registered, so they knew the exact range and they could hammer you with mortars as you crossed the river, and then of course you had to go up the other side against them. So you were hammered all over there, let's put it that way.

Crossing the Uso River over a Bailey bridge constructed by Royal Canadian Engineers. The ruins of the church of San Vito can be seen in the background.

As the 1st Division was relieved on September 21, the 5th Division moved across the Marecchia River and began its push north. The 11th Brigade led the way, moving up to the Fiumicino River, while the 12th Brigade fought its way to the Uso River. The journey was fraught with danger, as the 12th Brigade suffered 350 casualties in the four days that it took to reach the river. The 11th Brigade fared no better. Every river was a challenge to cross, facing German fire from the elevated riverbanks and having to find a way across. To make matters worse, in the last few days of September the rain became extraordinarily heavy, flooding the area and making the roads nearly impossible to use. Vehicles slid off the roads and became mired in the mud. The advance slowed to a crawl, and days turned into weeks with minimal gains. They took Casale late in September, but the conditions forced the Allies to shift the offensive inland, where the British took advantage of the better roads in the highlands. For the time being the Canadians protected the flank.

By October 11 the 1st Division was ready to return to action. They had spent those weeks in Cattolica and Riccione resting and refitting. While not completely up to strength, the units were in much better shape than when they had left. The 5th Division was promptly pulled back into reserve after several weeks of tough fighting. The 1st Brigade continued their slow advance, taking Sant'Angelo in Salute and Bulgaria Village in mid-October.

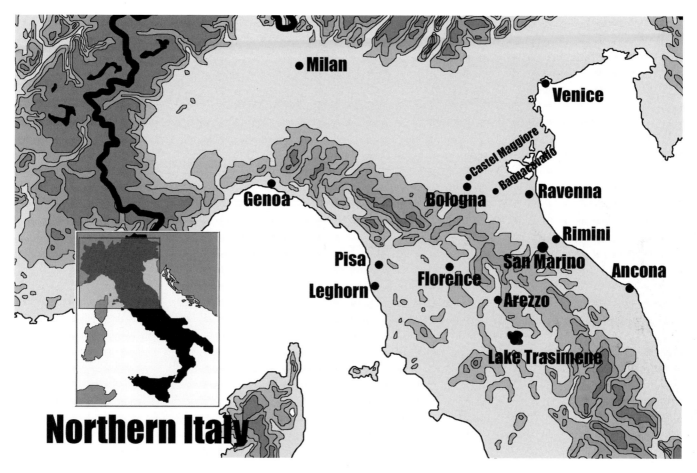

Northern Italy

Harry Fox (Hastings and Prince Edward Regiment)

They captured this little village Bulgaria, and it was a company commander's place I guess because the telephone rang. One of our men picked the phone up and says, "Go to hell you square head bastard," and then he was bragging about it. "You did the wrong thing," I said, "you should have let it ring, and the Jerries back there would have said, 'Those people up at the front are asleep again, send a patrol up!' and we would have caught two more!"

Jim Holman (48th Highlanders)

We got to this village of Bulgaria. I walked down the street maybe a few hundred yards, and the Jerries suckered us right in, they were waiting for us. As soon as we got in this town, they poured the mortars, just

8th And 5th Near Hookup As Allies Take Italy Pass 15 Miles From Bologna

Yanks Have Clear Access Into Po Valley After Smashing "Impregnable" Nazi Stronghold

Rome, Sept. 25—U.S. troops drove through Futa Pass to-day to Castel del Rio, 12 miles from the Bologna-Rimini highway, paving the way for a junction with the British 8th Army fanning up the Po Valley along the Adriatic coast.

Advancing northeast of the important road junction of Firenzuola, the 5th Army was in an unaccustomed position of fighting down hill instead of up, and had before them clear access across the eastern slope of the Apennines into the Po Valley.

Northwest of Rimini on the Adriatic sector, the Germans were using the cover of trees and vineyards on farms for delaying action, but Canadians of the 8th Army made steady advances Saturday to reach Pedrere Grande, five miles northwest of Rimini.

In support of that push northward, the British destroyer Loyal heavily bombarded German gun positions seven miles north of Rimini yesterday, pouring more than 400 rounds into the enemy-held coastal area.

Driving through the Gothic line at Futa Pass, strongest German position in all Italy and one they thought was impregnable, the 5th Army forces were reported yesterday to have been 15 miles from Bologna, greatest city of the rich Po Valley.

To-day's report did not pin-point the advance, but merely disclosed that the Allied troops were 12 miles from the Bologna-Rimini highway and within 21 miles of Bologna at their most forward stabilized positions. Official sources explained that yesterday's report that Americans were within 15 miles of Bologna was based on forward reconnaissance elements who came that near to Bologna on Saturday on patrol and then retired.

Fanning out from conquered Futa Pass, the Americans reached a point just south of Roco, six and a half miles due north of Firenzuola, and captured Monte Alafine, six miles northeast of Firenzuola, west of the highway following the Santerna River into the Po valley.

They also captured Monte Della Croce, eight miles northeast of Firenzuola, east of the highway, and Monte Cucca and Monte Porarra in the high ground immediately west of the highway between Monte Alfine and Monte Della Croce, all on an arc two miles south of Casteldel Rio.

Brazilian expeditionary troops fighting with the army in the western sector, made a small advance and suffered a few casualties. Ending its first week in the front lines, the Brazilian force had made a net gain of 10 miles north of Pisa.

Nazi Forces Attempt to Halt the Fifth Army Drive Toward Bologna

ROME, Oct. 12 (BUP).—German troops, reportedly bolstered by reinforcements from northern Italy, waged an all-out defensive battle in the foothills of the Apennines today in a desperate attempt to halt Allied Fifth Army columns driving toward Bologna and the Po valley.

Bitter fighting raged in the southern outskirts of Livergnano, less than 10 miles south of Bologna, all but halting the main American force pushing northward on the main highway from Florence.

The Germans, who were believed to have received reinforcements from Verona, were fighting desperately as the Fifth army offensive neared Bologna and the Po valley's open plains.

Increasing enemy resistance also was encountered by two other American columns east and west of the Florence highway after they had reached points approximately 12 miles from Bologna, gateway to the Po valley and the key point on the superhighway to Rimini.

While the Germans built up pressure against the Fifth army front before Bologna, Eighth army forces in the Adriatic sector were reported meeting weakening enemy resistance.

The Eighth army line was moving ahead along the entire 15-mile front stretching from Savignano southwestward to the town of Mercato Saraceno on the Savia river.

One unit succeeded in establishing a new bridgehead over the Fiumcino river and occupied the villages of Gatteo and San Giovanni in Competo, respectively one mile and a half mile northwest and west of Savignano.

West of Montigallo ridge, United Kingdom troops captured the town of Longino and pushed one mile beyond, while another force seized the village of La Crocetta, a mile north of Montigallo, to straighten the line between Longiano and Savignano.

To the southwest, however, the Germans counter-attacked all day yesterday, trying unsuccessfully to recover an unnamed peak, two miles west of Roncofreddo, and Monteleone, another mile farther west, but the Eighth army troops held firmly to their newly-won positions.

On the west coast, Brazilian troops of the Fifth army resumed their advance up the Serchio valley, with leading elements reaching the town of Barga, 16 miles north of Lucca.

Synthetic

Far left: *On September 25, 1944, the Allies are reported to be on fifteen miles away from Bologna.*

Left: *The Germans defend the route to Bologna and benefit from reinforcements in October 1944.*

poured them in. That's where I got it. I was off one side of the road, I'd be fine if I had stayed where I was, but there was a house opposite me, it was blown out but there was a doorway. I thought, "Gee, if I can make that doorway" and I got about three hops across the road, and me and the bomb hit the door at the same time. It hit right beside my foot and blew my foot off. The tendons were hanging there. It must have knocked me clean out, when I started to come to, I thought I was dead. I could hear music and I had this most peaceful feeling, it was just unbelievable the way I felt. I couldn't believe it, I thought, "This has got to be it" it was so wonderful. Then all of a sudden I could hear these bombs again, so I got up to run and I fell down, I didn't know my foot was off, and then I realized I was on fire — my hair had burned off, all my clothes were smoldering — so I try and put this out, and I look at my foot and it's sticking out on the side there. I had my putty on — I still have my putty with a hole in it. I unrolled the putty, and oh gee, what a mess. I looked at it, I tried to straighten it out a little bit, and then I started to feel sick, and I brought up. By this time I was screaming for a stretcher-bearer, and a fellow by the name of Glen Denny looked after me. Yeah, that was the end for me. Almost six months fighting and that was enough.

Albert Wade (Royal Canadian Dragoons)
We moved right up to this canal just east of Cesena, and we set up shop in an abandoned blockhouse, which was used I guess to keep animals in at one time. We went in and relieved the New Zealand infantry unit. They put me in a corner in this blockhouse and it had a big pit in underneath this barn, and they were using that as a bomb shelter. They stuck me in the corner facing a roadway, wide open, and I was joined in company by a dead pony. The dead pony and I sat with a Bren gun, so-called guarding from any attack from across this river. During the time that we were there the Seaforths, the Carleton and York, the RCR, the Hastings Prince Edwards, and the 48th Highlanders attacked Cesena and liberated it. The Princess Pats, they moved on from there and they got up on October the twentieth, they liberated a town called Martorano.

The 3rd Brigade then took the lead and on October 20 seized control of Cesena. The 2nd Brigade moved off to the right, battling the Germans as they crossed the Pisciatello and began the push towards the Savio River.

Albert Wade (Royal Canadian Dragoons)
It was west of Ceseno and we were doing a bit of infantry work. We were trained in that capacity, as support. My longtime driver — John Maitland, he was from Toronto — he volunteered go up on a reconnaissance

venture on foot. I couldn't leave the troop, and they asked for volunteers, and he was one of six that went with an officer. They went up towards this canal and he got struck in the back of the head. A bullet. It went through his helmet and it creased his scalp at the back of his head. He was taken out of action, but before we went to Holland he came back to me. He was once again my driver. He and I spent a lot of the war together. We really were a good team. I think he saved my life one day, he told me to sit down. I was standing up in the scout car and the Jerries were hiding in a house, and they were firing on us and I was watching it go by. I shouldn't have. He says, "Sit down, Wade!" Heh heh heh. I sat down — pfsssh! We had a lot of different exciting moments together.

As the Canadians arrived at the Savio River, they faced their greatest challenge yet in the Po Valley. The Germans had established excellent defensive positions along the far riverbank, which stood five metres tall. To get across would require moving through the muddy shore, where every step sank deep into the quagmire, slowing down the advance and becoming easy targets for the Germans above. Then they would have to cross the river, which was swollen and running fast. It was about fifteen metres across, and in some places it was waist deep and could be crossed. In other areas it was too deep and the current too dangerous to make an attempt. If the men made it that far, they would then have to contend with the mud again, attempting to scale the high riverbank while the Germans fired down on them. On October 20, that is exactly what the brave men of the PPCLI did.

Sydney Frost (Princess Patricia's Canadian Light Infantry)

It was a brutal, dirty campaign. And some of us were a little upset with the staff from time to time for throwing us into these battles without proper preparation. In this particular operation we had crossed several rivers beforehand, and we came up to the Savio River. It wasn't much of a river, but it was raining, and the general told our brigadier, "Throw a company or two across this river, just throw them across, no trouble, old chap" — very British. Well, the CO said, "We better make a reconnaissance." "Oh, there's not any time to make a reconnaissance." "Well, we'd like to line up a fire plan." "No time for the artillery to line anything up — get on with it!" So we tried it.

The crossing did not go well. The artillery hit the Germans along the west side of the Savio River. The Patricias had been given short notice for the attack, and when the artillery let up, the Germans moved back into their defensive positions and hit the Canadians hard.

Sydney Frost (Princess Patricia's Canadian Light Infantry)
So this first company, without any preparation at all, tried to get across and just before they got to the river, of course they ran into a minefield. The Germans weren't stupid, and they had both sides of this river mined. People were blown up, and finally the platoon commander decided that we can't go any further this way. We have to go around to the left. But a few men did get across, believe it or not — they had to swim. There was no time for assault boats or the engineers. They swam and got across to the other side, then the commanding officer put through another company, and it did a little better, but suffered terrible casualties. So at the end of the day, under Major Cutbill, who was in charge of one of the companies, I think there was something like 13 men out of maybe 150 who made it to the other side. They're supposed to attack a German position. Well, it was suicide. So we sent back a runner, I'll never forget it, his name is Sergeant Sparrow — because his wireless set had been knocked out. "Please send us up ammunition and more men." So they sent up another company. Well, there's four companies and three are already committed, and they had a tough time too, but they finally got there. Well then these wonderful men, they fought the Germans tooth and nail and killed a lot of them, but they were just overwhelmed, there was just too many of them. So finally the general in the rear realized that this is a failure. "Well, we'll fix that — this time we'll throw in two battalions instead of one — throw them in." They were the Seaforth Highlanders and the Loyal Eddies.

The next phase of the plan was for the Seaforth Highlanders to pass through the PPCLI position and to forge ahead to the Cesena-Ravenna road. The objective was situated fifteen hundred metres beyond the Savio, and would be key to the success of the operation. The Seaforths witnessed the fate of the PPCLI, and without enough room to build a bridge to their small bridgehead, the Seaforths decided to cross further down the river. In the meantime, the rain became torrential, and by the night of October 21, the river had raised two metres in only five hours. The Seaforths made the crossing anyway, fording the dangerous river a few hundred metres from where the PPCLI were hanging on against intense German fire. The rain turned the mud into very soft sludge, dashing any hopes to be able to erect a bridge across the Savio at the new bridgehead. The infantry were on their own, but the brave men of the Seaforth Highlanders were not to be denied, and they broke through the German defences along the riverbank.

Sydney Frost (Princess Patricia's Canadian Light Infantry)
The Seaforth Highlanders and the Loyal Eddies advanced over the same ground that we had fought over, but this time there was time to plan, to make a reconnaissance, line an artillery plan up, and that sort of thing — even air support. So that went into action the next day and it was a success. It was difficult, but they managed to get across the river and assault the Germans, and take the position. It was touch and go.

While the Germans fought the Seaforth Highlanders at their point of crossing, other German units were unaware of the situation. A short distance up the river a group of defenders left their posts along the riverbank to go have breakfast. When they returned, a company of Seaforths had taken their position and promptly took them prisoner. Not to leave it at that, the Canadians then cut the communications line to that sector. When the Germans sent a repair crew to fix it, the Seaforths captured them as well. With the establishment of a bridgehead, the men moved inland, seizing the road and preparing to defend it. As tough as it was for them to cross the Savio and to capture the road, it was nothing compared to what they would face in order to hold it.

Harry Fox (Hastings and Prince Edward Regiment)
So the 2nd Brigade did get the bridgeheads over, that was fine, that was a pretty swell piece of work, and then it rained heavily and the river come up and isolated them. So there were three or maybe four small bridgeheads on the opposite side of the river, and there was no way to get reinforcements over to them.

The Germans quickly counterattacked, sending three Mark V Panther tanks, two self-propelled guns, and nearly thirty infantrymen to the Cesena-Ravenna road. They arrived just as the Seaforths were preparing their defences, armed only with machine guns and PIATs. The situation was grim for the Canadians, but they were not willing to give up the road, no matter how badly the odds were stacked against them. Private Ernest "Smokey" Smith took the initiative and led his PIAT group to the road and hid in the ditches. As the first tank approached, spraying the ditches with machine gun fire, one Canadian was wounded. From ten metres away Smith jumped up and fired the PIAT at the German tank, neutralizing it. Part of the German infantry contingent were riding on that tank, and they immediately jumped off and charged at Smith, who promptly cut them down with his machine gun, killing four and driving the rest back. One of the self-propelled guns was destroyed, and Smith was under intense fire as he fought beside his wounded friend. The Germans were driven back, and as another tank moved into the area to fire on the Canadians, Smith destroyed it with another PIAT shell. At that point the Germans withdrew and the position was held until reinforcements arrived, securing the bridgehead.

For his bravery, Smith was awarded the Victoria Cross. He was the third, and last, Canadian to receive the honour in Italy. Smith was the last surviving recipient of the VC in Canada until he passed away in 2005. Such gallantry was inspiring to the men, as Smith had faced the enemy at point-blank range and turned them back.

Fred Scott (Perth Regiment)
We went with the British Columbia Dragoon Guards, and we went around where Smokey Smith won the Victoria Cross — it was a terrific battle, but things were moving so fast then, and we had the Germans on the move and we kept them on the move. I wouldn't say it was the toughest battle I was ever in in Italy, but it was sure as hell one of them.

The fighting continued for several days, and on October 24 the Germans began to pull back to their defensive line, which spanned across the Italian peninsula from Bologna in the west to Commacchio in the east. All across the front the Germans were under pressure. The Americans were pressing hard towards Bologna, forcing Kesselring to move two divisions from the Adriatic coast to counter their success. At the same time the British and the Poles were making headway near the Via Emilia, and the Canadians had breached the Savio River defences. The withdrawal to the next defensive line was the Germans' only choice, but as usual, it would be a fighting retreat. By October 25 the Savio bridgehead was securely in Canadian hands and they were in pursuit of the Germans up to the Ronco River. Three days later the majority of Canadians were put into reserve, with the exception of the 1st Canadian Armoured Brigade, which was still fighting in support of the Americans and British in the Florence area. The rest was well deserved, as the Canadians had fought for thirty-three days to advance the fifty kilometres from the Marecchia River to the Ronco. That short strip of land had cost them two thousand casualties. For the Allies, it was clear that they were not going to make it to the Alps that winter, so they altered their objectives and focused on taking Bologna and Ravenna.

Peter Routcliffe (Governor General's Horse Guards)
I remember quite a bit of the floods north of Rimini. We had to walk maybe three or four miles up to our chest and carrying your weapon over your head until you could even get through it. You couldn't tell where the road was because the flood was right over the road, and if you walked off one side or the other you'd be in the ditch, so you tended to follow

Top left: *Inscription of the sergeants' party photo.*

Bottom left: *Sergeants' party of the Governor General's Horse Guards in Dopo Lavoro Cervia.*

the line right through. Sometimes they put a rope or a ribbon along so you could tell where the road was. I think the driest place I ever got to was Cervia. After we took Cervia we went further along to Ravenna.

On November 5 the Canadians went through a change in command as Lieutenant-General Burns was replaced by Lieutenant-General Charles Foulkes as the commanding officer of the I Canadian Corps. The campaign in Italy had ground to a halt, with small skirmishes creating minor results. Each side tested the other, but it was clear that nothing major was in the works. For the Allies it was important to keep the enemy engaged so that they would not be able to transfer their troops elsewhere. Late in the month, a number of Canadians worked with Italian partisans behind the lines to create havoc around Ravenna prior to the main assault on the town, which was to be part of the Canadians' next assignment.

Sydney Frost (Princess Patricia's Canadian Light Infantry)

Well, you must remember that Mussolini came from the north and Fascism was born in the north, and so as the farther north we got, the more resistance we got from the Italian population. They were still Fascists to a great extent. They weren't like the southerners, who welcomed us with open arms, we didn't see any of that at all. They were a surly bunch, because they knew that they were losing the war. In fact, there were still Fascist brigades fighting with the Germans in northern Italy. Not too effective, but they were. On the other hand, we had partisans working for us. The partisans were awfully good, they were braver than anything. They'd go out at night and grab a German or two and bring them back. I asked one, "How do you do this?" "Oh," he said, "it's very simple. We sneak up very close to the German lines and we start cooking up a nice soup or stew, and the Germans come out to grab it and we grab them!"

Jim Holman (48th Highlanders)

There were Italian partisans. All of a sudden you'd run into these guys, and man, they were doing a real job. They didn't look like soldiers — they were a mess. Wearing bandanas on their heads and they'd be off some place, you wouldn't even know where they were, just doing their job on the Germans. I saw them a couple of times but never got to talk to any of them, most of them didn't speak English. The Italians were so glad to get away from the Germans, although there were a lot of Italian collaborators, especially the young girls. Of course, the girls were doing it because they would get something to eat. Whenever they found one of these prostitutes, they used to shave their heads. Whenever you saw a girl with a bandana on, you knew she had her head shaved and she didn't want anyone to see that.

John Richardson (Ontario Regiment)

So after Florence we holed up in Borgo San Lorenzo, that's what it was, Borgo San Lorenzo, about twenty miles north of Florence. That's where we wintered because with the mud and everything in the mountains, there was no way you could move around. Just little skirmishes was about all that we were doing.

Joseph Reid (Calgary Regiment)

We had a worse plight when we got to the Apennines north of Florence. When it was frostier weather, all the crew would be out walking. Sometimes you'd be surprised how we were holding the tank up as it started to slide down, and eventually you couldn't hold it up, so one time it went over the bank and down the back there, so you'd say goodbye to the driver. That was a hazard practically all through Italy because we would ruin every road we got on, eventually. And there are hairpin turns all over Sicily and Italy.

Sydney Frost (Princess Patricia's Canadian Light Infantry)

It's wintertime and we're still in our tropical uniforms that we had been issued in England, and we were all frozen to death. So what we would do is we would take German equipment and German uniforms. Myself, I wrote home a letter once that I can remember saying that I'm a marvellous-looking specimen now — I have an Italian shirt, a German sweater, a pair of Australian boots, and so on — because we didn't have any proper clothing. Finally it arrived! And along with it something we had requested way back in Sicily, and that was margarine that wouldn't melt. Well, of course it wouldn't melt in the winter either, so we had our problems. But we persevered.

Al Sellers (Governor General's Horse Guards)

We were never too crazy about our rations because we had that lousy MV — meat and vegetables. We had bully beef, and I think it came from old beef, and sometimes it would be so old that the stuff would be dried up in the cans. Spam — we finally got Spam, which was a whole bunch of different kinds of meat made into one kind. It tasted good, but you got awfully tired of it. The hardtack, you could do wonders with hardtack. You could cut and break it up and mix it up with the meat, just cook it up over a gas fire or a cordite fire. Sometimes you'd take a shell and take the projectile out of it, put the cordite in the ground and put some rocks around it, get a can and light a little trail, and put the can of whatever you were cooking on this bunch of rocks and light it. Phssst! Cooked. It was pretty good really, but sometimes the cans melted before the stuff got cooked. Our potatoes — sometimes they were good, but a lot of times they were soft, but they were still edible. And then we finally got them in cans, and that was good. There came a time when some pigs or some cattle would get killed in action, and they would be quartered and dressed, and the cooks would do a good job with it. It was catch as catch can.

Herb Pike (48th Highlanders)

The rations were terrible. M & V was in a can. You know we actually had stuff given to us down there that was First World War food — been in cans, can you believe it?! I remember a pile of bully beef about the size of a table and nobody would eat the stuff. One time a mortar bomb come in and hit this stuff and thank God it was gone!

Jim Holman (48th Highlanders)

I was born and raised in Thorold, right on the outskirts, and we knew right from kids which berries to eat, we knew what weeds to eat. My mother was raising us in the Depression, mom would know what to pick out of a field to feed us. There was lots of times you went into an action and they would outfit you with maybe a can of bully beef and some hardtack and your water bottle full of water and that was it. Well, a few days and nothing to eat and so you had to kind of scrounge, and I always had the guys say, "Hey, Holman, what are you eating now?" There was one time we were really hungry and we went through this field and somebody had planted corn and the corn wasn't mature. There was nothing you could eat off the corn, so I knew that if you take the corn and split it open, you can eat the pit that's inside. Boy, we were hungry, so I got my knife out and start cutting chunks out, and it's kind of on the sweet side too. I'm eating this and "Hey! What are you eating?" Well, they all tried it but there was some of them got a heck of a stomachache. The day after, we met the Princess Louise Dragoon Guards, and we hollered at them did they have anything to eat? So they threw us out a box of bully beef. We were really, really hungry, and the Germans had just about cleaned all the food out as they moved out. Once in a while you'd find a farm that had maybe a couple of chickens and maybe a little farmer who would give us some eggs. I remember one day one guy got a hold of a small piglet and a goose. We had one guy who did all the cooking, he wanted to be the cook, and nobody walked near him because he was always picking up pots and pans and hook them on his belt. He clanked too much, so we always made him walk at the very back. So he made up this stew, and I got all kinds of stuff, and we ate it, and nobody realized that you can't eat fresh pork. With pork you can't kill it and eat it right away, and it made everybody yellow and so sick.

Peter Routcliffe (Governor General's Horse Guards)
There was always some good hot stew or something coming up for you. In the mornings you'd get up and we'd have an ounce of rum and a cigar or something and call that your breakfast. All sorts of things were done that were more or less inventions by certain people — like one guy, he took a can of bully beef and cut it up, and he dipped it in batter and then fried it, and it was a hell of a nice dish to have with your meal.

On December 1 the Canadians were returned to the line, albeit not at full strength. The lack of reinforcements continued to haunt them, and the men were forced to go into battle with less and less support. The Allies wanted to take Bologna during the winter, and General Alexander devised a plan where the U.S. 5th Army would attack the city from the mountains while the British 8th Army would attack from the Romagna in a pincer move. The British would

launch their attack from the Santerno River, but that was twenty-five kilometres behind the line in German territory. The task of advancing to the Santerno was given to the Canadians, and it would be no mean feat. The plan was to use both the 1st and 5th Divisions, crossing the Lamone River, the Senio River, and finally the Santerno River, while capturing the towns of Russi and Bagnacavallo along the way. The three rivers were major obstacles, swollen and fast moving, and crossing the frigid waters would not be easy. Between the rivers was the ever-present mud, as well as canals, ditches, and ten-metre-high dykes that the Germans would dominate the battleground from. The plan was called Operation Chuckle, the name having been inspired by Dante's *Divine Comedy*. What the men were facing was no laughing matter.

Canadian soldiers prepare for the attack on the Lamone River by digging in a position for their 3-inch mortar.

The operation was launched at 0900 on December 2 as the artillery and air force bombed the path that the infantry would take. The West Novas and the Vandoos moved towards Russi and encountered fierce resistance, so they waited until dark to make their move. At that point a large group of Germans withdrew, and the Vandoos pursued them to a railway line beyond the town. The West Novas cleared the rest of the town through the night, taking control of Russi by the next morning. The 5th Division launched their attack by moving around the town of Ravenna, outflanking it. Sensing that they were about to be surrounded, the German defenders withdrew. The Princess Louise Dragoon Guards were stalled beside the Montone River, but the Westminsters were able to make the crossing and attacked the German defenders, quickly defeating them. The action allowed the battalion to make the crossing and surge forward.

On December 3 the Westminsters captured San Pancrazio and continued on to take Piangipane on December 4. That same day Ravenna was taken by elements of the 5th Division without a fight.

A Calgary Regiment tank moves through a narrow street in San Pancrazio.

A Calgary Regiment tank enters San Pancrazio amid the ruins.

The 1st Division was to secure a bridgehead over the Lamone River, and the 3rd Brigade made the push directly to the river, but suffered many casualties in the process. Even after sending in its reserve regiment, they were unable to make the crossing and secure a bridgehead. The task was then given to the 1st Brigade. The RCRs and the Hasty Ps were to make the crossing, even though they did not have an opportunity to do a reconnaissance of the area. They went through several changes of plan over a short period of time, including a different location to cross. The crossing was to go in at 0100 on December 5, preceded by a short bombardment. Tragically it came up short, decimating two companies of the Hasty Ps, so the RCRs went ahead with the crossing first, making the trip in collapsible canvas boats. One platoon was wiped out crossing the ruins of a bridge, but the rest faced scattered resistance. The RCRs got to the

Collapsible canvas boats were widely used in the Italian Campaign, similar to this one being trained with by the Vandoos.

other side and dug in, knowing that the Germans would counterattack at any time. Soon the survivors of the Hasty Ps made their way across the Lamone and protected the right flank of the RCRs.

The Germans launched their counterattack at dawn, during a light fog. They held an elevated railway line that stood six metres above the rest of the battlefield. From this position the Germans struck hard, eliminating the rest of the platoon by the bridge that was meant to protect the left flank. They fired down on the Canadian positions and used their self-propelled guns to fire airbursts over the men taking cover in the slit trenches. Methodically the Germans inflicted heavy damages on the RCR companies, forcing them to withdraw back across the Lamone while taking thirty-one prisoners. They then focused their fire on the Hasty Ps, driving them back over the river as well.

Sydney Frost (Princess Patricia's Canadian Light Infantry)
Another awful mess was the Lamone River where the RCR and the Hasty Ps were decimated. Throw a company across this river. Well they did, and they were just annihilated. My good friend Captain Hertzberg, his father was the commandant of the RMC, he was a good friend of mine and he was killed in that crazy assault.

By the morning of December 6 the 5th Division had pressed forward to create an eight-kilometre front along the Lamone River, having cleared out the area behind them. Foulkes was determined to force a way across the river, and he set about planning an assault utilizing both divisions. The 1st Division would cross at the same place that the RCRs and Hasty Ps were driven back from, while the 5th Division would cross several miles north of there. The attack was to go in on the night of December 6, but it ended up being delayed due to bad weather. Days passed and the weather did not let up, but the Canadians used the opportunity to do reconnaissance on the objectives across the river, allowing them to be fully prepared for battle — a luxury that the first assault regiments did not have. While they waited for four days, the Germans harassed them with constant shelling. It was a miserable time along the Lamone River, but the Canadians would soon be able to pay back their foes.

At 1930 on December 10 the Cape Breton Highlanders and the Perth Regiment quietly boarded their canvas boats and crossed the Lamone in stealth. The moon was obscured and the night was particularly dark, so they were not detected by the German sentries. The men of the 11th Brigade scrambled up the riverbank and quickly overtook the enemy defences. The Cape Breton Highlanders swiftly captured the town of Villanova, while a mile to the south the Perths were accomplishing the same thing at Borgo di Villanova.

Fred Scott (Perth Regiment)

I think the toughest battle I was ever in was crossing the Lamone River. Mud. Getting up to the river, crossing the river, and I know we were about the first to cross. An artillery shell landed in the water right beside me and the concussion knocked me unconscious. I've never seen my steel helmet from that day to this. As far as I know it's still at the bottom of the Lamone River. Well, I was unconscious from that explosion — this was about seven o'clock in the morning, and I didn't come to until about noon, and I was not with it. I could see way off in the distance a whole bunch of men coming to me and I didn't know whether they were Germans or Canadians. I was on the bank and I could kind of hear a motor running. I didn't know whether it was a tank, so I crawled right down beside the water and I sat there for about a minute and I kind of got my senses. I could see the water was flowing this way, and I thought to myself, well, the water's flowing that way so the Adriatic's got to be out there, and I knew we were about eight miles inland from the Adriatic, so I was getting my bearings back. My uniform was half off me from the explosion. I went down because I was going to see where this motor was, and here it was a fellow with a bulldozer — it was the Engineers building a roadway so they could build a bridge to cross the Lamone River. These fellows were coming up, it was a bunch of Cape Breton Highlanders. So they took a look at me, and I guess I was some fine-looking character, with half my uniform blown off, kind of on the stupid side, and I told them what happened. So they said just come with us, we're going up through the Perth Regiment anyways, so that's how I got back to the regiment. I was sent out for three or four days to get patched up a little bit. That was a tough battle, and the conditions were pretty rough.

Right behind them came the Westminsters and the Irish Regiment, fanning out to expand on the gains of the 11th Brigade. These new units were intended to protect the flanks of the newly established bridgehead, but they were so successful in their advance that they captured a bridge over the Fosso Vetro ditch before the Germans could blow it up. Twice the Germans counterattacked in an attempt to destroy the bridge, but the Canadians were resolute in their defence of it, and actually pushed the enemy back to the next ditch, Fosso Vecchio. There the Germans managed to destroy the bridge, and the advance had to stop so that the Canadians could consolidate their gains.

John Richardson (Ontario Regiment)

During the winter we were up in the mountains — now we're under the Americans, we're working under the 5th Army at this time. So we went up and relieved them, and I remember holding onto the tail of this little pack mule and climbing up the bloody mountain up to this place. We got up there and the Americans there got up and out, didn't say hello, goodbye, watch for this, watch for that, no conversation whatsoever.

Bang! Away they go. I just stood there with my mouth open. You know, usually anybody taking over, you talk about things, what's bad and what's good, its just common sense. I'll never forget that, I wish I could meet that guy sometime because I'd hammer him, because later on when I went down the side I got hit with shrapnel in the arm. It was a nasty place, because we couldn't move around at all. This was just over the mountain and going down into the Po Valley, and that's as far as the Americans got. We took over three of their tanks — the guns were full of water and no electricity in them at all.

While the 5th Division made its successful foray into enemy territory, the 1st Division was accomplishing the same thing a few miles south. In contrast to the 5th Division's silent approach, the 1st Division preceded its crossing of the Lamone with a massive bombardment of the German positions. For thirty minutes the deafening roar of the big guns and the resulting explosions filled the air.

Herb Pike (48th Highlanders)

The last real big artillery support we had was at the Lamone River. It was the first time they used artificial moonlight, the big spots. That turned out to be a fiasco because all you did was silhouette yourself on the dikes. The barrage was to come down on the other side of the river where Jerry was dug in. It would concentrate there, then it would lift, probably back maybe five hundred yards. Normally that's called a creeping barrage, and normally that was when it would stop and you would make the attack. But this time when they got back to five hundred yards it stopped, then they came back down onto the starting point again on the Jerry's side. On the thought that Jerry would now pop up again, once the barrage passed him he figures he's safe. Now it comes back down. That's the last time that we had any extensive barrage in Italy. Because we were just not getting the ammo.

The second bombardment caught the Germans out in the open as the shells exploded all around them. The night was lit up with "artificial moonlight" as floodlights caught the Germans in their glare all along that part of the river. At 2130 the infantry crossed the river in canvas boats, with the West Novas in the centre, with the Carleton and Yorks on the right and the 48th Highlanders on the left. For the Germans, the second bombardment ended only in time for the Canadians to appear right on top of them.

Gord Outhwaite (48th Highlanders)

When we crossed the Lamone the river was way up. Well, I went over the falls of a boat trying to get across the river. Herb was already across or trying to get across, and we had a couple of tanks, or SP guns actually. Fired a few shots on them and backed up out of the way. Well, I'll tell you, you're sitting there and all you can see is the barrel of this damn gun coming over the hole. What's that?

Herb Pike (48th Highlanders)

That was the old Tiger tank. Big 88 in front of her — massive weapon. Funny thing, the boats we crossed there were canvas. They were collapsible, and you'd pull them up and put a stay across and hold them up. It would hold nine men. By the time you'd get over a rifle butt went through or a guy would kick one of them with his toe and put a hole in the side and you were lucky to get across the river!

Jim Holman (48th Highlanders)

A couple of times you had to use those crazy assault boats. With two pieces of board stuck together, and when you pulled them open they had a canvas bottom and a couple of slats across to keep the two sides apart. I think some of them even pulled it up about halfway across. We had some weird things.

Herb Pike (48th Highlanders)

I remember when we crossed the Lamone I got on the other side and my PIAT man was John Woods from Buffalo. It was quite a heavy rig, and he had this on his shoulder, and he had a box which carried three projectiles, and he stepped on the bank as he was getting out of this canvas boat that we crossed in — we're under fire! He slipped and he fell into the river, and luckily enough I was standing beside him and I reached down and grabbed him by the webbing and I hauled him out and he still had this thing over his shoulder and he still had the box of bombs in his hands. He should have dropped them really, but there's dedication. Jerry makes a counterattack and there was a parallel road to the river. I got a couple of the sections in my platoon and we're lying in the verge of the ditch, and down this Tiger tank comes. Now the verge of the road is probably fifteen feet away from where this tank is coming down, and I said to the guys, "Christ, keep quiet, don't let them know we're here." Lucky enough the gun can't traverse that low, and his machine guns can't come that low, so I said to my PIAT man, "Make sure you hit this guy with one of your projectiles, but make sure you hit him dead-on," because the projectile of the PIAT had a detonator in the front that had three springs on it. Unless you hit correctly on this thing, the thing bounced off. That's how good the weapon was. I use the term loosely. He got one going and it bounced off the tank, and it stops and the gun comes over, and again you look at the muzzle cap. The thing was so big, and I said, "Well, geez, what are we gonna do now?" What we did, we got some smoke grenades and we threw two of them into his air intake. Now, luckily, this thing didn't have baffles in, because the majority of tanks had a baffle and you couldn't do that. We threw the smoke grenades into his air intake, and he had to get out to breathe. So as they come out the top we managed to hit them. But it was funny, when you think of it … projectile hits the side of the tank and it bounces off, now what are you gonna do?

The Carleton and Yorks led the charge up the riverbank, firing into the German positions and throwing grenades into the trenches and pits. The Germans were disoriented from the dual barrage and were caught completely by surprise. The 48th Highlanders overwhelmed their opposition quickly; while the West Novas met some resistance, they quickly neutralized it. Where the Germans appeared to be mounting a counterattack, the Canadians shelled them, eliminating any action that might repeat the disaster of the previous week. With minimal losses, the 1st Division had successfully established a bridgehead, and by the next morning bridges were in place across the Lamone. Tanks and self-propelled guns poured in, and the troops advanced against the retreating Germans. On the night of December 11 the enemy had moved back to the Naviglio Canal to prepare a defensive line there.

The area between the Lamone and Senio Rivers was crisscrossed with numerous canals. While the Canadians reached the Fosso Vecchio, elements of the German army waited for them on the other bank. To the west was the Naviglio Canal, dominating the terrain with its six-metre-high dykes. The approach to this imposing landmark consisted of flat, treeless fields, making for an assault a deadly charge without any cover. To make matters worse for the Canadians, the Germans reinforced their two divisions, defending the area with the 98th Infantry Division and the elite Kesselring Machine Gun Battalion. The Canadian success at the Lamone was being countered, and the Germans were determined to stop them at the Naviglio Canal.

On December 12 the Canadians prepared for the assault on the canal. As darkness descended that night, the Princess Louise Dragoon Guards and the Lanark and Renfrew Scottish moved up on the right, while the Carleton and Yorks moved up the left with the Hasty P's. A light rain fell as the men approached the canal, with its slope seeming to rise at an impossibly steep angle. As the Lanarks scaled the canal's dyke and reached the top, they came face to face with the German defenders. All hell broke loose as gunfire broke out and grenades exploded all along the canal. The Lanarks were pinned down, but held fast under intense German fire.

The Princess Louise Dragoon Guards fought their way over the canal, finding that the waterway was dry (due to the Germans having diverted the water elsewhere), so they were able to get across. They were immediately bombarded by the Germans, and after four hours of enduring the shelling, and with mounting casualties reducing their ability to hold the ground, they withdrew. A group that was holding out in a house fought valiantly until they had run out of ammunition, and then they surrendered.

Off to the left, the Carleton and Yorks faced equally fierce opposition, but they successfully cleared their section of the canal near Bagnacavallo and captured forty-five prisoners in the process. Once the bridgehead was established by the Carleton and Yorks, the Hasty Ps surged forward and enlarged the holding to the right as additional companies of the Carleton and York expanded the left side. The Canadians had taken a foothold, but it was small and they would be hard pressed to hold it. The Germans launched their counterattack at dawn, with a sizable force of tanks and infantry. The Carleton and Yorks withstood the onslaught through the morning, but the pressure was too much to bear and they withdrew to the canal to fight from there. The Hasty Ps were also being battered mercilessly, and they eventually withdrew. A small group of Carletons held out in a house in the field below the canal, bravely fighting back tanks with small arms and machine guns. They desperately hung on until several Sherman tanks and Fireflies arrived at 1500 to dispatch the German tanks, and the sliver of a bridgehead was saved.

At 1600 the Loyal Eddies along with the B.C. Dragoons launched an attack to restore the bridgehead in their area and to drive the Germans out. As daylight waned the "artificial moonlight" was used to flood the battlefield with light, and the Canadians continued their task. The Seaforth Highlanders moved into action, and by midnight all of the territory was regained by the Canadians.

Sydney Frost (Princess Patricia's Canadian Light Infantry)

Ah yes, the Naviglio Canal. That's where Lieutenant Frost gets his third wound. By that time I was in command of the machine gun battalion and we were following up a road, preparing for an attack on still another river. The Germans started to shell this road. I was in an open jeep mixed in with a bunch of tanks so I thought, "Well I'll be safer if I get in between two tanks — they'll shield me a little bit." But it didn't work that way because the Germans had a mortar called a Moaning Minnie. This was a six-barreled mortar that fired six quick bombs — boom boom boom — like that. And as I was going along my driver says, "Sir, I just saw six dirty black flashes up ahead there, that's a Moaning Minnie, and the next one may get us." And by God it did! I was blown out of the Jeep and the driver was killed. A few other people were killed from these Moaning Minnies, and I was going down the road, sort of limping a bit trying to help these guys that had been wounded, and one of the soldiers said, "Sir! You've got a helluva tear in the ass of your pants there," and sure enough I absorbed one of these hunks of lead, and believe it or not — I still have it. So I was evacuated to the hospital and operated on, this one hit me in the rear end. Not the hip that had taken the bone out, but the other hip, just to even things up a bit. I woke up in hospital and dangling from my arm in a vase was this little bit there [shrapnel], and that's what they dug out just next door to the spine. If it had gone another quarter of an inch I would have been a dead man. You see, what happens [is] it hits the ground and explodes into a thousand pieces, some small ones like that one — but imagine if you get hit with a large one — you haven't a hope. You're a dead man. It wasn't a serious wound, I was only in hospital for about six weeks, and finally it cleared up and they took out the piece and sutured it together. Very painful sitting down though for a while.

On the morning of December 14 the Germans launched yet another counterattack, but this time the Canadian artillery was ready for them and stymied their assault. By midday the 5th Division was using the 1st Division's bridgehead to get across the Naviglio Canal in order to achieve their objectives north of it. First the Westminsters moved across and with the support of the Lord Strathcona's Horse, they advanced north and drove the Germans away from the canal. Later in the day the Lanarks made the crossing and took the village of Osteria. By the next morning the 5th Division had secured their section of the canal.

The situation on the battlefield was turning into a stalemate. The Germans wanted to drive the

R. Hill and A.D. Hiebert man a slit trench with a Vickers machine gun.

Canadians back across the Naviglio Canal but were unable to dislodge them. The Canadians, on the other hand, were attempting to advance, only to find that they could not make any headway against the reinforced German forces. To overcome the situation, General Foulkes determined that they would have to take Bagnacavallo. The Canadians began to shell the town in preparation for an attack. The Germans still held the Fosso Vecchio as well as a portion of the Naviglio Canal south of the Ravenna-Lugo railway line. Foulkes wanted those positions taken as well. On December 16, the 48th Highlanders moved towards the Fosso Vecchio and called in artillery barrages to destroy German positions. The next

Newspaper review of the Canadians' first year in combat in Italy.

day they were withdrawn in order to launch a large-scale attack by the RCRs and the Hasty Ps. Both regiments had been decimated at the ill-fated first crossing of the Lamone, and they lacked both manpower and necessary officers to fight another major battle so soon. But their new divisional commander, Harry Foster, insisted on it, and into battle they went. The results were devastating as the two crippled units struggled through the battle, with only one company crossing the Vecchio. They were driven back by a German counterattack of considerable strength. The RCRs and Hasty Ps were badly mauled, with many of the men who were re-mustered ending up wounded or dead. The ranks of officers were depleted to a few men, and with a severe lack of reinforcements available it Italy, it was questionable how the regiments would be brought back up to fighting strength in the near future.

At that point the Canadians focused their efforts on clearing the Fosso Munio, where the Germans still held a portion of the Naviglio Canal by the railway line. It was an odd-shaped position, in the shape of an "S," which provided the Germans with an exceptional defensive location. On December 19 the Loyal Eddies and the PPCLI launched the attack at 2000, taking a silent approach. They moved through mined vineyards and had to overcome every small house that the Germans had set up as a stronghold. They cleared the surrounding area by the afternoon of December 20. Meanwhile, the Irish and Perth Regiments had to approach the Fosso Munio across a vast flat area without any cover. Both got pinned down by German fire, but one company of the Perths found a way through the German defences and moved towards Casa della Congregatione and took the farmhouse. They fought off German counterattacks while the Canadian Engineers created a road for the Strathcona tanks to take to the Casa. The Perths paid a high price for taking and holding their objective, but the Casa was a key strategic location, and with the Canadians in control of it, the Germans withdrew from the Fosso Munio and Bagnacavallo that night. On the morning of December 21 the Carleton and

Just southwest of Bagnacavallo the route is lined with ammunition to be used to overcome the German defences in the Adriatic area.

Yorks entered the town of Bagnacavallo without a shot fired, while other Canadian units pursued the Germans up to the Senio River.

As Christmas approached, the two combatants dug in along the Senio River. In many areas the two sides were separated by the river, but in others the Germans still held the near riverbank, which rose high above the flat land surrounding it. In other areas they held small pockets of land. The offensive had come to a halt, as both sides were battered and fatigued from the fighting and the appalling weather. The two sides prepared for a static winter line. The month of December was once again a cruel one for the Canadians. Like the carnage of 1943, the toll for the month in 1944 amounted to 2,500 casualties. The stress continued on the men as the enemy was only a matter of a few metres away. The bitter weather conditions did not help either. Between of the losses, the conditions, and the lack of reinforcements, it was a tough time for the Canadian soldiers in Italy.

Peter Routcliffe (Governor General's Horse Guards)

I was ordered at four o'clock in the morning to go up and help them at the Senio River. We just got to the edge of the river when we had a voice on the radio said that we were to get off the road. The regiment was coming through. So we went to get off the road and we hit a mine and it blew out the front of the tank. The driver bounced out of the tank and I fell out the front and I don't know what happened to them. I crawled through the embankment to a house there and I was lucky it was our troops in there. So I stayed there a while and then they put me in an ambulance and took me back. That put me behind the line for about three days. That was just about the twenty-fourth or twenty-fifth of December, just at Christmas. I didn't realize what the hell had taken place at all.

FROM SOMEWHERE IN ITALY

1944

CHRISTMAS GREETINGS

MISS. MARIE SPENCE.
140 MARCHMOUNT, Rd.
TORONTO (4) ONT.
CANADA.

A Christmas letter from Italy, 1944. Note the "From Somewhere in Italy" heading to maintain secrecy about the specific location of the Canadian troops.

Christmas Day was quiet along the Senio River as neither side was inclined to fight. Men were rotated back to enjoy a hot Christmas dinner, and along the front carols were sung in English and German. For one day the cruelty of war lifted, and thoughts turned to home and loved ones. That peaceful respite ended all too quickly, and the Canadians spent the next week aggressively patrolling the Senio.

Gord Outhwaite (48th Highlanders)

We had an advance position on the Senio River. Again the Germans had all the high areas, the tall buildings and stuff like that. They could see across, and we had three positions up there, so our officers said, "Okay, we need six men to get up there and man these three slit trenches to keep an eye on things." The Germans took off because it was Christmas. Our company commander said to me, "Gord, I want you to take five men and go down there," and I said to him, "Sir, are you mad at me?" and he looked and he said, "What do you mean?" He took everything serious. I said, "You just sent six men down there yesterday and the Germans got them, now you're going to send six more and you're going to get rid of me! But it's all right sir, we'll go." Well, we went down there and I thought, "Well, we're going to have to do something," so I got two pieces of rope. I connected all three trenches, and I said to them, "Now look, I don't care what it is, if you think you heard something, just pull that line, then all the trenches will know something is up." Sure enough it was the real thing, and we fought our way through it. I got all five back. They didn't take us but we were ready for them. They cut our phone lines, there was a phone going down there. I was as scared as anybody — in fact, I was terrified. We ran out of ammunition and all we had left was a box of grenades, but the battle was over. Fortunately, if they had come at us again, we were lost. So that was good, and when it got a little lighter they sent a fellow down with some ammunition for us. There were patches of snow around, so he donned the white suit and everything was fine until he hit the patches where there's no snow! Heh heh heh. But in the daylight time you didn't stick your head up at all, because they had the high spots on the other side and their snipers were just knocking people off just like that. We got out of it and I was as happy as hell.

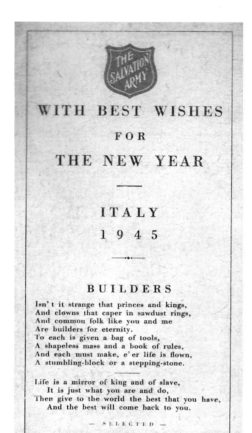

Program for the New Year's service held by the Salvation Army for the men as they ushered in 1945 in Italy.

Sydney Frost (Princess Patricia's Canadian Light Infantry)

So there I has again, back in hospital when the other troops were fighting their way forward. I had the joys of celebrating Christmas and New Year's in hospital again, my second Christmas in hospital! I got back after Christmas. At that time the regiment had finally got to its Senio River winter line. By that time the high brass realized there was no point in trying to fight any further. It was wintertime, the Germans were ensconced in all these rivers, and they were ready to fight and we weren't, we didn't have the men. The attrition had been terrible because you see at this stage the second front was getting all the men and equipment — we were getting nothing. So the generals decided this was enough, and we'll wait until the spring and then we'll deliver the final push. Thank God for that! It no doubt saved endless lives by that decision. So we sat there for about two months facing the Germans — sort of like the first war — Germans on one side, us on the other, staring down each other. But it certainly was a lot better than trying to ford rivers or swim across icy rivers.

Joseph Reid (Calgary Regiment)

We spent our whole winter in Florence. We were billeted in a place just outside of Florence. We went into Florence for lectures that the professor at the university would talk on something. Have a dinner in town, but you had to go back and it was the whole winter of us sitting still.

On New Year's Eve the 1st Canadian Armoured Brigade began a trek across Italy to rejoin the rest of the Canadians in Italy. The Calgary, Ontario, and Three Rivers Regiments had spent a great deal of the campaign supporting the British and Indian troops. Located near Bologna, the brigade headed through the Apennines in a snowstorm and carefully negotiated the dangerous mountain roads en route to the Senio.

John Richardson (Ontario Regiment)

I guess our brigade had probably a longer time in the line than any formation in the war. Two hundred and sixty five days we were in the line. I don't know if that's the exact figure, I know it was two hundred and sixty-something — that is the Ontario's, the Calgary's, or the Three Rivers were committed and fighting.

Prowling Amidst Enemy Toronto Troopers Learn War Still Has Its Thrills

Cross River and Land Between Hun Sentries, Then Spend Three Nights Creeping Into Nazi Secret Places, Seeking Information For G.G.H.G. Planning Attack

By MAJOR BERT S. WEMP, D.F.C.
Telegram War Correspondent

With the Canadian Corps, Italy, Jan. 4 — When it comes to thrilling war experiences, the blood-curdling hair-raising kind, you can hand the cake to Lieut. Bob Murray and Trooper D. J. Davies of the Governor-General's Horse Guards, Toronto.

As a recce information and observation party they spent three nights and two days behind the enemy lines playing hide and seek with the Huns, had two radios go out but made contact with the regiment by stuffing a note in a bottle and throwing the bottle across the Lamone River to their waiting pals.

The G.G.H.G.'s took part in the Canadian Corps advance from the Montone River, the capture of Ravenna and the advance of 12 miles up country north of Ravenna to the Senio River.

BEHIND ENEMY LINES

It was while facing the Lamone that two G.G.H.G.'s crossed the river, entering enemy territory. With a radio they packed themselves into a small collapsible boat with rope attached. In the dead of night they paddled across, landing between two German sentry posts. Their boat was then pulled back to the other side.

Climbing the high dike unnoticed they crossed a field to an Italian house where they made an assault entry, ready to blaze away with tommy guns. Backed against the walls were only frightened Italians. Seeing they were Canadians, the Italians were as much relieved as were the Canucks to find the house only occupied by Ities.

They slept there that night, but the radio refused to work, having received a splash or two of water in the river crossing.

Next day they prowled around and found Hun locations, strength and gun positions. During the night with the radio out, they again made the river dike, throwing a message across in a bottle. It was received. Another radio came, but it also got wet.

The second night they occupied another house in which some Huns ate but this was discovered too late. They locked themselves in the attic. The Huns knocked and kicked at the door but didn't force an entrance. As they knocked at the door, Murray and Davies stood in opposite corners of the room with their fingers on the triggers of their tommy guns. They sweated but were ready. The Huns went downstairs, had their meal and departed.

FIND GOOD TARGETS

The second day, the two Canadians secured much valuable information including pinpoints for artillery and tank shoots, returning to their attic for a good sleep early in the evening. During the third night they again passed between the German dyke sentries, had their signal acknowledged from the op-

the artillery was given some excellent targets which they successfully blasted.

In the 12-mile advance over rivers and quagmire fields, the G.G.H.G.'s were part infantry, part tank and part artillery.

When it was necessary to completely dismount, the boys were infantry. When only half dismounted, the movable tanks supported the men on foot. At other times, the tanks turned into artillery. Nothing stopped them in carrying their share of the fighting.

In the advance toward Alfonsine, north of Ravenna, the Germans held out desperately in fortified Italian stone houses.

ALL ARMS TOGETHER

In one bad spot air, tanks and artillery worked together. The artillery took on enemy batteries and mortars. As dive-bomber strafers went in, tanks would roar up, blasting the enemy positions with all they had. As the air withdrew, so would the tanks. The Huns received quite a pasting. In one attack the tanks alone took 12 prisoners.

In another "dust up," a squadron under Major G. A. Burton, D.S.O. effected complete surprise, did a lot of shooting, killed 30 Germans and captured 11.

For part of the time the G.G.H.G.'s were on the right flank of another well-known Toronto regiment as they went in to attack in clearing up the banks of the Senio River, where the Huns attempted to hold out. Both were successful in their operations and their objectives were secured.

The regiments in the Alfonsin area ran into many minefields, around and back of which the Germans were dug in, armed with bazookas.

Some officers and men who have again upheld the glorious tradition of the G.G.H.G.'s are Majors W. Alex Boothe, A. A. Hugman, C. F. Baker; Captains Bud Waas, M.C., George Brown, Duggan Hood, H. W. F. Appleton; Leuts. Bob Irwin, P. F. Nieukirk, T. R. Richards, W. G. Base, William J. Duthie, W. S. Jamieson, Adjutant Harry Tye, Intelligence Officer D. J. Chant, M.C.; Sergeants N. A. Beeston, R. H. Buchanan, B. J. O'Brien, O. Paterson, R. H. Webber, C. R. Dobson, L. G. Elinsky, T. W. Ruff, M.M., D. L. G. Mullett; Corporals A. R. Lang, L. R. Castello; Lance-Corporals E. W. Wilson, J. L. Bacon; Troopers W. K. Forsythe, N. Toffan, V. W. Matthews, R. A. Johnston, B.E.M., and E. K. Dalton.

HAVE THEIR TURKEY

Ordinary army rations were delivered by jeep-trains to the G.G.H.G.'s in the line on Christmas, but a sit-down turkey dinner was the order of the day for New Year's.

A regimental parade and memorial service at which a Toronto commanding officer took the salute and gave the salute to the fallen was held

Credit Toronto Regiment With Comacchio Mop-Up

Governor-General's Horse Guards Fought Brilliant Action on Adriatic Coast

By MAJOR BERT S. WEMP, D.F.C.
Telegram War Correspondent

With the Canadian Corps, Italy, Jan. 15—Sunday's communique revealed that it was the Governor-General's Horse Guards of Toronto that cleared the Comacchio Spit on the Adriatic in a blinding snowstorm Friday morning.

I described that action in full in Saturday's cable, but the name of the regiment was withheld at that time.

It was a brilliant action on the part of the G.G.'s, not one German escaping, it is believed. Forty-eight prisoners were taken and added to the bag of six hundred and sixty-eight taken since the Canadians and British advanced to the Lake Comacchio.

It is estimated the Germans have lost two thousand five hundred in this area in two weeks, seven hundred and sixty dead having been counted on the ground.

The wounded and those dive-bombed and strafed by flyers on the escape routes must be added to these figures.

Since the Canadian advance to San Alberto along the Reno river and southern end of Lake Comacchio and the blasting of a German counter-offensive, the enemy has continued to send over fighting patrols but with disastrous results.

After one of these skirmishes Saturday night, thirty dead Germans were counted on the ground in one place Sunday morning.

A mile or so up river from there the Germans dug through the Senio River dykes, entering our territory for a look-see. They did, but under the watchful eyes of Canucks. In the meantime our lads mined their return passageways. The Huns were wiped out in the middle of them.

An Eastern Ontario regiment with boys from the watchful Quinte district have always been known for their dead-eye Dick snipers, but Germans in trees have been giving them some trouble. When our snipers didn't get them, the Piat boys took a hand. They not only got snipers with their bombs but trees and all.

The Piats and their bombs were designed as death for German tanks, so the Hun snipers got a sure-fire blasting and then some.

To meet winter conditions, snow, ice, rain and snow again and keep advancing the Canadians are now sending new socks to the boys in the line with their rations and nothing is so welcome.

As the boys get mud-plastered and soaked through, they are brought back a short distance, given a sleep in a warm bed and awakening find everything new and clean clothes laid out for them. It's war, but nothing stops our grand fighting lads.

Thursday night the ground was frozen hard to be covered by a blinding snowstorm Friday morning. The snow was inches deep. Rain blew in Friday night and it has been raining now for two days. Everything is a quagmire and rivers and streams are rising.

Newspaper coverage of the advance of the Governor General's Horse Guards along the Adriatic in January 1945.

While the line had become static, the Canadians decided to clear out the remnants of the German positions on the near side of the Senio in early January. At the right end of the Canadian sector the Germans held an area north of Ravenna near Lago Comacchio, while on the left end they held a strip of land down to the town of Granarolo. The 5th Division would take out the enemy positions at Lago Comacchio while the 1st Division and the British 56th Division would deal with Granarolo.

On January 2, 1945, the 5th Division launched its attack at 0500 with a massive barrage, followed by the advance of the Irish and Perth Regiments along with the 8th New Brunswick Hussars. They descended on the German defences between Conventello and Fosso Basilica and cleared them out by the early afternoon. Then the Cape Breton Highlanders, the B.C. Dragoons, and the 8th Hussars pushed towards Sant'Alberto on the south shore of Lago Comacchio.

On January 3 the Vandoos attacked the Germans near Bagnacavallo, creating a diversion from the main attack on Granarolo by the PPCLI. The Patricias attacked

from the south and surprised the Germans, capturing many prisoners along the way. At midnight the Seaforths moved north around Granarolo to outflank the Germans. The Germans withdrew that night, and the Loyal Eddies entered the deserted town in a magnificently executed plan by the 2nd Brigade.

That same day, the 5th Division came under attack during their advance towards Lago Comacchio. The Germans were determined to recapture Conventello, which would trap the units moving north of there. At 0500 on January 4, the 16th SS Panzer Division roared into action, striking against the Westminster Regiment at the Fosso Basilica. It was the only time that the Canadians in Italy fought the SS, the most fanatical of the German forces. The 16th SS Panzer Division was rated as the strongest combat division in all of Italy. The Westminsters opened fire on the elite German division with everything that they had. For once the Canadians held the high ground and raked the flat fields with a deadly onslaught, while the Germans struggled to reach the dyke and to attempt to cross it. It was in stark contrast to the fighting all through Italy where the Canadians had to fight at a disadvantage. Facing the same obstacles, the Germans did not fare so well. The bulk of the division was stopped dead in its tracks by the Westminsters. Further along, where a few of the SS had made it across the dyke, the Irish

A group of Canadian soldiers admire the view from Gradara Castle, which had been used by the Germans to combat the advance up the Adriatic.

A Canadian Sherman tank rolls through the streets of Ravenna during a light snowfall.

The Lanark and Renfrew Scottish Regiment's anti-tank platoon trains with 6-pounder guns.

Regiment and a squadron from the 8th Hussars crushed them. By early morning the German attack had failed, and 180 prisoners were taken.

The German defences south of Comacchio were in a shambles after the rout of the SS, they were utterly demoralized by the easy defeat of their best division. The Cape Breton Highlanders and the B.C. Dragoons advanced to Sant'Alberto and took the town uncontested. The fifty Germans there simply gave up. The Cape Breton Highlanders pushed on north until they reached the Reno River, while the B.C. Dragoons joined the Perth Regiment in moving east to link up with the British near the Adriatic coast. The Senio was cleared in the Canadian sector, and as a result, they had taken 600 prisoners and soundly defeated the best that the Germans had in Italy.

Harry Fox (Hastings and Prince Edward Regiment)

As far as prisoners goes, the RSM is responsible for them. All prisoners are turned over to him and he has to see that they're searched and held for questioning and then taken back to brigade. So all prisoners passed through me. Well, their attitude was they told you their name and their number, and that was it. No more information from them. They were very well drilled on that, and it seemed to me that they didn't make any attempt to escape. Once they were taken prisoner, it was our job to look after them. Some of them were cocky, but most of them were name and number, that's all. They didn't know anything.

The fighting in Italy more or less ceased for the winter, with the men digging in on their side of the Senio. Patrols were sent out to maintain the vigil, but the weather limited their range and effectiveness. The Canadians were stretched thin across a forty-three-kilometre front, and they were defending with severe rationing of ammunition. If the Germans had launched a major attack, the Canadians would have been in a bind with their lack of supplies. The marginalizing of the Italian Campaign put the men at risk, and their bravery to hold their positions while inadequately supplied cannot be overstated.

Fred Scott (Perth Regiment)

One time in one battle we were rationed five bombs a day because of lack of material. I guess everything was going into the D-Day business, and it was kind of scary there for a while.

Gord Outhwaite (48th Highlanders)

One time we were pinned down and we said, "Holy Hannah, how are we going to get through there?" There wasn't much cover. "That's all right, you're going to have a barrage." Okay, we had six mortar bombs, four HE, and two smoke. They were there, and the guy says, "Well c'mon, let's go!" And we said, "Where the heck is our barrage?" Heh heh.

Herb Pike (48th Highlanders)

Artillery would send up what we would call a FOO, a forward observation officer, and we had a guy we nicknamed "Six round Harrison" — that was a barrage! Six rounds! I'll be quite frank with you, it was damned disheartening, you're trying to do a job and you don't have the tools to do it with. That was only because everything was being saved for the Second Front. That's what made the Italian vet a little upset.

While there were minor skirmishes along the Senio that winter, the biggest one was launched by the Germans on February 24, 1945. They had

Three members of the Vandoos try to stay warm around a small fire.

bombarded the area for an entire day before 150 Germans put in the attack. Armed with flamethrowers, the Germans rushed the Canadian positions held by the Loyal Eddies and the Seaforth Highlanders. While the Eddies were successful in repelling the assault, the Seaforths were overrun by the Germans. The dire situation was remedied by the Seaforths when they called in artillery fire on their own position. The Canadians ducked in their slit trenches while the Germans got torn apart by the barrage. By the next morning the Germans had left the east shore of the Senio.

Canadian soldiers plod through the mud and endure miserable winter weather in Italy.

Al Sellers (Governor General's Horse Guards)

It was wet. Our last action was as a police squadron at the Comacchio salient. That was a wet, sorry, sleety day when we sent these prisoners back and we got forty-five or fifty or so, and it was not too far from where we stopped at Lake Comacchio. That pretty well finished I think the 5th Division's action. It was very static. It was just a case of sitting there and waiting for something to happen. We weren't looking for trouble, and neither were they.

OPERATION GOLDFLAKE

FOR MONTHS THE CANADIAN GOVERNMENT AND military leaders were pressing for the unification of their troops in northwest Europe. At the end of January the decision was made at a meeting of the Combined Chiefs of Staff that the Canadians would be transferred to the Netherlands to join the rest of the Canadian Army. This had more to do with the British desperately needing reinforcements in northwest Europe than it did with fulfilling the Canadians' request. The plans were drawn up, and it was given the code name Operation Goldflake. It was a monumental task, planning the rotation of two divisions and a brigade out of the line, transporting them to a port, and the organization of shipping all those men and their equipment to another country. The operation was conducted in secret, and the Allies deceived the Germans into thinking that the Canadians had withdrawn from the line to prepare for a spring offensive. For the Germans, the appearance of the Canadians in the Netherlands would be a huge surprise. The first contingent of Canadians moved across Italy to the western port of Leghorn (Livorno) and shipped out on February 15. The 5th Division went first since they were in reserve, then as the month progressed, the 1st Division made the journey. A total of 58,172 Canadians made the trip, boarding ships and naval transports of all kinds. They left Leghorn and travelled to Marseilles in the south of France. From there the massive convoy of men and machines headed north, ending their journey in Belgium. There they reorganized and moved up into the line in the central region of the Netherlands, finally joining their countrymen as one single unit. There they would end the war and save the Dutch from starvation.

Fred Scott (Perth Regiment)

Well, things began to slow down for us, and in February they had plans for us. They sent us back, getting us prepared for the move from Italy up into northern Holland. And the brigade that took over from us was an Italian brigade.

Radio operators of the Governor General's Horse Guards. Their communications with HQ were vital for relaying intelligence and maintaining a coordinated effort along the front.

Al Sellers (Governor General's Horse Guards)

I can recall when our regiment was finished up in the Lake Comacchio area, I was the last tank out of there. When the regiment pulled back they pulled the radio operator in our tank and gave me another operator, and we sat there for about two days, just broadcasting messages. So when the Italians moved in, well, it was terrible. They just ran around as if there was no war at all, they were having a good time. They'd drive their trucks with full headlights, they had open fires, and when we got the signal to leave to rejoin the regiment, I was happy to get out.

John Richardson (Ontario Regiment)

The Italians always had a lousy reputation, but the poor Italians were poorly led. Most of the Italian officers bought their commission. So they weren't necessarily top-hole soldiers that they had fighting with them. You could almost feel sorry for the Italian soldier. I'm sure some of them looked after themselves pretty well. But the Germans didn't treat the Italian people very nicely, they were pretty damn rough on them.

Herb Pike (48th Highlanders)

Quite frankly not the best troops in the world, but of course they weren't interested in fighting. We pulled out of the line and we were replaced in our positions by an Italian brigade. Jerry pushed them back. We

Loading equipment on an LST bound for France during *Operation Goldflake. Eventually all of the Canadians would participate in the liberation of the Netherlands.*

A Sherman tank prepares to load onto an LST for Operation Goldflake.

had to go back in and take the area again and then we moved back and we were told we're heading out of Italy.

Sydney Frost (Princess Patricia's Canadian Light Infantry)
So the emphasis then was on the second front, let's finish them off there. And to finish them off they needed more troops in France, in Germany. So who do they call up, of course? The First Canadian Division as well as the 5th Division.

Herb Pike (48th Highlanders)
We were leaving Italy at Leghorn, and I forget the general's name, he had us all in a big valley and he had speakers going, and they told us we were going to be ridiculed when we get up to the Second Front. We were going to be called D-Day Dodgers and this sort of stuff. He said, "Never mind, fellas, just show them when you go into action what the D-Day Dodgers can do." That's exactly what we did. When you stop to think of it, you know, it's sad. The chain of events when you're told that you're going up to another place and you may be ridiculed for the front you were on, and you'd been down there for close to two years, twenty-two months actually.

Gord Outhwaite (48th Highlanders)
Yes, they were long months. Wow, were they ever long.

Herb Pike (48th Highlanders)
Italy was either so hot or so cold, and not a lot of snow, but damp and wet, and oh, the wintertime — terrible.

Al Sellers (Governor General's Horse Guards)

We were just outside of Leghorn and we were just sitting there thinking, "We're just back on a rest" but then we started getting our equipment ready to board boats. They labelled all the equipment. God, I can remember measuring the tank, the height and width and the order that we would get in these things. You know, it was well done when I think of going on that landing tank craft, and I thought, "This damn thing is going to sink with all these tanks in here," but you know they loaded them up. You'd chain them down in what they called "bear traps" — with the thing you could tighten the chain up. We took about three or four days to get up from Marseilles. At that time I thought, "Well, where do we go now?"

Sydney Frost (Princess Patricia's Canadian Light Infantry)

So the entire corps were transported, right from under the noses of the Germans, across the Italian peninsula, from Leghorn to Marseilles by ship, and up the Rhone valley and up into Germany, and do you know it, the Germans hadn't a clue what had happened. I'd have to emphasize that the secrecy, the security arrangements were just incredible on our side. The Germans had no idea about this operation until we

Canadian tanks ready to load onto transport vessels at Leghorn harbour.

Preparing to ship the Sherman tanks of the Governor General's Horse Guards through France on flatcars during Operation Goldflake.

were finally in Holland, fighting. I remember I captured a German officer, he said, "Hell, you're supposed to be in Italy still!" and I said, "Sorry, chum, you're my prisoner."

The departure from Italy was a bittersweet experience for the men. For some, it was a happy occasion, leaving behind the miserable conditions, the tough terrain, and the memories of some of the most vicious fighting that Canada would ever participate in. For others, it was a sad occasion. Many had made enduring friendships with some of the Italian populace, while others mourned the comrades that were being left behind, buried in the war cemeteries. They also felt a sense of disappointment in leaving before achieving a final victory in Italy. The men had fought so long, and had paid so dearly, to wrestle Italy free from Fascism, that to leave it without a resolution was difficult. As they departed, the outcome was assured thanks to their monumental efforts, but they were not to revel in the celebration of victory in Italy. They would, however, enjoy that joyful taste of victory in the Netherlands, where the celebrations would exceed anything that they would have experienced in Italy.

Above: *Group photo of the Governor General's Horse Guards.*

Right: *Tanks of the Governor General's Horse Guards advance through a town in the Netherlands.*

Al Sellers (Governor General's Horse Guards)
Thank God we're out of here. I think every guy in the 1st and 5th Div were just glad to get out of Italy. It wasn't the job. It was something that you didn't like about Italy.

Y̲ou are now saying farewell to 5 Canadian Armoured Division. Soon the Div will be disbanded. Many of us have come a long way together, others a lesser distance. For none of us has the road been easy but for all of us there has been the compensation of friendships made and the satisfaction of working together to see a job well done. It is hoped that we will have many opportunities to renew and maintain these friendships in civil life. We have made an enviable reputation for ourselves in which every man shares and in which he can well be proud. We wish you good luck and great happiness in the future.

I. S. JOHNSTON, BRIG.
GENERAL OFFICER COMMANDING
5 CANADIAN ARMOURED DIVISION

Top left: *Cover of farewell program distributed for the departure of the Canadian 5th Division from Europe in 1945.*

Top right: *Included in the farewell program was a map tracing the path of the Canadian 5th Division through Italy, Holland, and on to victory.*

Left: *Brigadier Johnston's message to the men of the 5th Division in the farewell program.*

Fred Scott (Perth Regiment)

To be honest with you by the time we moved from Italy all the way up there, we were hoping the damn war would be over. Everything was going good in the Western Front, and the Americans were moving along, and the British and Canadians were moving up into Belgium and Holland. Everything seemed to be going fairly well on our side, and we were kind of hoping the everything would be over by the time we got up there. But it wasn't.

Peter Routcliffe (Governor General's Horse Guards)

I think everybody thought that the job was finished, because the Italians had taken over and the British forces had gone on ahead. American forces were there, so I don't think they needed the Canadians, so they just put us where they thought was the best place to put us.

Sydney Frost (Princess Patricia's Canadian Light Infantry)

I think the Italian Campaign was a campaign where initiative of junior officers and men really played an important role, whereas in the fight in France, it was such a massive thing, I don't think there was that area of improvisation that we had to do. And of course we didn't have the kind of weapons they had in the second front. We were relegated to second-class status, but we survived, we made do. The spaghetti and vino were very good too. They made up for it.

THE LEGACY

THE ITALIAN CAMPAIGN STANDS OUT AS the longest offensive of the Second World War for the Allies, and yet the nations that fought in it fail to give their veterans their due for this long and bitter war. Perhaps the reason is that there are varied perspectives about the necessity of the campaign: some feel that it was crucial to create an additional front to divert German divisions away from the Soviet Union and Normandy, while others feel that it was strategically unnecessary. The very nature of the campaign may have relegated it to a lesser position of recognition — it was intended as a diversion, to prepare for the "big show" in northwest Europe. It was never intended to be the main event, and unlike the other two fronts, it never directly attacked Germany itself. Another issue is the fact that Italy was a member of the Axis, and that the Canadians were not part of a liberating force but a conquering force. They were not greeted with the same warmth as they were in France, Belgium, and the Netherlands. That resonates today in Italy, where there are precious few monuments to the Allied sacrifices, especially in comparison to the multitude of them in northwest Europe.

Fred Scott (Perth Regiment)

I think the most important part of it — we kept two of the best German armies, the best the Germans had, out of D-Day. Those fellows didn't have to face the 10th German Army and the 14th. It could have been a different story.

John Richardson (Ontario Regiment)

We had a job to do there, and we had General Kesselring who was one of the better German generals. We were holding down at one time about twenty-eight German divisions, but they thinned that out once they got the lines organized. We faced better divisions, most were a lot better than the divisions involved in D-Day. They didn't face nearly as good as the troops as we did in Italy, not by far. We didn't have any of the young fellas or the old fellas that they had to fight. The German's a good soldier, no doubt about it. I mean, as much as you hate their guts, when it comes to that they're a good enemy.

Peter Routcliffe (Governor General's Horse Guards)

Well, it's been overlooked more or less. The general public feels that was finished and that was it. That doesn't belong to today, in this generation, forget about it. Go on with something else.

Herb Pike (48th Highlanders)

Resentment? I think it would only be understandable, why sure there was. Mind you it's dissipated over the years, but it still lingers.

Sydney Frost (Princess Patricia's Canadian Light Infantry)

I have no resentment about it, it's just a fact of life, and I can understand why it went that way. Of course there's no hope today because no one studies history in the schools or anywhere else — just a very cursory examination of the wars, it's not really part of our heritage anymore. So I understand the reason for it, although I don't agree with it. Certainly we haven't been given the credit that we should have been given. It was a very difficult campaign and six thousand Canadians died in Italy. Six thousand — that's the population of a small town. I have no resentment, that's the way it goes. If I can do anything to change that opinion, I'd be very happy to!

Fred Scott (Perth Regiment)

There was this lady in Mitchell teaching a history class, and I was just shocked at these kids — we're talking sixteen-, seventeen-year-old kids in grade ten in high school. They didn't know. Well, I was telling them about being down in Italy and they didn't know what I was talking about. This one fellow says, well the turning point of the Second World War was D-Day, and of course right then I had a notion to say bull, but you couldn't do that in the school. But they had no idea, the turning point of the Second World War to me was the battle of El Alamein and the battle of Stalingrad. They were the two turning points of the Second World War, and nobody will tell me any different. Well, that was pretty near a year before D-Day. But that's when things started to roll for the British and the Russians was those two battles. And they say, well that was the first landing in Europe, and I said another word **** — Sicily was the first landing in Europe, and you must remember the city of Rome was the first capital city to fall to the Allies — before D-Day. Juno Beach — I was over there about a year or so ago and I never felt so small in my life. "You weren't on Juno Beach?" No, I wasn't on Juno Beach, but I had about eleven months of war before they ever heard tell of Juno Beach. They don't know this. Well, I guess we are second-class citizens when it comes to the Second World War.

The marginalizing of the role of the Canadians and the Allies in the Italian Campaign essentially started during the war. It was evident in the lack of supplies and reinforcements. Once the invasion of Normandy took place, the press relegated the stories from Italy to secondary status. Officers transferred to Italy considered it a form of exile, tantamount to punishment or demotion. The men felt as if they were forgotten while they fought in Italy, performing in a sideshow that no one cared about. For the Canadians it was particularly difficult, as they had committed a large force to the campaign, yet not large enough to have a say in the overall planning of it. They were attached to the British Army and were merely a part of their success, but would be singled out for any failure. The Canadians were accomplishing great victories in Italy, and no one was noticing.

Fred Scott (Perth Regiment)

I know Bradley, Montgomery, and Eisenhower — they all had a whole press travel with them. This is why down in Italy we had no press. I was just looking at the Legionnaire — important days of the Second World War. The most important day was D-Day — okay, but for a year the First Division and part of the Fifth Division had done a heck of a lot of work to prepare for that, and this makes you feel like a second-class citizen. We had no press there, and the people at home like my dad and mother asked, "What are you doing?!" — so even the people at home were feeling we were not doing anything.

John Richardson (Ontario Regiment)

Italy was all they had to talk about until the landing. I don't know about the publicity. I sometimes think we don't make enough of Ortona. I wasn't there, I'm not sorry I missed it because it was a real dirty slugging match down there. We lost quite a few people, but when you consider the casualties we had at Ortona versus the D-Day landing, I think they lost somewhere around three hundred and some-odd killed on the landing — but in Ortona they slugged it out house to house with the toughest troops in the German Army and they had over a thousand killed. That's nearly three times what they had in the D-Day landing. That was a major, major offensive.

Lloyd Williams (Royal Canadian Navy)

Normandy took over, really. That's basically the reason. In those days it wasn't overlooked. If you saw the headlines of North Africa and Sicily, they were very large, especially in the U.K. papers. These were big battles and just as fierce as anything that ever happened in Normandy, probably more fierce. It must have been a hell of a war for these guys.

Sydney Frost (Princess Patricia's Canadian Light Infantry)

The second front stole our show. It was unavoidable. Couldn't be helped. If we hadn't have been there, we would have been in France and a part of the great Canadian Army, but we weren't. We were fighting under British control completely, and it didn't make any news because it was unspectacular for one thing. One river crossing was just the same as another. And the reports used to come back and they would annoy us a bit — "Well, last night the Canadians crossed another river, there were only a few hundred casualties" — you know that used to just burn our ass no end. One casualty is too much as we know today so well, they make such a fuss out of one casualty. But then what's another hundred casualties, it didn't seem to mean much. Regrettable, but that's the way it was.

The insult was ultimately symbolized by the infamous Lady Astor incident, which led to the nickname D-Day Dodgers being given to every Italian Campaign participant. Lady Astor was the first woman elected to British Parliament, and she often corresponded with the soldiers serving overseas. One such letter arrived where the soldier glibly signed it "D-Day Dodger," which she mistook to be a nickname like the Desert Rats, so she replied, addressing her letter "Dear D-Day Dodger." It was a mistake that would find Lady Astor vilified by the proud men fighting in Italy, while some turned the phrase around to be a symbol of the misconceptions about the tribulations that they were facing. A song was penned about the D-Day Dodgers in Italy, sarcastically bragging about the "easy time" that they were having there. It was sung to the tune of the popular "Lili Marlene":

We are the D-Day Dodgers, way out in Italy,
Always on the vino, and always on the spree.
Eighth Army skivers and their tanks,
We go to war in ties and slacks,
We are the D-Day Dodgers, in sunny Italy.

We fought into Agira, a holiday with pay;
Jerry brought his bands out, to cheer us on our way,
Showed us the sights and gave us tea,
We all sang songs, the beer was free,
We are the D-Day Dodgers, in sunny Italy.

The Moro and Ortona were taken in our stride,
We didn't really fight there, we went there for the ride.
Sleeping till noon and playing games,
We live in Rome with lots of dames.
We are the D-Day Dodgers, in sunny Italy.

On our way to Florence, we had a lovely time,
We drove a bus from Rimini, right through the Gothic Line.
Then to Bologna we did go,
We all went swimming in the Po,
We are the D-Day Dodgers, in sunny Italy.

We hear the boys in France are going home on leave
After six months' service, such a shame they're not relieved,
We were told to carry on a few more years,
Because our wives don't shed no tears,
We are the D-Day Dodgers, in sunny Italy.

We are the D-Day Dodgers, way out in Italy,
We're always tight, we cannot fight,
What bloody use are we?

Sydney Frost (Princess Patricia's Canadian Light Infantry)
They blame it on poor Lady Astor, not true. What happened there, this was way back early in the campaign, a soldier in the Buff regiment, that's a British regiment, wrote to Lady Astor and told her how things were there — grim, we wanted more rations, more everything, and signed it: "Private Smith, D-Day Dodger." Well she got the letter, and she thought that this was a common expression that they used. So she wrote back "dear D-Day Dodger" and that's where that phrase came from. So many people have blamed her for it — not her fault at all!

The term "D-Day Dodger" has been embraced by the Canadian veterans of the Italian Campaign, who use it to set them apart from those who served elsewhere during the war. It is a badge of honour, earned through harsh conditions that only those who were there can relate to. Underlying all of that, it remains as a reminder to the Italian Campaign veterans that they have never received the recognition that they so richly deserve. Annually they congregate in Orillia for the D-Day Dodgers Reunion, honouring their fallen at the cenotaph then marching to Legion Hall Branch 34, where they have a feast and raise a glass to toast their comrades. They are the proud few who remember what so many Canadians have forgotten, or have never known about. They may be called the D-Day Dodgers, but they dodged nothing.

Sydney Frost (Princess Patricia's Canadian Light Infantry)
We latched onto that thing and that was one of our big songs. We are the D-Day Dodgers … and we had a lot of fun with it. It didn't mean anything to us, but to this day I run into people who say, "Oh, you were a D-Day Dodger" with a negative connotation. No, we just laughed it off.

John Richardson (Ontario Regiment)
We call ourselves the D-Day Dodgers, everybody just treats it as a lark. It's kind of stupid, but you get stupid remarks from people like that, you know. We weren't dodging, when you joined up like we did, we signed a piece of paper and we went where we were told to go, and do the job that we were told to do, and that's all there is to it.

Above: In silent remembrance during the D-Day Dodgers Reunion, May 2006.

Top right: The D-Day Dodgers Reunion is held annually in Orillia, Ontario, starting with ceremonies at the Cenotaph, followed by a parade to the Royal Canadian Legion hall (Branch 34).

Centre right: The 28th annual D-Day Dodgers Reunion parade, May 2006.

Bottom right: The veterans on parade during the D-Day Dodgers Reunion, May 2006.

Herb Pike (48th Highlanders)
We're called the D-Day Dodgers.

Gord Outhwaite (48th Highlanders)
Ha ha — right!

Herb Pike (48th Highlanders)
We had a couple of D-Days before that happened! Not to take anything away from D-Day, but the fact was we were the forgotten front. Up until prior to D-Day we were big sweats, as it were, but once D-Day went, they forgot about us. And things were hot and heavy, let me tell you.

Gord Outhwaite (48th Highlanders)
We're over on the other side, we're having just as hard a time because they have all our support, and they completely forget about us at all.

Herb Pike (48th Highlanders)
At about half strength too.

Gord Outhwaite (48th Highlanders)
Yeah, and that's no good. You just can't forget about these two invasions going in. Two D-Days, so to speak.

Jim Holman (48th Highlanders)
Well, you know there was a lot of camaraderie. You know your buddies are with you in your platoon or your section — you're all together, you're for each other, and I think that does something to you that when you get later on in life, you want that back. You kind of miss it, I guess. Life is so fast, like coming home, getting married, having a family, working your whole life to get something, and then all of a sudden you're old! And when you get older you seem to have that little more time to sit around and think. There are so

many aspects of war that is horrible. It's not just soldiers getting killed, it's the civilians, and the mess — you see kids, little kids blown apart, and the hunger and all that kind of stuff. It was just awful. I don't know of any idiot who would want to start a war. It is just awful.

Al Sellers (Governor General's Horse Guards)
We were the forgotten army. Well, I think that history will never recognize Italy. Certainly they recognize the desert war, that was very important because the oil was to be considered. Italy was a go-between, that was a stepping stone up to Germany. We just resigned ourselves to everything, at least I did. We don't care, but we actually were forgotten. I don't think any of those fellows are resentful. We don't have to answer to anybody.

The Canadian role in the Italian Campaign was pivotal. They led the attacks, facing the best that the Germans had, and continually succeeded. They fought through the hell of Sicily's heat and the quagmire of Italy's mud. They coped with the high waters of innumerable river crossings and constantly fought from a position of disadvantage. The brave Canadians persevered through the most vile conditions with a shortage of men and *matériel*, making history at places like Ortona, the Liri Valley, and the Gothic Line, to name but a few. Despite the adversity, the Canadian soldiers never faltered. They were part of an all-volunteer army, having joined up out of a sense of duty and a desire for a bit of adventure. No other country committed so much of itself to the war effort as Canada. One in ten joined up out of a nation of 11 million, and of those, 92,757 served in the Italian Campaign. For twenty months they battled the enemy, with more than 3,500 locations of engagement.

Herb Pike (48th Highlanders)
I'll give you an example: as far as Italy was concerned, where the majority of our regiment's casualties occurred — we lost close to four hundred men. Which is almost half of a regiment, and wounded in action — not only once, again remember we were hit and go back to the hospital, patched up and sent back again, so there was just in excess of twelve hundred wounded, at least once. At least once. So that's only one regiment that lost that number of men, we weren't the only ones.

Al Sellers (Governor General's Horse Guards)

There's very little written about the Italian Campaign, and there's so much to be said about what we went through. First of all the lack of equipment — poorly equipped. Absolutely appalling, the junk that we had to take over and keep running, whether it was a transport troop — whether it was troops in your own regiment or whether it was the army service corps. Worn-out equipment.

Harry Fox (Hastings and Prince Edward Regiment)

Canadians should know more about it. The newspapers could print a few things like sixty-eight years ago today so-and-so happened, and give a little story on it or something like that. The same with TV. But other than that I think it's too late.

Sydney Frost (Princess Patricia's Canadian Light Infantry)

I think I did my duty. I had a lot of different appointments in the army. I started out in 1940 — I graduated from RMC on my twentieth birthday, by the time I was twenty-one I was on the way to Italy and Sicily. I was in charge of a platoon at first, and then I was given the scouts and snipers, later I was put in charge of the machine gun platoon. I became acting second-in-command of the battalion at twenty-two — not bad. Of course it was just a matter of luck, everybody else was dead or gone. Well, I came home.

John Richardson (Ontario Regiment)

All the guys I joined up with, we all went and did what we were supposed to do, so I would say that I was very satisfied. I got wounded but not very badly. I came through with my skin intact, and most of my men came through, and that was the important thing. Your job is to do what you are supposed to do and keep your casualties to a minimum or nil, and that's what I planned on doing and that's what I did. I had a few badly wounded, had a few killed, but on the whole I kept the guys intact, and we did what we were told to do and asked to do. And maybe a little bit more.

Jim Holman (48th Highlanders)

I'm really, really proud that I was able to do it as far as I did. And that I had the guts and the courage — can't call it courage, but guts — to do it day after day after day. It was an experience — it's one I'm glad I did.

CANADIANS' CEMETERY IN ITALY WET, WEEDY

Rome, May 1—(CP)—Two fine Canadian cemeteries for the dead of the 1st Canadian Corps have been completed in Italy, except for headstones to replace the present wooden crosses, but elsewhere in Italy the graves of Canadian soldiers bear signs of at least temporary neglect.

Agira cemetery in hilly central Sicily and the Moro River cemetery near Ortona, where the Canadians fought one of their biggest engagements, are well-kept prototypes of other cemeteries now being built by the Canadian War Graves commission in France, Belgium and Holland.

But the 5th Canadian Armored division cemetery at Villanova near the banks of the Lamone canal, west of Ramenna, is depressing. The graves of more than 225 soldiers there have obviously received no attention since the 1st Canadian Corps left early in 1945.

Parts of the cemetery lie under more than an inch of water, with weeds growing freely not only between the graves but in the aisles between the plots.

So far no Canadian cemeteries have been made in the Gothic line area south of Rimini or around Ravenna. The Canadians are buried in British cemeteries at Gradara and Coriano Ridge, where the 8th Army fought through the Gothic line.

An early newspaper report on the state of the Canadian War Cemeteries. This would change after the war, and today the sites are immaculately maintained.

Harry Fox (Hastings and Prince Edward Regiment)

Well, Canada did very well in the Italian campaign. We had more men than the Greeks, the New Zealanders, and the South Africans, but the Brits and the Americans had more men than we did, so we didn't get all of the hype that some of the other armies got. The Canadian 1st Division was good. We held up our end, there's no doubt about that. We did very well in Italy.

Albert Wade (Royal Canadian Dragoons)

We had the best army in the world, I don't care what anybody says. The Canadian Army never, never retreated, never! I am very proud of the fact that I was there. And that's the best I can do.

Joseph Reid (Calgary Regiment)

The campaign that brought out the best of Canadians was the Italian Campaign. They used every tactic you could think of to get by.

Gord Outhwaite (48th Highlanders)

We did a good job. We did what we were there for. It's costly, but at least we made a name for Canada, we fought for freedom, and we have freedom. That name will live forever now. They know Canada's around.

Herb Pike (48th Highlanders)

I'll tell you there's a helluva lot of guys that are left over there that could have been great citizens. A great asset to come home.

Al Sellers (Governor General's Horse Guards)

Well, I like them to remember we were there, and that there was Canadian representation down there, and anyone of those guys that I rubbed shoulders with don't have a thing to be ashamed of.

THEY ARE AT PEACE

They shall live, though we no longer
    see them,
    For their souls have returned to
        God;
And we shall not weep at their leav-
    ing,
    For they walk where the angels
        have trod.

They walk in the bright shining
    valleys,
    Where the white clouds of Heaven
        look on;
They appear in the grey of the even-
    ing,
    And shine in the colors at dawn.

You can see them whene'er there's a
    rainbow,
    They are near in the warmth of the
        sun,
They are watching your daily labor,
    And rest with you when you are
        done.

Do not sorrow because they have
    left you;
    God will let them be close to you
        still.
It may be for only a moment,
    According to His blessed will.

But you'll see them in each morning
    sunrise,
    In the beauty, when sunset re-
        turns,
In the shadows of gathering twilight,
    In the sound of the bells' distant
        chime.

They are close in the darkness at
    midnight,
    You can feel their presence so
        near.
They are trying to say not to worry;
    "Everything is alright with us
        here."

And those who have had no loved
    ones,
    No parents to cherish and care,
They shall walk by His side in their
    glory,
    Forever His love to share.
    This poem was written by Pte.
L. F. Rowdon, who was wounded
last summer, and who is still in
hospital overseas. He is a son of
Mr. and Mrs. E. Rowdon of 50
Dacotah street, St. Catharines.

Fred Scott (Perth Regiment)

I'm proud to be a D-Day Dodger. We don't have to take a back seat to anybody as far as I'm concerned. When you talk about these nineteen cemeteries, there's this one little cemetery, I have a couple of good buddies buried in, a little cemetery at Villanova. I think if my memory serves me correctly there are 212 graves in that little cemetery, and out of them 206 are Canadians. I'll never forget that little cemetery. Freddy Smith, my buddy, and Bill Faucet are both there. But anyway, that's my story.

Peter Routcliffe (Governor General's Horse Guards)

All those fellas that stayed over there, never came home, are still remembered as Canadian soldiers, and its pretty hard when you think of it. So many people left over there.

Herb Pike (48th Highlanders)

Well, the first time I went back to Italy I was amazed at some of our cemeteries, how well kept they are, the Canadian War Graves are responsible, but the populace, even in Italy, were looking after them. People out there with flowers on them, on the graves. It amazed us.

John Richardson (Ontario Regiment)

Every time they play that Last Post I — it's all I could do … It seems that all the ones we lost were the good guys. It always seemed the way. War isn't a pleasant thing, but you can't give any more than your life, can you?

Poem "They Are At Peace" eulogizes the fallen soldiers, written by Private L.F. Rowdon of St. Catharines, Ontario. Clipped from newspaper.

The Canadians fought some of the worst battles in some of the most extreme conditions of the war in Italy, where 19,486 were wounded. More Canadians made the ultimate sacrifice in Italy than anywhere else in the Second World War. More than 5,900 Canadians remain in Italy and Sicily today, buried in the eighteen war cemeteries that are located throughout the country. They are the Agira Canadian War Cemetery (Sicily), the Assisi War Cemetery, the Bari War Cemetery, the Moro River Canadian War Cemetery, the Sangro River War Cemetery, the Caserta War Cemetery, the Cassino War Cemetery, the Beach Head War Cemetery (Anzio), Rome War Cemetery, Florence War Cemetery, Ancona War Cemetery, Montecchio War Cemetery, Gradara War Cemetery, Coriano Ridge War Cemetery, Ravenna War

Cemetery, Casena War Cemetery, Villanova Canadian War Cemetery, and the Argenta Gap War Cemetery. There were 192 Canadians who died in the Italian Campaign without a known grave, and they are commemorated at the Cassino Memorial, which lists the names of 4,054 Allied men who were lost in the war.

Left: *The Italy Star medal.*

Right: *The Italian Campaign commemorative stamp was issued by Canada Post in 1993 to mark the fiftieth anniversary of the major events of the Second World War in 1943.*

The Canadians who fought in the Second World War did so for freedom, eliminating the tyranny of Fascism and ensuring that the world was a better place. Canada did not stand idly by while others shaped the future of the world. The country stood up for what was right, and its citizens made personal sacrifices to guarantee victory. Those that joined the armed forces made sacrifices that are unimaginable. They gave up nearly six years of their youth, leaving behind their homes and loved ones, willingly and selflessly fighting for the benefit of others. Some sacrificed their health, their limbs, or even their lives to do the right thing. The Canadians who fought in the Italian Campaign deserve to be honoured for their role and remembered for the incredible hardships that they endured. Through hell and high water, they brought victory — and a better world.

Lest we forget.

APPENDIX

CANADIAN ARMOURED CORPS

1ST ARMOURED BRIGADE
11th Armoured Regiment (The Ontario Regiment)
12th Armoured Regiment (Three Rivers Regiment)
14th Armoured Regiment (The Calgary Regiment)

1ST INFANTRY DIVISION
1st Armoured Car Regiment (The Royal Canadian Dragoons)

5TH ARMOURED DIVISION
3rd Armoured Reconnaissance Regiment (The Governor General's Horse Guards)
5th Armoured Brigade:
     2nd Armoured Regiment (Lord Strathcona's Horse (Royal Canadians))

5th Armoured Regiment (8th Princess Louise's (New Brunswick) Hussars)
9th Armoured Regiment (The British Columbia Dragoons)

FIRST CANADIAN ARMY TROOPS
A, B, and G Squadrons, 25th Armoured Delivery Regiment (The Elgin Regiment)

ROYAL CANADIAN ARTILLERY

1ST INFANTRY DIVISION
1st Field Regiment RCHA
2nd Field Regiment
3rd Field Regiment
1st Anti-Tank Regiment
2nd Light Anti-Aircraft Regiment

5TH ARMOURED DIVISION
17th Field Regiment
8th Field Regiment (Self-Propelled)
4th Anti-Tank Regiment
5th Light Anti-Aircraft Regiment

1ST CORPS TROOPS
7th Anti-Tank Regiment
1st Survey Regiment

FIRST CANADIAN ARMY TROOPS
No. 1 Army Group RCA:
    11th Army Field Regiment
    1st Medium Regiment
    2nd Medium Regiment
    5th Medium Regiment

CORPS OF ROYAL CANADIAN ENGINEERS

1ST INFANTRY DIVISION
2nd Field Park Company
1st Field Company
3rd Field Company
4th Field Company

5TH ARMOURED DIVISION
4th Field Park Squadron
1st Field Squadron
10th Field Squadron

1ST CORPS TROOPS
9th Field Park Company
12th Field Company
13th Field Company
14th Field Company

GHQ AND L. OF C. TROOPS
1st Drilling Company

ROYAL CANADIAN CORPS OF SIGNALS
1st Armoured Brigade Signals
1st Infantry Divisional Signals
5th Armoured Divisional Signals
1st Corps Headquarters Signals

CANADIAN INFANTRY CORPS

1ST INFANTRY DIVISION
The Saskatoon Light Infantry (MG)

1st Infantry Brigade:

    The Royal Canadian Regiment

    The Hastings and Prince Edward Regiment

    48th Highlanders of Canada

2nd Infantry Brigade:

    Princess Patricia's Canadian Light Infantry

    The Seaforth Highlanders of Canada

    The Loyal Edmonton Regiment

3rd Infantry Brigade:

    Royal 22nd Regiment

    The Carleton and York Regiment

    The West Nova Scotia Regiment

5TH ARMOURED DIVISION

11th Infantry Brigade:

    11th Independent Machine Gun Company (The Princess Louise Fusiliers)

    The Perth Regiment

    The Cape Breton Highlanders

    The Irish Regiment of Canada

12th Infantry Brigade:

    12th Independent Machine Gun Company (The Princess Louise Fusiliers)

    4th Princess Louise Dragoon Guards

    The Lanark and Renfrew Scottish Regiment (1st Light Anti-Aircraft Regiment RCA until July 13, 1944)

    The Westminster Regiment (Motor)

1ST CORPS TROOPS

1st Corps Defence

FIRST SPECIAL SERVICE FORCE

1st Canadian Special Service Battalion

ROYAL CANADIAN ARMY SERVICE CORPS

1st Armoured Brigade Company

1st Infantry Divisional Troops Company
1st Infantry Brigade Company
2nd Infantry Brigade Company
3rd Infantry Brigade Company
5th Armoured Divisional Troops Company
5th Armoured Divisional Transport Company
5th Armoured Brigade Company
11th Infantry Brigade Company
12th Infantry Brigade Company
No. 31 Corps Troops Company
No. 32 Corps Troops Company
1st Corps Transport Company
No. 1 Motor Ambulance Convoy
No. 1 Headquarters Corps Car Company
No. 41 Army Transport Company

ROYAL CANADIAN ARMY MEDICAL CORPS

1ST ARMOURED BRIGADE
No. 2 Light Field Ambulance

1ST INFANTRY DIVISION
No. 4 Field Ambulance
No. 5 Field Ambulance
No. 9 Field Ambulance

5TH ARMOURED DIVISION
No. 7 Light Field Ambulance
No. 8 Light Field Ambulance
No. 24 Field Ambulance

1ST CORPS TROOPS
No. 4 Casualty Clearing Station

No. 5 Casualty Clearing Station

GHQ and L. of C. TROOPS
No. 1 General Hospital
No. 3 General Hospital
No. 5 General Hospital
No. 14 General Hospital
No. 15 General Hospital
No. 28 General Hospital
No. 1 Convalescent Depot

CANADIAN DENTAL CORPS
No. 1 Dental Company
No. 3 Dental Company
No. 8 Dental Company
No. 11 Base Dental Company

ROYAL CANADIAN ORDNANCE CORPS
No. 201 Infantry Ordnance Sub-Park
No. 205 Armoured Ordnance Sub-Park
No. 1 Corps and Army Troops Sub-Park

ROYAL CANADIAN ELECTRICAL AND MECHANICAL ENGINEERS
1st Armoured Brigade Workshop
No. 1 Army Tank Troops Workshop
1st Infantry Brigade Workshop
2nd Infantry Brigade Workshop
3rd Infantry Brigade Workshop
5th Armoured Brigade Workshop
11th Infantry Brigade Workshop
12th Infantry Brigade Workshop

No. 1 Infantry Troops Workshop
No. 5 Armoured Troops Workshop
1st Corps Troops Workshop
No. 1 Recovery Company

CANADIAN PROVOST CORPS

No. 1 Provost Company (RCMP)
No. 3 Provost Company
No. 5 Provost Company
No. 1 L. of C. Provost Company
No. 35 Traffic Control Company (35th Light Anti-Aircraft Battery RCA until June 15, 1944)

MISCELLANEOUS

Canadian Section GHQ 1st Echelon A.A.I.
Canadian Section GHQ 2nd Echelon A.A.I.
No. 1 Base Reinforcement Group:
No. 1 Base Reinforcement Depot
No. 2 Base Reinforcement Depot

ROYAL CANADIAN AIR FORCE SQUADRONS

No. 331 Wing
No. 420 (Bomber) Squadron
No. 424 (Bomber) Squadron
No. 425 (Bomber) Squadron
No. 244 Wing
No. 417 (Fighter) Squadron

BIBLIOGRAPHY

Cameron, Craig. *Born Lucky: RSM Harry Fox MBE, One D-Day Dodger's Story*. St. Catharines: Vanwell, 2005.

Canada-Italia 1943–1945. Veterans Affairs Canada, 1991.

Dancocks, Daniel. *The D-Day Dodgers*. Toronto: McClelland & Stewart, 1991.

Frost, Sydney. *Once A Patricia*. Nepean, Ontario: Borealis, 1988.

Hayes, Geoffrey. "The Canadians In Sicily, Sixty Years On." *Canadian Military History*, 2003.

McAndrew, Bill. *Canadians and the Italian Campaign*. Art Global, 1996.

"The Governor General's Horse Guards 1939–1945." *Canadian Military Journal*, 1945.

Sources

Canada At War (wwii.ca)

Canadian War Museum (WarMuseum.ca)

Juno Beach Centre (www.junobeach.org)

Loyal Edmonton Regiment Museum (www.lermuseum.org)

National Archives of Canada

Veterans Affairs Canada (www.vac-acc.gc.ca)

War Amps (www.waramps.ca)

www.canadiansoldiers.com

www.regiments.org

THE MONTE CASSINO SOCIETY

NA15141

THE MONTE CASSINO SOCIETY IS DEDICATED to furthering an interest in the experiences of those from all nations who took part in the Italian Campaign of the Second World War. Our aim is to collect and encourage access to the accounts, memoirs, recollections, and associated information about the campaign.

If you are an Italian Campaign veteran, or a son, daughter, or relative of one who served in the Italian Campaign, we would like to hear from you.

For information, and to receive our quarterly newsletter, please contact us at info@themontecassinosociety.org; write to us at The Monte Cassino Society, RR 5, Orangeville, Ontario, Canada, L9W 2Z2; or visit our website at www.themontecassinosociety.org.

Special Thanks

Jan de Vries

Rosalind Galloway (The Monte Cassino Society)

Andrew Irwin

Jack Martin

Jim Parks

Veterans' Affairs Canada